Queer Temporalities in Gay Male Representation

Routledge Studies in Rhetoric and Communication

1. Rhetorics, Literacies, and Narratives of Sustainability
Edited by Peter N. Goggin

2. Queer Temporalities in Gay Male Representation
Tragedy, Normativity, and Futurity
Dustin Bradley Goltz

Queer Temporalities in Gay Male Representation

Tragedy, Normativity, and Futurity

Dustin Bradley Goltz

NEW YORK AND LONDON

First published 2010
by Routledge
711 Third Avenue, New York, NY 10017

Simultaneously published in the UK
by Routledge
2 Park Square, Milton Park, Abingdon, Oxon, OX14 4RN

Routledge is an imprint of the Taylor & Francis Group, an informa business

First issued in paperback 2011

© 2010 Taylor & Francis

Typeset in Sabon by IBT Global.

All rights reserved. No part of this book may be reprinted or reproduced or utilised in any form or by any electronic, mechanical, or other means, now known or hereafter invented, including photocopying and recording, or in any information storage or retrieval system, without permission in writing from the publishers.

Trademark Notice: Product or corporate names may be trademarks or registered trademarks, and are used only for identification and explanation without intent to infringe.

Library of Congress Cataloging-in-Publication Data

Goltz, Dustin Bradley, 1974–
 Queer temporalities in gay male representation : tragedy, normativity, and futurity / Dustin Bradley Goltz.
     p. cm. — (Routledge studies in rhetoric and communication ; v. 2)
 Includes bibliographical references and index.
 1. Gay men in mass media. 2. Gay men in motion pictures. 3. Gay men on television. 4. Gay men in literature. 5. Gays in popular culture. 6. Gay men—Identity. I. Title.
 P96.H632U64 2010
 302.23086'642—dc22
                                                            2009028374

ISBN10: 0-415-87228-6 (hbk)
ISBN10: 0-415-89815-3 (pbk)
ISBN10: 0-203-86131-0 (ebk)

ISBN13: 978-0-415-87228-7 (hbk)
ISBN13: 978-0-415-89815-7 (pbk)
ISBN13: 978-0-203-86131-8 (ebk)

I dedicate this project to my cohort of queer friends with whom I spent the majority of my late teens and twenties in Phoenix, Arizona. Facing our days, nights, and lives without a clear map, we spent much time battling against, planning for, rejecting, thumbing our nose at, and contemplating the limitations and potentials of a "future" and "adulthood." That journey still lingers in my mind and my body. It continues to push me forward with this work, even as it pulls me backwards. No matter how far away from it I get, I sometimes—still—feel like that boy on the dance floor at Preston's, the club that was torn down long ago and continues to haunt and comfort me, leaving me to fear, seek out, wonder, question, and mourn our future from back then. ss

Contents

Acknowledgments ix

1 Introduction: "Deleted Scenes" and "Innocent Questions" 1

2 The Heteronormative Tragedy: Kenneth Burke and Queer Media Criticism 19

3 Victims in/of Time: Gay Aging as Ritualized Horror 47

4 Future Identification: Symbolic Mergers with Heteronormativity 81

5 The Dinner Party: Queer Gesturing to Time and Future 115

Notes 157
Bibliography 175
About the Author 187
Index 189

Acknowledgments

Many colleagues and mentors have helped to shape the ideas that appear on these pages, and I would like to acknowledge and thank Jennifer Linde, Sarah Tracy, Aimee Carrillo-Rowe, Dan Brouwer, Amira de la Garza, Karma Chávez, Linda Park-Fuller, and Kristin Valentine for their support and guidance in developing this work. I wish to acknowledge the generous support of the Arizona State University's Graduate Professional Student Association (GPSA) for providing a grant that assisted in the funding of this project. I wish to thank and acknowledge the work of Erica Wetter, the editorial staff at Routledge, and the reviewers of the manuscript in its earlier stages. Each helped shape, strengthen, and complicate the project in multiple ways. Thank you to Jackie Taylor and the College of Communication at DePaul University. Kimberlee Pérez walked through this entire project with me, and so many of the ideas, questions, and discoveries that emerged from our many wonderful talks are scattered across these pages. I wish to specifically mark the guidance and advisement of Cheree Carlson, David William Foster, and Frederick Corey. Cheree Carlson planted Burke into my impressionable undergraduate mind, many years ago, and those seeds have been working their way through my own ideas ever since. Foster expressed unwavering faith in the project, while challenging me each step of the way. The mentorship, advice, and investment of Frederick Corey has been a consistent and important presence in my life for sixteen years, and his comments, concerns, and assistance have inspired and directed many of the ideas put forth in this volume. In addition, I wish to acknowledge the love and support I have received from all my families throughout this process, specifically to Jason Zingsheim, who sat through hours of television and film, countless moments of frustration, dozens of messy drafts, and day-long theoretical ramblings where I refused to talk about anything else. In breakthroughs and roadblocks, we continue to do this future together. Whatever the thing is, I'm glad it is ours.

1 Introduction
"Deleted Scenes" and "Innocent Questions"

> The way to deal with the asymmetries and violent frenzies that mark the present is not to forget the future. The here and now is simply not enough. Queerness should and could be about a desire for another way of being in both the world and time, a desire that resists mandates to accept that which is not enough. (Muñoz, "Cruising" 365)

In the much-publicized announcement in mid-October of 2007, famed author and pop cultural phenomenon J. K. Rowling revealed to an audience of fans at New York's Carnegie Hall that Albus Dumbledore—wizard and headmaster of Hogwart's School of Witchcraft and Wizardry in her Harry Potter series—is gay. The statement instantly garnered international attention, spanning from news coverage on CNN, *Time*, and *Newsweek* to homemade tribute videos on YouTube, inevitably followed up by an avalanche of parody. The *Saturday Night Live* (*SNL*) "Weekend Update" reported Rowling's statement that Dumbledore was gay, followed by the punch line, "What's more, he has Hogwarts." In a later sketch, after the story had been circulating for a few weeks, *SNL* produced a skit where "J. K. Rowling" appears on "Larry King" to discuss the media firestorm. The Rowling impersonator comments, "Larry, there were scenes from the movie that were cut for time that if they remained, they would have clearly shown that Dumbledore was gay." The Larry King interview skit is a framing device to showcase three parody sketches—presented as "deleted scenes" from a recent Harry Potter film—that openly mark, as well as predictably mock, the gay Dumbledore. In the first "deleted scene," Albus sits miserably in his chambers, moaning in agony over a recent "booty owl" message he received from "he who shall not be named," his ex-boyfriend Gerry. In the second scene, Albus stands before a floor-length mirror, lamenting, "This robe is two things I'm not, young and fun." He questions, "Why don't they make an invisibility cloak for stomach poochies?" Minerva—the headmistress at Hogwart's—inquires about Albus's sad disposition, and Albus discloses a recent run-in with his ex-boyfriend Gerry at a gay bar. Minerva offers comfort to Albus, to which he replies, "Oh Minerva, if only you had a penis and balls!" The final "deleted scene" places Albus in a gay bar, desperately searching for his ex-boyfriend Gerry. Minerva follows Albus to the bar, hoping to prevent Dumbledore from making a fool of himself. Albus moans, "I don't want to die alone," yet is quickly distracted by the sight of a young boy off camera. He announces, "Check out that juicy little pork chop," tosses Minerva to the side, and breaks into an absurd and awkward dance, bumping and grinding with the now visible younger gay boy.[1]

The humorous premise of this *SNL* sketch claims to expose the deleted "gay scenes" that landed on "the cutting room floor," reportedly hidden from broader cultural discourse and circulation. This "never before seen" footage, however, is a succinct and accurate representation of the discourses that circulate around gay male aging across multiple film and television productions. Prior to being "outed," Dumbledore had been represented as a respectable, wise, and somewhat asexual character within the Harry Potter narrative, yet his gayness produces a significant discursive transformation. Albus is suddenly overly emotional, highly sexualized, attracted to younger boys, hyper-conscious of his bodily appearance, and consistently alone, depressed, and lacking a sense of completeness. Suddenly, through the mere mention of homosexual desire, Dumbledore is rearticulated as a developmental failure and a joke. The clips that "clearly" show Dumbledore's homosexuality pull together a quick assembly of cultural signifiers attached to the aging gay male body—sexual predation, isolation, regret—demonstrating the limited, violent, and stereotypical meanings assigned to the aging gay male. Coupled with the first "Weekend Update" report that suggests he "has Hogwarts," which in this connotation is a disease rather than the name of a school, these jokes rely on the cultural equation between the gay male, hyper-sexualization, and sexually transmitted disease. Whereas *SNL* is obviously a program geared towards humor and parody, the device of "deleted scenes" is merely a guise to mock Dumbledore, compartmentalizing him into a rigid framework of culturally produced meanings surrounding the aging gay male in mainstream media. The "never before seen" footage is, in actuality, a cliché that is seen over and over in film and television. The *SNL* skit does, however, beg the follow-up question, "If the 'deleted scene' is actually the mainstream representation, then what other narratives and stories of gay aging are lost to the cutting room floor?"

The Harry Potter franchise has been estimated to be worth $15 billion—surpassing both the Star Wars and James Bond enterprises (Harris 36)—leading Rowling to be championed for the timeliness and timelessness of her creation. Through the cultural appropriation and navigation of Dumbledore's recently marked sexuality, however, the notions of time and timelessness point to a discussion outside the international phenomenon of Harry Potter, the heteronormative foundations that dictate the cultural production of time, age, sexuality, and future.[2] As articulated in the Dumbledore parody on *SNL*, U.S. popular culture circulates a limited and problematic body of meanings of gay aging and future that have existed for decades. The televised representations of gay men in the late 1960s included psychiatric accounts such as "[t]he fact that somebody's homosexual . . .

automatically rules out the possibility that he [sic] will remain happy for long" (Hart 599). Russo claims the primary message that comes out of the film *The Staircase* (1969) is, "'Nobody loves you when you're old and gay'—not even yourself" (192). Michael in *The Boys in the Band* delivers "[t]he play's most famous line, 'you show me a happy homosexual and I'll show you a gay corpse'" (178). Through decades of gay and lesbian representations in Hollywood film, "self-hatred was the standard accessory of every new model" (136).

Derived from negative mythologies assigned to the gay male body, popular representations repeatedly cast the older gay male as doomed to a future of sadness, misery, isolation, and perpetual loss. Within the proliferation of "positive" images through the 1990s, the storylines of gay characters on television shows continually faced negative consequences (Hart 606), as "romantic happiness is not to be found" (605) and homosexuality remained a problem that other heterosexual characters must deal with (603). As articulated in the Dumbledore parody sketch, the horror story of the miserable and perverted aging gay male works to preserve the illusionary perfection and correctness of heterosexual models of romantic relationship building, procreation, and future scripting through depicting the aging gay male as a cautionary tale of developmental failure. *Queer Temporalities in Gay Male Representation: Tragedy, Normativity, and Futurity* breaks down and interrogates the rhetorical influence of heteronormative constructions of time and future in contemporary popular culture, exploring how gay male sexuality is positioned within a tragic cycle of aging. Always to the service of supporting heteronormative engagements with time and future, and foreclosing queered or nonnormative potentials for rethinking time and future, the aging gay male is cast as villain and constructed as sacrifice to hegemonic temporal modes. In other terms, the aging gay male is alienated from the very notion of future and denied access to a positive view of health, longevity, or aging.

TIME, AGE, AND FUTURE: GAY, STRAIGHT, AND QUEER TEMPORALITIES

> Younger gay men's awareness of popular, negative stereotypes of their older counterparts may contribute to their fear of aging, due to their fear of adopting such negative, stereotypical characteristics as they age. (Hajek and Giles 707)

This book begins with a simple and seemingly innocent series of questions. What does it mean to be an aging gay man in the United States of America? What cultural meanings are attached to the aging gay male body in contemporary media? What might a queer understanding or engagement with the future look like? How does the future look in the mind of "younger" gay men? Where do they see themselves in fifteen years? Thirty years? Where do those scripts come from, how are they constructed, what do they foreclose, and whom or what do they serve? How are gay men narrating their futures?

Media criticism and cultural studies scholars have established a growing body of literature exploring the importance of gay representation, charting a history of gay characters from villainous blood-thirsty monsters to fashion-savvy cosmopolitan leading men on "Must See TV."[3] In an age following *Brokeback Mountain*, *Queer Eye for the Straight Guy*, *Will & Grace*, and *Queer as Folk*, where NBA star John Amaechi has come out of the closet, the democratic party organized the first debate dedicated to gay and lesbian concerns, and LOGO and Here! broadcast exclusively gay-themed entertainment, why is the study of gay aging and future relevant? The short answer would be that the cultural construction of time and future operate under violent, exclusionary, and oppressive terms, marking gay male aging as a horrific and repulsive process that ought to be devalued, if not fully avoided. Contemporary media sets forth an ideological agenda of temporality, promoting limited conceptions of "aging," "future," and "time" that seek to punish and foreclose queer articulations of what "aging," "future," and "time" *might* potentially mean. As with most short answers, however, complexity is lost in the interest of brevity.

Perhaps it is best to stay with Dumbledore as an example, taking note of how this older and respected character's "gayness" shifts the ways Dumbledore is read and negotiated. What are the cultural meanings we assign to the older gay male which emerge in the wake of Dumbledore's "outing?" As demonstrated in the *SNL* skit, "deleted scenes" needed to be presented to situate Albus within frameworks of intelligibility for mainstream recognition of his "gayness." Albus's friendship with Minerva is recoded in the familiar narrative of the dismissive gay male and his lovelorn and codependent fag hag. Dumbledore suddenly introduces his body as a topic of discussion, marking it as no longer attractive or desirable, loathing his "stomach poochie." His sexuality is heightened, excited by the "juicy little pork chop," and his absence of a sexual partner becomes his primary narrative, scripted with misery, desperation, and the despair of dying alone. His personal chamber, which often has been associated with mystery and power, is recoded as a den of loneliness and failure. Furthermore, his age becomes the butt of the joke by relocating Albus in a gay bar in the final segment. In short, for *SNL* to "clearly show" Dumbledore as "gay," within the limited narratives and understandings available for what "gay" means, required a complete rewriting of Albus's relationship to time, future, and his own body.

Embedded within the *SNL* parody is a body of meanings designated specifically for the aging gay male body, marking the process of "aging" as culturally contingent and constructed. In this study, the concept of "aging" is approached as a collection of meanings assigned to bodies as they exist for longer periods of time within specific cultural contexts. Whereas the biological changes facing a human body as it accumulates age is a topic of research best suited for medical science, the cultural construction of age and meanings attached to aging processes are a discursive and a communicative phenomena, marking a separate area of inquiry. For example, medical science explores the ways bodies change and alter as they grow older from the perspective of biological processes. However, the signification of older bodies, definitions of what constitutes "old" or "older," cultural scripts of "successful aging," cultural expectations for "acting your age," values places on different ages, narratives for mapping and constructing future, and the ways sexual desire and attractiveness are constructed around discussions of age present socio-cultural points of inquiry.

For several decades, scholars in the fields of gay studies and gerontology have identified and worked to compensate for the absence in literature surrounding gay and lesbian aging processes (Barker; Berger, *Gay*; Cruz; De Vries and Blando; Ellis; Kimmel; Lee). This research asserts that the life stages and models of aging for homosexual populations work differently from traditional heterosexual models (Gorman and Nelson 88; Herdt and De Vries xviii; Kertzner, Meyer, and Dolezal 100; Kimmel 267; Kooden and Flowers; Rawls 118), marking gay and lesbian aging as a distinct area of study. Furthermore, this research challenges the logic of conflating discussions of gay male aging and lesbian aging (Gabbay and Wahler 3; Goltz, "Investigating"), as the construction of age and aging—as well as the values assigned to these concepts—are radically varied between gay male and lesbian cultures.

As this project examines how gay male aging and future are constructed in contemporary popular culture, while bringing together disparate bodies of literature, several caveats must be forefronted. Although queer theoretical work is central to this project, grouping gays and lesbians under the anti-essentialist "queer umbrella" needs to be approached with some caution. To lump together the representation of gay and lesbian aging in popular culture runs the risk of conflating complex cultural scripts and different systems of meanings, rather than parsing out the nuances of how the intersections of patriarchy, masculinity, whiteness, classism, and ageism function uniquely in gay and/or lesbian constructions. In serving a larger project of theorizing tensions between heteronormative and queer temporal engagements in popular discourse, this book opens up a much larger discussion. The critical examination of gay and lesbian aging requires a parallel project that examines how lesbian constructions are uniquely coded and shaped within discourses of age, future, meaningfulness, and heteronormativity. An additional project might also explore how aging and future for heterosexual females are articulated in popular culture and how these representations work alongside and against gay and lesbian constructions, as research suggests issues of "accelerated aging" and the emphasis on youthfulness are greater for heterosexual women than in lesbian communities (Gabbay and Wahler 6).

Forging a dialogue between gay and lesbian aging literature, queer theories, and media criticism brings forth some inescapable tensions, as the queer impulse to challenge essential identities runs counter to much of the gay aging research that relies upon gay identity and gay male culture as empirical categories of study. Whereas marking categories of "the gay male" or "gay male culture" is admittedly problematic, as it falsely implies a homogenous cultural group—while erasing additional axes of intersecting identities such as class, race, and gender—these tensions and erasures will be addressed in the theoretical work of this project. Critical studies of gay and lesbian aging have much ground to cover; however, this study focuses specifically on the representation of gay male aging, with the objective of offering a point of entry into a much larger discussion that continues to critique and complicate the foundations from which it works.

Turning to research of gay male culture, studies indicate an extreme value and privilege placed upon youth and youthfulness (Barker 48; Cohler 212; De Vries and Blando 20; Goltz, "Investigating"; Kooden and Flowers 28). The youth-centeredness or "youthism" (Berger, *Gay* 190) of gay male culture has been tied to numerous obstacles that problematize gay male aging, most notably an intense fear of aging (Kooden and Flowers 16; Berger, *Gay* 14), arrested development (Rawls 118), feelings of invisibility for aging gay men within gay communities (Barker 31; Ellis 43; Gorman and Nelson 79; Kertzner, Meyer, and Dolezal 99), accelerated use of drugs and alcohol (Gorman and Nelson 84), and feelings and fear of isolation and abandonment in older gay populations (Cohler 231; Hostetler 158). These complications are further heightened through issues of internalized homophobia (Gorman and Nelson 79), HIV survivor guilt (Gorman and Nelson 83), the trauma of loss from the AIDS pandemic (80), and internalized ageism (Kooden and Flowers 17).

A prevalent cultural myth in mainstream and gay cultural discourses paints the image of the "older" gay male as an isolated, miserable, and bitter sexual pervert (Berger, *Gay*; Berger, "Realities" 61; Cruz 27; Ellis 1; Goltz, "Investigating"). Varying manifestations of this theme can be seen in many popular films, such as *Death in Venice*, *Gods & Monsters*, and *Love and Death on Long Island*—as well as the recent *SNL* Dumbledore skit—where cultural ageism and homophobia intersect to present intergenerational relationships as inappropriate and the elder gay characters as "love starved and eager to recapture lost youth" (Yoakam 66). De Vries and Blando identify a unique stigma to gay male aging, reporting that older heterosexual men are commonly stereotyped as asexual, whereas older gay men are highly sexualized as "perverts and predators" (7; Kelly).[4] The depressed and isolated mythologies attached to older gay men, while ever-present in cultural discourses, have continually proven to be inaccurate reflections of the majority of older gay populations.

Multiple studies report that older gay men actually display less signs of depression than aging heterosexuals and are equally equipped to handle the challenges of aging (Berger, *Gay* 15; Cruz 16; Ellis 4; Hostetler 155; Rawls 120). Although research continually indicates the cultural myth of the miserable lonely gay man is not accurate (Berger, "Realities"; Berger and Kelly 62; Brown et al.; Dorfman et al.), the myth continues to circulate within mainstream cultural productions (Yoakam) and within gay subcultures (Goltz, "Laughing"; Hostetler 143). Berger argues that this cultural myth serves a "social control function" (*Gay* 15), inciting fear in "younger" gay men to sway them from the gloomy future that is guaranteed by living a gay life. The tragic sight of an older gay man in the youth-centered gay bar "provides a cautionary tale about developmental failure" to many younger gay men (Hostetler 160), as well as the broader heteronormative culture, marking gay aging as a process devoid of happiness or fulfillment.

SNL's rewriting of Dumbledore demonstrates this cautionary tale, reframing Albus as a tragic figure to the gay aging cycle. Now marked as "gay," aging becomes a ritual of punishment and exclusion, presenting the professor as penalized by time, as well as a fool to be mocked and belittled. The "gay" Dumbledore is denied self-confidence, his body is marked as unattractive, and his integrity is diminished, no longer resembling the once-respected headmaster. This tragic demonizing of Dumbledore demonstrates how heteronormative aging and gay aging are not completely discrete and autonomous processes, as they function in tragic relationship with one another. The mocking and punishment of Dumbledore, now a gay man, serves to reify the correctness and naturalness of heterosexuality—the assumed sexual categorization placed upon Dumbledore until he was explicitly labeled otherwise. As Berger suggests, mythologies of gay aging serve as a cautionary tale (*Gay* 15), a tragic framing of the aging process, which are used to rhetorically support and uphold heterosexuality. Gay aging mythologies operate as heteronormative endorsement.

The discursive construction of gay male aging is shaped in tragic relation to heteronormative narratives of "correct" and "natural" development, yet the terminology associated with aging processes fails to transfer without contestation. Terms such as "old," "older," "young," "youth," and "adult" mark negotiated, fluid, and culturally specific meanings. The term "old" is always relative, but "traditionally, gerontology and social science have taken age 65 as the chronological marker of being 'old'" (Barker 31). However, research within gay male culture locates the deployment of the terms "old" and "older" to describe gay men as early as thirty-five to forty years of age (Bergling; Hostetler 161; Kertzner, Meyer, and Dolezal 100).[5] The elevated predominance of youth-centrism and the cultural conceptions of what marks "old" identifies a distinct system of values and meanings that circulate around aging within gay male communities. It would be counterproductive and dangerous to assume the notion of "youth" or "old" function in predictable ways across cultural discussions, and so these terms must remain suspect and open to interrogation and contestation.

The crossing over from a "young" to an "older" gay male, and thus being marginalized from the youth-centered culture, is a transition that is closely observed, actively avoided, and even dreaded. Michael Weinstein, president of the AIDS Healthcare Foundation, stated, "I've heard a lot of young gay men say, 'You know, I would rather die of AIDS than grow old'" (Kooden and Flowers 16). Taken seriously, this statement spotlights a serious concern for gay health workers but also begs media critics to question how gay aging is constructed and perpetuated in popular culture. This narrative of the gay male approaching the future with fear and a sense of dread works to define the concept of "future" as a site of punishment that ought to be avoided and rejected rather than privileged and embraced. How has the gay male become positioned in negative relation to the unknown and yet-to-be determined future, cut off from narratives of possibility, optimism, or hope?

In approaching the dominant media construction of gay male youth-centered culture, it is important to examine the equation established between "youth" and beauty (Cohler 213). Kooden and Flowers deploy an economic metaphor, stating that "the [gay male] body is a form of currency in the free market of desire" (28). The extreme emphasis placed upon physical beauty as a cultural value instantly marks aging as undesirable and equated with loss. This sense of loss and dread of aging is further perpetuated by the absence of older gay representation within the culture and a lack of visible role models (Gorman and Nelson 88), resulting in the mutual loss of generativity (87). Erikson's concept of generativity in the development of human psychology describes the "contributions one makes to the generation that follows, and is especially salient in middle and later life" (Gorman and Nelson 87). Generativity marks a process of meaning construction for aging populations, most commonly discussed through intergenerational dialogue afforded through heteronormative reproductive systems. In heteronormative systems of marriage and procreation, generativity is assumed and constructed as "natural," as the social script creates the expectation of intergenerational relationships between child, parent, and grandparent. Whereas this absence has been used to discuss the obstacles that face some "older" gay men and lesbians (87), the reciprocal benefits of generativity are lost on gay youth, limiting their exposure to older representations of gay male aging (Berger, *Gay* 191; Berger, "Realities" 60) and punctuating their understanding of gay "future" with a question mark. The youth-centered values of many gay male communities, the cultural myths of gay aging misery, and the lack of counter-representations of "older" gay men have a negative impact on both "older" and "younger" gay males, assisting the perpetuation of negative aging myths, the equation of aging with loss, and a fear of the future.[6]

Several theories can be applied to shed light on this trend of age fear and negative future relation. Romàn argues that HIV-negative status in the gay community is viewed as temporal, suggesting a belief of the inevitability of seroconversion, "not *if* but *when*" (164). Romàn's rationale for this argument operates through the equation perpetuated in the early days of HIV where gay media representation was consistently tied to contracting the virus (Hart). Romàn argues that popular media constructions of HIV-negativity are depressing, providing limited discourses, and offer "little incentive to imagine a life worth living," whereas the culture of positivity in urban centers has become urban gay culture (166). The cultural emphasis on HIV/AIDS and the representations that equated gay men with HIV/AIDS for over a decade (Hart 600) have worked to create a perceived cultural norm that gay men die young. The expectation of dying at a younger age is further problematized by the cultural myth of the single, miserable, and bitter old queen, marking longevity as undesirable. These discourses of future and aging present a complementary self-sealing fate where one is not only taught to expect a shortened life, but is also told that the actual attainment of a longer life is hardly worth aspiring to. It echoes the cliché, "Live fast, die young, and make a beautiful corpse."

Contemporary discussions in queer theory have approached themes of sexuality and aging through a different theoretical vocabulary, yet these discussions are relevant to social scientific research on gay male aging. Echoing, yet rearticulating, the impact of HIV/AIDS on gay male engagements with temporality, Halberstam marks the outbreak of HIV/AIDS as an impetus for a queered understanding of time. "Queer time, even as it emerges from the AIDS crisis, is not only about compression and annihilation; it is also about the potentiality of a life unscripted by the conventions of family, inheritance, and child rearing" (*Queer* 2). Mirroring Romàn, yet considering the emergence of queer time as a potential for resistance, Halberstam calls into question the dangers and limitations of heteronormative temporal modes for how they confine and discipline queers into compliance. Following in a trajectory of queer theory—which seeks to explore the margins of discourse and intelligibility to locate potential queer modes of expression, resistance, and futurity beyond the foreclosures of heteronormative systems—Halberstam sets forth an exploratory project of theorizing queer time. Critiquing the adult/youth binary formation, culturally constructed notions of maturation, and the "conventional emphasis on longevity and futurity" (2), Halberstam theorizes queer time as stretching out dominant understandings of adolescence to rethink subcultural involvement as a lifelong commitment, rather than a "life stage" (174).

The theorizing of queer time and queer temporality marks an important and growing body of literature in contemporary queer theory, marking a contentious, complex, and radical rethinking about how time and future are articulated within heteronormative logics. Boellstorff problematizes Halberstam's queering of time through the stretching of adolescence, suggesting her notion of queer time remains faithful to a linear and heteronormative temporal engagement, or "straight time." Edelman argues that the future has been highjacked in the name of the Child, calling for a queer negativity that rejects investing in the future for all its trappings. Muñoz complicates Edelman's polemic, calling out the racial and classed undercurrents of Edelman's theorizing, refusing to either "hand over futurity to normative white reproductive futurity" ("Cruising" 365) or abandon hope and a "forward-dawning futurity" (357).

Although the terms "gay"[7] and "queer"[8] mark radically distinct lines of thought and engagements with identity, queer theoretical discussions of temporality and research on gay male aging inform each other in useful and productive ways. Boellstroff's conception of "straight time" defines the heteronormative script of aging and future, as well as the tragic cautionary tale of gay male aging discussed by Berger (as articulated through Dumbledore). Gay male aging myths rhetorically construct an evil that upholds and sustains heteronormativity's illusionary perfection, connecting gay male aging mythologies and gay cultural youthism as part and parcel of a straight temporal regime. In addition, the youth/adult binary and heteronormative script of maturation criticized by Halberstam are the very technologies that drive the negative connotations of aging within gay male culture. Mirroring gay aging researchers' interrogation of the culturally constructed nature of concepts such as "old" or "young," Halberstam locates these terms as faithful markers of a heteronormative temporality. Edelman's theorizing of reproductive futurism and the sacred Child provide the foundation for the ways future is constructed in popular discourse, to the tragic punishment and exclusion of queers. However, Muñoz refuses to abandon hope and futurity, calling for a more nuanced investigation of the raced, classed, gendered, and embodied dimensions of future. This book engages and extends these theoretical discourses through the analysis of popular culture, specifically mainstream representations and constructions of gay male temporalities and queer potentialities.

The broad theoretical discussions in this study cannot and should not be divorced from the lived experiences of queer lives, as gay cultural youthism, gay aging mythologies, and the temporal regime of straight time impact all sexual subjects moment by moment. For example, the material effects of youthism, aging mythologies, and straight time offer a unique perspective on the ongoing problem of gay "youth"[9] self-destructive behaviors. As the existence of self-destructive behaviors in gay "youth" has been documented for years (MacDonald and Cooper; Morrison and L'Heureux; Nicholas and Howard; Remafedi, *Death*; Remafedi, "Sexual"), indicating accelerated drug and alcohol abuse, depression, suicide, and suicidal ideation, it is logical to begin examining what the future and aging *means* to "younger" gays. As self-destructive behaviors indicate a devaluation of health, longevity, and future, there seems a logical concern to interrogate the very meanings that are constructed around gay future, gay aging, and gay longevity, regardless of arbitrary and heteronormative designations of "young," "adolescent," and "old." What role does the media have in shaping, restricting, or disciplining gay futures, as well as potentially queer futures? Who are these images and representations serving and validating, and what are they struggling to contain and prevent? This book project unites several bodies of literature to engage the questions it poses, bringing queer theory, queer media criticism, Kenneth Burke, and gay aging studies into the analysis of gay aging in mainstream popular culture.

The literature on gay cultural youthism, gay aging mythologies, straight temporality, and gay self-destruction locate a series of vital questions surrounding the construction of time, aging, and future in gay male communities, yet I—as researcher—have a personal history and rationale for my own investment in these questions. I am a thirty-five-year-old white, Jewish male who has self-identified as both gay and queer for over seventeen years. The topic of study, meanings of gay aging and gay future, is a personal one, stemming from many years of watching myself and others struggle with anxiety and ambivalence about our futures, our health, and any aspiration of longevity. Narratives have followed us around our whole lives. Narratives we pass back and forth to one another, but rarely interrogate. "It's a lonely life," "It's not the life I wanted for you," "It's a harder life," and dozens of other scripts that we internalize and perpetuate have very material effects. I have "known" for years that I needed to find a partner early, because I "knew" that once I was old, I would be deemed useless, undesirable, and repulsive. In my twenties, I spent countless nights in drug-induced discussions about the fear and dread of facing the years to come, as my gay friends and I fought to hold onto the last moments of the "prime" of our gay lives. The future for us was easy to see. There is a bar stool, there is a drink in front of us, and we will wait out the rest of our days. I come to this study with this history, these narratives, and the loss of loved ones who did not see any reason to take care of themselves, as the future was not something to look forward to, but a lingering sense of dread to be avoided. My objective is to interrogate the limitations of certain representations of future, but also, I hope to locate places of resistance and alternative strategies that assist gay men in rethinking and reimagining future in fulfilling and potentially exciting ways.

CULTURAL STUDIES AND IDEOLOGICAL CRITIQUE

> The visible presence of healthy, non-stereotypic lesbians and gay men does pose a serious threat: it undermines the unquestioned normalcy of the status quo. (Gross, *Minorities* 92)

Cultural studies theorists have long argued that media representation is always political, marking a major site for the production of cultural knowledges (Hall; Kellner). Media "contribute to educating us how to behave and what to think, feel, believe, fear, and desire—and what not to" (Kellner 9), and thus the media must remain subject to ongoing interrogation and continual skepticism to further uncover how mediated texts function (McKerrow). Cultural theorists aim to uncover the ways media serve vested interests, how media promote and maintain dominant ideological agendas, and how media encode relations of power and domination (Kellner 12).

Media take an active role in shaping and defining cultural groups and identity, yet gay male culture engages in a unique relationship with mainstream mediated representation. Warner argues that gay culture, more than any other minority group, is an identity shaped and constructed through consumerism ("Introduction"). Fejes argues that the gay community is defined by its niche marketing buying power, where "pulling out the American Express Card has replaced the raised fist" (213). Gay enculturation and the construction of gay values and identities are more reliant on the media than any other minority culture, as gay culture is not primarily passed down from parents and traditional family. Gay culture is driven by media consumption and is reliant on the media for much of its definition (Sender). Similar to de Lauretis's discussion of gender (3), sexuality is a representation, and that representation is the technology of its construction (Foucault). Regardless of essentialist debates, for the young boy growing up in a world where he does not know any "out" gay men, gay representation on television or in film constructs and reconstructs what "gay" means. For the mother or father whose child comes "out," and their only point of reference is *Will & Grace*, Jack and Will become representative. As many turn to popular culture, specifically television and film, to hear stories, to experience other's lives, and to see our lives reflected back to us, these representations shape discourse and identities.

Contemporary queer media criticism has theorized several problems with contemporary gay male representation, specifically the reification of misogyny (Shugart), normativity (Battles and Hilton-Morrow; Dow; Yoakam), and whiteness (Dow; Shugart), as well as the problematic deification of gay men suitable for straight consumption (Brookey and Westerfelhaus). Fejes marks a shift in representation, suggesting that "rather than being portrayed as pathetic, mentally ill sex perverts and child molesters who are threats to religion, home, family, and the state, they [gay men] are now portrayed as *young*, healthy, fun to be with, and having a lot of disposable income" (217, emphasis added). A key insight in Fejes's discussion is the marking of "young" as one of the desirable traits currently associated with gay men in contemporary media. The current study problematizes the "pathetic, mentally ill sex pervert" stigma as a thing of the past and argues that it remains a thing of the *future*, a stereotype reserved for "older" gay men.

What does it mean for "older" gay men that the more "positive" portrayals of gay men are focused on youth? What does it mean to define progress as youthful, when youth is temporal, fleeting, and in a perpetual state of loss? The mediated construction of gay aging, meanings of gay future, and their relationships to heteronormative temporality mark important areas of consideration in the mediated construction of the gay male, but have yet to receive close attention. This absence within the literature of queer media criticism marks a highly problematic silencing of one of the key components to understanding gay representation, as well as a major discussion in the critical examination of gay identity formation in gay aging studies. Paralleling the question of "what does an 'older' gay man looks like" would be "what does the future *mean* in gay male representation?" How is the future constructed, shaped, or anticipated? Cultural discourses of aging shape, dictate, and determine the meanings that circulate around future, and thus the discourses of aging and future are inescapably tied to one another. This project is a queer interrogation of the dominant ideological meanings attached to contemporary understandings of "time," "aging," and "future" through the rhetorical study of gay male representation within popular media.

In selecting the scope of texts for analysis, the objective is to study the dominant ideological constructions of gay male aging and future that circulate in mainstream U.S. culture. The projects aims to generate greater understanding of what meanings are circulating, how these meanings function, and what limitations or constraints these representations place on the potential ways gay and or queer futures might be envisioned. Given these concerns, the scope of the study needs to be primarily dictated by the dominant circulation of meanings (Sloop, "Disciplining" 169), looking at texts that are moving, being seen, most likely influencing mainstream audiences, and are readily available and widely distributed for mass consumption. This approach allows the access to dominant constructions of gay aging, but also these "mainstream discourses illustrate the rhetorically material ways that those who do challenge dominant ideology are ideologically disciplined" (Sloop, "Disciplining" 169). Observing how queer resistance is disciplined in popular media brings this project in line with the ongoing work of queer world-making—the seeking out and pointing to the presence of alternative meanings of aging and future—and interrogating how queer resistance is negotiated within the larger narrative.

This project seeks to explore current meanings of gay aging and future circulating in contemporary discourse, focusing on texts released from January 1, 2000 to December 31, 2007. Using the search terms "gay," "homosexual," and "queer" through IMDB-Pro Web service, a film industry database that tracks box office, video/ DVD sales, and rental information, every film from this search that grossed more than $500K in U.S. box office was included in the study. In addition, the weekly top-fifty rental charts for the U.S. from 2000 to 2007 were reviewed to make sure the box office reports did not exclude films that were highly successful on DVD but were not theatrically released. These criteria resulted in sixty-one feature films, which comprise the primary film texts to be studied. In addition to the sixty-one films compiled from IMDb-Pro, additional films were added for reasons of theme or circulation. For example, the film *Poseidon* was a summer Hollywood blockbuster that had a leading gay character that did not come up under the key term "gay" on IMDb-Pro. As a major Hollywood film with broad circulation, it was included in the analysis. In addition, over a dozen gay independent productions, such as *Hellbent*, *Shock to the System*, and *An Empty Bed*, are included in the study, as they directly engage with the themes of aging, future, and narratives attached to gay male identities.

The television programs included in the study were produced during or after January 2000 and need to have been released on VHS or DVD at the time of the study. The requirement of VHS or DVD release is for practical purposes of analysis as well as marking the continued circulation of these texts beyond their original broadcast. The following four criteria were set up to gather the greatest possible range of televised representation, and if any series satisfies any one of the four criteria, it was also included in the viewing list. First, the study includes all TV shows that have appeared on the weekly top-50 rental report from 2000 to 2007, which offer a regular gay character as part of the ongoing storyline, such as *Sex in the City* and *Entourage*. Second, the viewing list includes all TV shows in the top 20 Nielsen rankings for more than three consecutive weeks with a regular gay character, such as *Desperate Housewives* and *Brothers & Sisters*. Third, the viewing list includes all TV shows in wide circulation that depict an explicitly self-identified gay character, such as *Will & Grace* and *Dawson's Creek*. Fourth, the viewing sample includes any TV series that has a *leading* character that regularly identifies as gay, such as *Dante's Cove*, *Queer as Folk*, *Noah's Arc*, and *Rick and Steve: The Happiest Gay Couple in the World*.

Over a hundred films and twenty-five television series were analyzed for this book, ranging from sitcoms, primetime police dramas, family drama, animated parody, screwball comedy, romantic comedy, historical drama, and horror, to soap opera, reality television, and biography. Rejecting the hierarchal premise that seeks to mark rigid distinctions between high and low culture—the educated and the masses—this project is based in a cultural studies tradition, where culture is located in the ordinary (Williams). Approaching popular culture as synchronic—a site that is always "moving between resistance and incorporation at any given historical moment" (Storey 11)—the texts in this project are engaged as a location of ideological struggle and negotiated meanings. Identifying and theorizing emergent narrative themes across a broad selection of texts, television shows like *South Park* and *Degrassi: The Next Generation* are analyzed alongside more critically lauded cultural works such as *Six Feet Under* and *Quinceañera*. By placing these cultural texts into discussion with one another, this study is clearly not designed to discuss or debate the aesthetic merit of these texts,[10] but rather embraces an orientation of ideological criticism that seeks to interrogate the vested interests and politicized meanings actively working within and through the texts (Wander).

QUEER MEDIA: TRAGEDY, HOMONORMATIVITY, AND ELSEWHERE

> Mysterious thing, time. Powerful, but when muddled with, dangerous. (Dumbledore, *Harry Potter and the Prisoner of Azkaban*)

The invisibility of gay futures marks a new form of "symbolic annihilation" (Gross, *What* 143) as tamed and assimilated images of gays and lesbians offer limited potential to younger gays and lesbians who often grow up with "little or no help in understanding or defining themselves as gay or lesbian" (Fejes and Petrich 396), not to mention potentially queer. Chapter 2 presents an overview of the history of gay media criticism and the movement into contemporary queer media criticism. Whereas early gay media criticism was committed to reclaiming subtext and theorizing resistant audiencing strategies, the proliferation of gay representations since the late eighties into the new millennium shifts the attention of critics to the politics of popular gay representations and how they function. Queer media criticism is faced with new obstacles in the wake of "positive" or "progressive" representations, as these representations enlist a series of rhetorical strategies to garner normative identification and assimilation (Brookey).

Chapter 2 introduces the writings of Kenneth Burke, specifically his concepts of orientation, tragedy, comedy, perspective by incongruity, and the bridging device. Burke is a rhetorical and social critic whose work in literary criticism, symbolic systems, narrative critique, and the study of motives offers a theoretical framework that challenges temporal narratives of progress and compliments and extends queer critique (Goltz, "Perspectives"). Enlisting a Burkean framework of tragic and comic systems, Chapter 2 situates gay and queer media criticism within a Burkean system, laying out the theoretical foundation for the study that seeks to problematize a linear trajectory of "progress" within mainstream gay representation. Adopting a Burkean model of sacrifice and redemption, the progress narrative of gay Hollywood is redrawn within a narrative of circular tragedy, symbolic merger, and comic corrective.

Chapter 3 argues that the cultural representation of the gay male enacts a tragic ritual of torture and sacrifice, repeatedly scripting cautionary narratives of horror and punishment for those who deviate from socially sanctioned codes of normative sexual desire. Although this model of gay male vilification and sacrifice has been present in the cultural production for decades, the cultural construction of gay male aging processes offers up the gay male as a tragic victim to time and future. Mirroring and reinforcing the youthist worship located within gay male communities, gay male characters in contemporary film and television are cast as inevitable victims of/in time. Aging is crafted as a ritual of punishment, where worshipped and admired gay youth are haunted by the ticking of the clock, forever aware that aging and future are to be actively avoided. In turn, older gay male representations repeat the story of Albus Dumbledore, where the meanings of gay aging are confined to sexual predation, isolation, depression, and social mockery. The gay male, both young and old, are constructed as the victims of time and future, yet these tragic rituals of gay aging are determined by the exclusionary logics of heteronormative temporalities—victims to a limited conception of "straight time" (Boellstorff). The governing temporal logic in mainstream popular culture is tied to heteronormative constructions of time, serving to reify the correctness of straight temporal maps to future, offering up gay males as tragic sacrifices to straight time's illusionary perfection.

Situated within a false tragic binary of assimilation or punishment, Chapter 4 interrogates the rhetorical processes for the mainstreaming of white and middle-class gay males into dominant frames of identification with future. As heteronormative tragedy constructs the future through limited signifiers of child and spouse—while casting those outside these systems as aliens to the future—there is a trend in contemporary media to offer up a homonormative (Duggan) gay male who pledges deep allegiance to the corrupt and exclusionary systems of domination that drive a complex intersection of social oppressions. Exemplified in popular characters, such as *Will and Grace*'s Will Truman and *Six Feet Under*'s David Fisher, Chapter 4 examines how white, middle-class, and masculinist systems of identification become sites of symbolic merger, where the "normal" gay male pleads their case of assimilation before the heteronormative court of mainstream audiences. Herein, a future is accessed through allegiance to straight temporal frameworks, reifying and sustaining heteronormativity's governance over meanings of age, future, and time.

The final chapter is presented on an exploratory register, enlisting the Burkean concept of perspective by incongruity to locate and theorize queer temporal ruptures within the cultural production. Rejecting straight time's construction of gay male aging as a tragic ritual, as well the homonormative mandate that limits the future to the process of assimilation, this chapter looks to de Lauretis's "space off" at the margins of mainstream represented space to theorize nonnormative engagements with time, aging, and future. Situating this discussion in such texts as HBO's *The Wire*, Todd Haynes' *Far From Heaven*, and the Cole Porter biopic *De-Lovely*, gestures to queer articulations of future are located through expanded notions of community, generativity, family, relationships, aging, and futurity.

Queer Temporalities in Gay Male Representation offers a foundation for critical and queer studies in gay and lesbian aging. This project places multiple important and emerging areas of inquiry into discussion with one another, fostering an interdisciplinary convergence of previous research as its point of departure. This volume offers contributions to queer theory and queer media criticism by bridging discussions of gay male aging and youthism with contemporary queer theorizing of time and futurity. As the topics of ageism and youthism have yet to be given concentrated attention in the area of queer media criticism, the project places the culturally constructed process of aging alongside identity discourses of race, gender, sexuality, and class for the purposes of demystifying the oppressive function of heteronormative temporality. Deeply indebted to the work of gay aging scholars, queer media critics, rhetorical criticism, the writings of Kenneth Burke, and queer theorists of temporality, this discussion forefronts the interworkings of age, heteronormativity (as a raced, classed, and gendered institution), and mediated representation in the cultural production of future, meaningfulness, and sexual citizenship. Beyond the theoretical contribution, this study forefronts the objective of cultural pedagogy to foster a greater critical consciousness of how age, future, time—in relation to sexuality—are constructed through popular media in oppressive and violent configurations. Time and future, as articulated through a heteronormative temporal map of mainstream representation, work to punish queer sexualities, actively diminishing and foreclosing queer imaginaries of futurity. Interpellated into a mediated flood of cultural representations, which position queers in opposition to the very concept of future (Edelman), it is not surprising that age, health, and longevity are found to be devalued in the study of gay male cultures. The cultural screen repeatedly narrates the gay male in limited and tragic frames, claiming the future as something for the gay male to fear and actively avoid.

Through interrogating the rhetorical function of these representations—the tragedies they enact, the violences they promote, and the foreclosures they perform—this book hopes to challenge the limited ways gay lives are narrated through "the harder path" and "the miserable life." It casts a utopian gesture to rethinking about time in queered and creative ways—following in the tradition of Halberstam, Boellstorff, and Muñoz—actively seeking out queer articulations of future that work against violent systems of racial, sexual, gender, and class-driven oppression. On the most grounded and pragmatic of levels, it asks the reader to think twice before regurgitating a litany of cultural narratives that inflict violence, often without intention. Whether to friend, son, daughter, colleague, sibling, stranger, or self, there is an oppressive and disciplinary heteronormative subtext in the most innocent of questions and statements:

It's just that, this wasn't the life I wanted for you.
I'm just worried about you. It's a hard life you have ahead of you now.
I can't imagine my life without children.
I just don't want you to end up alone.
Where do you see yourself in twenty years?

How old are you?
Aren't you a little old to be. . .?
When are you going to grow up and start thinking about the future?

Whereas these statements and questions may appear innocuous or seemingly harmless to some—a response that marks an uninterrogated access to privilege—to many queers, these statements and questions are the source of tremendous anxiety, frustration, resentment, or even anger. Embedded in each of these utterances is the assumed compliance and commitment to a temporal regime that seeks to assign meaning to age, future, aging, and sexuality in predetermined, tragic, and oppressive ways. Conceived through heteronormative systems, time becomes a tool of great violence. Queer poet and novelist Dennis Cooper articulates the violent, oppressive, and mundane construction of time, arguing that time serves an exclusionary social and political function while enacting "a blasphemy on forever" ("Time"). How might we think of time otherwise? How might we locate the future elsewhere, a future that has yet to be written or remembered?

2 The Heteronormative Tragedy
Kenneth Burke and Queer Media Criticism

> A cavern opened in my mind, black, full of rumor, suggestion, of half-heard, half-forgotten stories, full of dirty words. I thought I saw my future in that cavern. I was afraid. (Baldwin, *Giovanni's Room* 9)

Popular culture has repeatedly scripted the "coming out" scene. Two hands of shame are lowered to reveal a queer face, wiping one stagnant tear, before peering deep into the camera. Music drips into the background, building with intensity. Fear is swallowed in this moment, as the words begin to form, first with conflict and apology, but with a flourishing momentum, matched only by the soundtrack. "I'm gay." A pause, as the camera lingers on the eyes of a queer, who looks to us, the film and television audience, awaiting our response. Their eyes communicate an uncertain fate. Regardless of how the mother, brother, father, or friend on screen responds to our queer hero's disclosure—whether acceptance or rejection—this is a moment of triumph for the queer viewer. Our hero has looked shame in the eyes and declared, "I will not be afraid of who I am, nor will I apologize! Now look me in the face, oh monster of my shame, and draw your sword!" The resolve of the queer hero's stare is matched by the triumphant music, pleading with us to embrace the hopeful and dangerous insanity that times have changed and the hours we face will weigh less heavily on our shoulders.

Anyone with the lived experience of "coming out of the closet" has a firm grasp on this narrative's limitations. Most importantly, the line between "in the closet" and "out of the closet" is not as stable or fixed as prime-time dramas would wish us to believe. Working within the closet metaphor requires an understanding that the closet is a daily and moment-by-moment negotiation, contingent upon context, social assumptions, and shared social cues. Short of the moments when we are holding hands with a same-sex partner, who happens to be wearing their favorite "I'm not gay, but my partner is" T-shirt, the positions of "in" and "out" are rarely marked with clarity. The ambiguity of lived experience does not lend itself to the heroic triumph of crafted coming-out tales, and like most Hollywood productions, ambiguities are often sacrificed for dramatic effect. Hollywood has recounted numerous coming-out tales, but also has a coming-out story of its own, one that is much more complicated than a singular declaration and a heroic musical score.

20 *Queer Temporalities in Gay Male Representation*

Once upon a time, gay Hollywood was confined to the claustrophobia of Giovanni's room. Its camera lens was smeared with white cleaning polish, blending gayness into a foggy backdrop, obscuring the lives and existence of homosexuality to outside viewers. Gayness was drenched in darkness—dark rooms, dark bars, dark alleys, and dark endings as the lingering shame required a sacrifice. The director calls for a lighting shift, as the stone walls that encased Giovanni's room are torn down, demanding visibility for all of the lives confined to blackness. Darkness turns to rainbows and sunshine, as the heroic story moves "out of the closets and into the streets." Closet doors become thresholds, bridges into pride, acceptance, and triumph. The coming-out story sprints into forward motion, progress, and liberation, charting a trajectory beginning sometime before *Suddenly Last Summer* and ending in the prime-time visibility of *Will & Grace*. The monumental footprints of that forward sprint from the closet seem to move in both directions now, abstracting each other, softening a well-worn, rhetorical path.

The historical space between *Boys in the Band* and *Brokeback Mountain*, for many, offers a narrative of progression, of moving forward, of coming out of the closet. Yet applying the closet metaphor to popular representation is riddled with problems, as the concept implies a unidirectional, collective, linear progression that obscures greater complexities (LaCroix and Westerfelhaus 12; Seidman 42). Like many of Hollywood's stories, the "coming out" of Hollywood constrains gay representations as much as it promotes them. Closet logics would suggest we have moved past shame and the claustrophobia of *Giovanni's Room*, marched through the streets of *Philadelphia*, and emerged (buff and tanned) on the dance platform of *Queer as Folk*. The closet places shame and victimage in the past, creating a distance between where we were and where we currently are, the relationship of past and present removed through linear time and physical space.

Upon reflection of his gay-themed film, a popular film director expressed his desire to "[t]ell the private love story of two people who happen to be men and whose relationship is systematically destroyed by their environment, which gives them no chance. In this way, perhaps, it just may be possible to change the public sentiment; it's only a hope. I don't know if it will happen" (qtd. in Russo 206). The rhetorical strategy enlisted in this statement of "merely a love story" between two people "who happen to be men" was commonplace in the discourse surrounding Ang Lee's 2006 film *Brokeback Mountain*. These words do not belong to Ang Lee, but were spoken by Wolfgang Peterson in reference to his 1977 film *The Consequence*. Thirty years later, the discussion is far more similar than linear progress narratives might account for. Yet the well-worn path is often mistaken for unexplored terrain. This argument is not implying that representation has not shifted or greatly increased in thirty years, as surely gay and lesbian representations are engaging mainstream audiences in unprecedented numbers. The question at hand is a matter of change, or progress, within these representations. What rhetorical strategies have dominant media enlisted for the mainstreaming of gay men into larger cultural discourses?

Whereas the history of gay representation is a well-worn path, this chapter seeks to defamiliarize the trajectory through a shift in perspective, queering the temporality of the story to challenge progressive views and highlight "the extent to which things have *not* changed" (Luciano 251). This chapter takes a step backwards, or perhaps sideways, providing the foundation for the project of investigating gay future construction by retracing the movement of gay media criticism through a Burkean framework. Placing the "coming out" narrative of representation to the side, linear logics of invisibility to visibility are reconsidered as rhetorical practices for garnering mainstream acceptance. In short, how have gays achieved the mainstream presence in popular media over the last few decades, what tactics were enlisted, and what sacrifices were made? This shift in focus bridges the work of queer media criticism and queer theory with the work of Kenneth Burke, approaching representation as a circular—rather than linear—narrative. The chapter first examines gay media representation as an active site of cultural discourse that shapes and defines gay culture, gay identity, and meanings attached to gayness. Second, the chapter provides an overview of the history of gay media criticism through the Burkean lens of tragedy. Problematizing the notion of linear progress in gay representation, this section asserts that much of the "progressive" representation further privileges heteronormative orientations. From doomed villains to the "normal gay" of the 1990s, mainstream images of gayness perpetuate a tragic cycle through punishment and exclusion. Finally, queer theory and Burke's comic corrective provide a theoretical and methodological basis for interrogating future construction in contemporary media, enlisting the tool of perspective by incongruity and the guiding ethics of fallibility and musement (Cornell).

REPRESENTATION MATTERS: TELEVISION MADE ~~ME~~ MY "GAY"

> Almost any film starts off with the burden of trying to redress an imbalance. (Russo 243)

In the classic memoir, *The Best Little Boy in the World*, "John Reid"[1] recounts his experiences in the 1970s, where the first two people he "comes out" to ask him an identical question. "Have [you] seen *The Boys in the Band*?" (101). Afterwards, John goes to see the film, from which he reflects how

> an unrealistic amount of emotion and unhappiness must be crowded into a two-hour gay birthday party. But at least I would have learned a little about gay life, become familiar with some gay lingo. I would have

seen a perfectly straight-looking, dignified pipe-smoking man who was gay, and that would have made an impression on me. (106)

Two key ideas are embedded in this passage. First, whether straight or gay, the media plays a significant role is constructing what audiences understand "gay" to mean. Second, whereas those meanings are constructed through popular media, if you put five people—gay, straight, or label-resistant—in front of a gay film, you will get a minimum of five different responses.

Illusions of transparent, "accurate," or unbiased representations in the media have long been criticized, both in and out of the academy (Brookey 40). Yet this does not discount the power of media in influencing dominant perception. Media are active in their work, not merely reporting or reflecting cultural experience and meanings, but shaping, molding, constructing, selecting, omitting, framing, characterizing, weaving, judging, and moralizing the culture, moment by moment. Put simply, media has effects, but when this statement is made in the classroom, students' hands will race to the air in protest, jumping right to the discourses of the day: Columbine, pornography, video games. "Video games don't make people shoot other people." Heads begin to nod with a growing momentum. "I watch pornography and I don't go out and sexually attack women!" The class will quietly chuckle at this self-disclosure. "In fact, my girlfriend watches it with me." "If somebody watches a Pearl Jam video and then goes and shoots up a school, that isn't Pearl Jam's fault! It's the parents' fault!" Already the class is resistant to considering the influence of media on their lives and their perceptions. Ironically, however, the very media that they argue has no effect has shaped their arguments and their framing of the discussion.

Suggesting that the media has effects is a very different assertion from the argument that the media has a predictable and systematic effect. This discussion requires the carving out of a space between the completely rational enlightenment subject and the subliminally programmed assassins of *The Manchurian Candidate*. The either/or binary fails to provide an effective frame to broach the discussion of media. We are neither independent thinkers, impervious to the media we consume, nor remote controlled robots who finish watching *Commando*, mechanically rise from our sofas, walk blankly to the closest gun store, only to unleash a sea of bullets on the local shopping mall.

Rather than simply arguing that media have effects to a resistant classroom, a second entry point to the discussion has proven more effective. "Imagine you or someone in your family, however you define that term, has a child whom you grow very attached to and care for very much. For the sake of discussion, imagine this child expresses to you that he or she is gay. What is your response?" Again, hands will shoot to the ceiling, but the responses will likely vary. "Homosexuality is a choice." "No it's not, and I'd love the child just the same." "I'd say the kid was just confused." "My best friend is gay and I adore him." "I'm a lesbian and I'd be thrilled to have a queer child." Whereas the responses range from homophobic scripts to the quoting of Cyndi Lauper's "True Colors," the class will likely have one common theme running through their reactions. Whether or not they know someone who identifies as gay and regardless of whether they make moral judgments about gay persons, the class believes that the road ahead of that child is a harder one. "It's a miserable life." "I wouldn't want a child to go through that." "I'd feel bad for the kid." "I'd want more for someone I love than *that*."

This script of the "harder" and "miserable" life presents an entry point into the discussion of the relevance of mediated representation of gay culture, identities, and future. Whereas representation may or may not directly shape specified behaviors, the media is an active agent in constructing cultural scripts and meanings of normative and nonnormative positions (Hall; hooks; De Lauretis; Gross "Out"; Wilson and Guitiérez; Kellner; Pieterse). In short, representation *always* has a political dimension. Cultural studies and media scholars have developed a dense and continually growing body of literature that seeks to interrogate and problematize the ways media representations normalize and privilege constructions of race, gender, heteronormativity, ability, middle-class economic positions, religion, and age.[2] These identifications are normalized in popular discourse, constructing the illusionary, homogenous, and invisible norms of society. In turn, nonnormative identities are marginalized through absence or through representations that work to reify and support the assumed superiority of normative values, beliefs, and identity formations.

Specifically in the area of sexuality, there are numerous accounts[3] that chronicle the emergence of gay and lesbian representation from a "closeted" 1950s all the way to the explosion of visibility of the 1990s (Gross, *Up*; Russo; Seidman; Tropiano; Walters). These critical projects faced a unique urgency, for unlike most minority groups, younger gays and lesbians commonly grow up in an environment with "little or no help in understanding or defining themselves as gay or lesbian" (Fejes and Petrich 396).[4] Gross referred to the invisibility of gays and lesbians in the mainstream media as a "form of symbolic annihilation" ("What" 143) that functions to contain and cultivate the images of groups "about which there is little firsthand opportunity of learning" (144). For this reason, the media has taken on a more prominent role in defining what it means to be gay or lesbian. Gross argues that "the visible presence of healthy, nonstereotypic lesbians and gay men does pose a serious threat: it undermines the unquestioned normalcy of the status quo" ("Minorities" 92).

At the beginning of many research projects on gay representation, the author begins with a personal narrative that situates the author as a consumer of media. Often openly queer, the researcher recounts a childhood self, watching film and television with a desperate hope of seeing themselves within a hetero-washed culture. Stories of thrill, confusion, and disappointment narrate how *Boys in the Band*, *Making Love*, *Dynasty*, and

Cruising became pivotal moments in history, where the queer researcher first identifies his or her queerness reflected back at them. Seeing a gay character on the television, in my home, being watched by my entire family—who may or may not have known that I was "like" that person—creates a nervous excitement. An intense shame accompanies the witnessing of a ruthless, perverted, miserable homosexual killer on the movie screen, while hearing the audience applauding as the heterosexual hero slaughters the "fag." Times have changed, somewhat. As gay representation increases, excited narratives about spotting the rarely depicted gay or lesbian in popular media will likely become less prominent, preserved only in books and relayed histories of "back when." Perhaps if John Reid were to have come out in 2007, leaping to the question, "Have you seen *Boys in the Band*" might seem slightly more ridiculous, if not extremely narrow, in this historical moment. However, would it only seem ridiculous because everyone is assumed to have seen *Will & Grace*, *Brokeback Mountain*, and *My Best Friend's Wedding*? Are we less reliant on mediated gay representation, or is there just more of it out there?

Differing from issues of race, sex, or economics, queer sexuality does not always signify its presence in visible or readily apparent ways. The closet, as the governing metaphor for sexual identity, presumes one is straight until "proven" or "declared" gay. Herein is where discourses of sexual identity get tangled into discussions of "choice," "flaunting," and "throwing it in our face," as heterosexuality is coded through the absence of visible transgressions of gendered performance. Flaunting heterosexuality (and it happens everywhere) blows past mainstream audiences like a moderate breeze. It is room temperature and taken for granted as "just there" until the sexual temperature shifts. As gays are a "self-identifying minority" (Gross, *Up* 16), behaviors or statements that mark the existence of alternative modes of sexual expression suddenly have the audience fanning themselves in sweaty frustration. Is that air conditioner on? Passing is a performance of gender and sexuality that plays along with the homogenous cultural assumption of heterosexuality, the metaphoric closet.

The closet is what makes the significance of gay and lesbian representation unique, as many people's first (knowing) encounter with an *actual* gay person is mediated (Gross, *Up* 11). For this reason, audiencing[5] *Soap*, *Brothers*, or *That Certain Summer* are potentially life-changing moments. Mediated gay men and lesbians take on a greater burden of role modeling, as gays "are rarely born into minority communities in which parents or siblings share our minority status" (Gross, *Up* 13). Media representations of race, gender, or economic positions, while highly influential, rarely provide the sole outlet for locating self-representation. This argument is not intended to downplay the significance of media representation for other minority populations, but suggests the closet constructs a unique relationship between gays and the media. For example, Billy Douglas, who was played by Ryan Phillippe on *One Life to Live*, came out in the summer of

1992. This singular representation elicited hundreds of fan letters, about half of which were from gay teenagers who were not thought of as the target audience of the program. Gross reprints a handful excerpts from these letters ("Gideon"), many expressing their gratitude for and identification with Billy's experiences. Whether closeted or dealing with homophobia in their own communities, these letters attest to the validating and inspirational effect of seeing gay lives reflected back to us, of not feeling alone. In short, gay representation works to construct "how members of a group see themselves and others like themselves" (Dyer, *Matter* 1).

Growing up "closeted" or "feeling different," without a model or representation to make sense of one's feelings, can produce a very different way of engaging with the world. Coupled with a sense of isolation, this engagement with the world can take the form of a quest, a double consciousness that things may not always be as they seem. The subtlest of statements, glances, or nonverbal behaviors become the crumbs to follow. Queer audiencing is prefaced on this quest, this complex set of codes and clues that hint to alternative sexualities and desires, which are easily passed over by those who are not actively looking. In keeping with the tradition of several gay and lesbian media critics, I will provide my own "as a child" personal narrative, my own personal quest.

John Hughes's *The Breakfast Club*, now viewed as a classic 1980s teen angst melodrama, marks a moment in my life where I realized I was watching a completely different film from those seated next to me. Andrew, portrayed by Emilio Estevez, played the stereotypical jock, star wrestler, and all around "popular" guy. In the second half of the film, Andrew confesses the reason he was in Saturday detention, as the film is centered around five high school students, forced to endure Saturday detention together. In this microcosm of high school life, the rebel, the school princess, the geek, the recluse, and the athletic Andrew suddenly begin confessing their greatest fears to one another. Andrew was punished for "taping Larry Lester's buns together." He slowly recounts the experience of watching Larry undress in the locker room, commenting on Larry's weak body and excessive body hair. Andrew, deeply shamed and confused by his actions, leapt to his feet, jumped on top of Larry, and starting "wailing on him." I knew what Andrew was confessing to the detention gang, as well as to the audience. It was upsetting, familiar, and painful to listen to, although admittedly erotic in an uncomfortable way. No one in my family seemed to think twice about this monologue. My eleven-year-old buddies thought that part was "stupid." Whereas I had seen a handful of gay male representations by that time in my life, this one was significant to me. Andrew was closer to my age, grew up in suburban Chicago, played sports, and carried a painful secret I understood. A secret that was safe with me, as he did not seem to tell anyone else. I have often wondered what happened to Andrew, and even attempted to pen my own sequel to the *Breakfast Club* at different times in my life. Even though the film alluded to his pairing up with Ally Sheedy in the end, where all of her wonderful dark eye make-up and baggy clothes were unjustly discarded for lip liner and a girly white blouse, it seems clear to me that she was as queer as Andrew. The film attempted to "save" her by disguising all of her wonderful dyke-ness, but I understood their relationship was about coalition, not romance. I wait anxiously for the day that sequel is made—fully aware that I will be disappointed when it comes.

Absence of visibility promotes these quests for identification in the media, creating shared secrets between mediated characters and gay and lesbian audiences. While not marked as specifically gay or lesbian, queer characters have always been there (Russo). For several decades queer images lingered beneath the surface of explicit mainstream representation, forcing queers to dig deeper into the mediated texts for sites of identification. This practice seeks to "uncover subtextual queer experience in mass mediated texts that do not appear to explicitly represent said experience" (Brookey and Westerfelhaus 142). In the absence of representation, the practice of reading "between the lines, and—if need be—to 'rewrite' scripts, characters, and cinematic moments" (Walters 132) provided the foundation for queer reading practices.[6] Marking a queer sensibility and resistant audience position, queer audiencing claimed a space for queer identification in the, assumed to be, lukewarm heterosexuality of mainstream media. In a violently homophobic society, the dark multiplex and the home television provided safer spaces for queers to embark on their quests to locate "others like me."

One area that is rarely broached in gay representation literature is how age factors into gay media visibility (Yoakam 65). As discussed in the introduction, aging models in gay culture differ from both heterosexual aging models, as well as how aging is constructed in lesbian communities. Whereas media are active in shaping and defining gay culture and gay identity, the media also takes on an active role in defining gay aging processes and meanings. Asking a self-identified heterosexual to describe what an older heterosexual looks like seems somewhat absurd. The absurdity is fueled by the consistent exposure we have to older men and women in our culture, who are mostly assumed to be heterosexual. Parents, grandparents, teachers, politicians, aging actors, and neighbors are, once again, straight unless that room temperature heteronormative breeze is violated. Several other factors complicate the visibility of older gay aging representations. For one, the notion of being "out and queer" has been commonly linked to a younger queer sensibility, whereas many older gays have lived their lives through passing as a means of survival and protection (Fox 48). Also, cross-generational relations and dialogue is greatly impeded in many gay communities (Cohler 221; Fox 55; Gorman and Nelson 83), limiting the interaction and exposure of younger gays to older gays. This is perpetuated by the youth-centeredness of gay culture and the cultural mythologies that demonize older gay men. In the absence of visibility and first-hand experience, both gay and mainstream audiences rely on mediated representation to fill in the missing stories and images of gay aging. Unfortunately, even within the 1990s boom of visibility, representations of older gay men are few and far between.

The 1990s introduced an unprecedented proliferation of explicitly gay and lesbian representation (Gross, *Up*; Seidman; Shugart; Tropiano; Walters), mainstreaming—and perhaps downplaying—the needle in the haystack thrill of discovering there are "others out there like me." Explicitly marked gays and lesbians have "entered the ranks of our culture's permanent cast of characters" (Gross, "Gideon" 124), appearing in newsprint, television, film, and popular discourse in ways unfathomable just a few decades before. For the first time in history, detailing gay media representation had become an exhaustive effort. Gay characters were accompanied by sitcom laugh tracks, assisting Julia Roberts with her romantic dilemmas, being martyred by bigoted lawyers for their HIV status, raising children with Madonna, teaching violin lessons on primetime drama, and assisting countless heterosexuals in overcoming their own homophobia. Suddenly, the quest to find reflections of gay life in popular media became easier than ever, although scholars are quick to point out that this visibility comes with a price (Brookey and Westerfelhaus; Dow; Erni; Seidman; Shugart)

Mocking the film industry of the 1970s, Russo argued, "Homosexuality had become a fact of life, and Hollywood ballyhooed it as though the movies had invented it" (170). Twenty years later, in the wake of increasing gay representation in media, this statement ought to be reconsidered. Whereas it is quite obvious that homosexuality was not invented[7] by Hollywood, popular culture has become a driving influence in the discursive production of *a* gay culture, one constructed with the comfort of dominant populations in very much in mind (Becker; Brookey; Dow; Shugart; Seidman). This gay culture, as produced in popular media, is as fun and playful as Robin Williams, as sexy and stylish as Rupert Everett, as loveable as Tom Hanks, as white as Ellen, and as wealthy as the whole lot. Suddenly, the gay male friend was the fashion accessory of the 1990s, which no hip Carrie Bradshaw–wannabe or liberal minded metrosexual male should be without. The kooky and ever-so-stylish gay character spiced up any party, sitcom, or romantic comedy with witty banter and sound advice for getting that heterosexual relationship back on track. It was the Tickle Me Elmo craze for the hip 1990s heterosexual who was "straight but not narrow." The gay community, however accurately, has been pegged as a new niche market (Fejes) with disposable dollar bills blowing from every pocket of their Hugo Boss sport coats. Gays have received the greatest honor America has to offer, direct advertising (Gross "Gideon" 125).

The limitations of this 1990s visibility are explored later in this chapter, but in terms of representation, the 1990s presented an important shift in the presence of gays in mainstream entertainment. In a climate of "Out of the closet and into the sitcom," suddenly "gay youth (and adults as well, of course) turn on the TV and see some version of themselves served up for

28 *Queer Temporalities in Gay Male Representation*

prime-time consumption" (Walters 22). In a context where younger gays were exposed to images of homosexuality in mainstream entertainment like never before (Seidman 22), media claimed greater definitional power over gay lives.

The importance of media representation has always rested on the claim that "[w]e come to know ourselves and to be known by others through the images and stories of popular culture" (Walters 13). Rather than discussing whether or not representations are accurate, as this line of inquiry is essentialist and problematic (Brookey), representation matters for its rhetorical function—the realities it creates, the ideologies it promotes and reifies. Older generations of gays and lesbians will likely view the 1990s explosion with a different perspective from younger gays, one of comparison based on life experiences and previous representations. "What do we say now about growing up with reasonably common news and entertainment presence" (Gross, "Gideon" 121)? With the illusion that Hollywood has come out of the closet, and thus has nothing to hide, what kind of complacency does this foster, in terms of reading between the lines, the once-prized quest for self that cultivates a gay sensibility? What was once sought out through coded and resistant audience strategies is now openly marked and visible. If these offerings of gay representation are now in abundance, does this foreclose the search for alternatives, the quest for seeking an "elsewhere" (De Lauretis) not visible, but still present? What foreclosures are presented by repeated and seemingly definitive constructions of "this is what a gay man is, looks like, acts like, and desires." As *The Boys in the Band* was once taken as "the gospel" of what it meant to be gay (Russo 175), how has the gospel shifted and to whom is it preaching? Whom is it preaching for?

These inquiries pose a new set of challenges to queer media scholars, suggesting that increased exposure is not the end of the critical road. Representation matters, perhaps now more than ever before. However, the marking of gay representation in a temporal chronology of past/present/future, mirroring a coming-out narrative and linear timeline, needs to be problematized. Understanding the gospel of the gay, currently produced in popular media, requires a step backwards because visions of the future are more telling about where we have *been* rather than where we are actually going (Gilbert 123).

HISTORY PART 1: THE IRON LAW OF GAY TRAGEDY

> They are afraid of what they know is somewhere in the darkness around them, of what may at any moment emerge into the undeniable light of their flashlamps, nevermore to be ignored, explained away. The fiend that won't fit into their statistics, the Gorgon that refuses their plastic surgery, the vampire drinking blood with tactless uncultured slurps, the bad-smelling beast that doesn't use their deodorants, the unspeakable

that insists, despite all their shushing, on speaking its name. Among many other kinds of monster, George says, they are afraid of little me. (Isherwood, "A Single Man" 26–7)

During the years of the Code,[8] explicit mention or depiction of homosexuality required censure and revisions for the purpose of upholding "moral standards," presenting "correct standards" that in no way sympathized with violations of natural or divine laws (Russo 122). For several decades leading up to the 1960s, explicit reference to homosexuality was, literally, in the closet, if not dropped onto the cutting room floor. Whereas homosexuality was always present in the margins of Hollywood productions, providing a "lurking reminder of an alternative truth" (Russo 32) through coded references and subtle significations, explicit representation of same-sex sexual desire was actively omitted from Hollywood for the moral good of society. The 1960s marked a turning point for representation, as homosexuality came "out of the closet and into the shadows" (122). A far cry from a film like *Sweet Home Alabama*, where the supporting character of Bobby-Ray is publicly "outed" and then quickly embraced and supported by his community, Hollywood's coming-out story took a much darker turn. Homosexuals were now appearing on the screen, but confined to a limited typology of roles that were "pathological, predatory and dangerous; villains and fools, but never heroes" (122). The 1960s Hollywood homosexual was a creature of the night, existing in "the cultural space inhabited by unhappiness, murder, despair, freakishness, and invisibility" (Peele 6). The homosexual was painted as a self-loathing, depraved, excessively promiscuous monster (Fejes and Petrich; Gross, "What"; Seidman; Walters), who—like Isherwood's "unspeakable"—dared "to speak its name." The coming-out party for Hollywood looked more like a public lynching than a celebration, as gays and lesbians became criminals on "wanted" posters in movie theaters across the country.

The "wanted" poster conjures a familiar narrative of the Wild West and the ruthless gun-slinging outlaw. In these old western narratives, the villainous faces plastered across those cities-in-ruin were the assumed cause for the corruption that plagued those "once peaceful towns." Once a villain was marked, it was time for some good old-fashioned George W. Bush–style heroism to save the day. What is that riding over the mountain on a big white horse? It is the presumed-to-be heterosexual (white, male) hero! The evil infestation is then captured and punished, providing a cautionary tale for the townspeople about the price of straying from the path of the righteous. Hollywood's coming out was a story of heroism and triumph. It just was not a triumph for gays and lesbians. By stepping into the limelight of explicit representation, homosexuality gave heterosexuality its coherence, its heroism, its opportunity to "save the day" and further construct homophobia as virtuous. However, the homosexual and the Wild West villain fail to provide a perfect parallel, as the homosexual was seen as far more sinister and dangerous than the cold-blooded outlaw. As screenwriter Abby Mann stated, "[I]t's easier to be accepted in our society as a murderer than a homosexual" (qtd. in Russo 169). Childhood experience testifies that, whereas many neighborhood kids were overly willing to play the cold-blooded murderer in a game of "shoot 'em up," asking who wants to play "homosexual" received less-than-positive responses.

Hollywood's coming out provided the tragic formula for a whole new crop of exotic and fascinating villains to capture, punish, and publicly denounce, perpetuating what Burke refers to as "the iron law of history" (*Religion* 4). Kenneth Burke is a literary and social theorist whose body of work interrogates motivation in symbolic systems. Using drama as a governing framework for his project, Burke argues that humans are separated from their natural condition as a result of their complex symbol systems, so that drama is no longer a metaphor for human experience, but the human experience is inherently dramatic (*Language*). The foundations for these ideas are developed throughout several volumes of Burke's writings; however, *Permanence and Change* provides an entry point through the development and elaboration of the Burkean conception of orientation. Burke defines orientation as a form of reality training, an understanding of relationships, where past experiences limit and define our expectancy (14) and "affects our choice of means with reference to the future" (18). In other words, orientation marks our training but also our trained incapacities by limiting our ability to grasp or imagine experiences outside of our orientation, frame of reference, or reality. For example, orientation can be demonstrated through the concept of heteronormativity,[9] which centralizes and naturalizes—and thus privileges—heterosexual scripts and relationship formation as the assumed organizing principle of sexual life (Warner, *Trouble*; Yep). Whether conscious or unconscious, heteronormativity normalizes hegemonic heterosexuality through its constructed and taken-for-granted correctness (Yep 18), articulating public decency and order as synonymous with heterosexuality (Peele 59). In Burkean terms, all society is operating under the same sexual orientation (Goltz, "Perspective"), which is defined through the unmarked and invisible trained incapacity of hegemonic heteronormativity.

The utility of orientation is extended in *Attitudes toward History*, where Burke suggests that orientations are more than simply ways of understanding the world, but are fundamental to the construction of motives. More directly, orientations build motives, and so Burke furthers his project by breaking down a series poetic frames that work to organize and analyze the workings of orientations. Primary to this discussion is the acceptance[10] frame of tragedy. The tragic frame, or the tragic motive, tells a story that gay men in Hollywood have experienced for decades, as tragedy is the governing framework for negotiating any minority representation into mainstream film and television. In any critical account of gay and lesbian representation from the mid-twentieth century to the 1990s, the words "villains," "predators," "murderers," "depressed," and "psychopaths" are as common as shoulder pads in a 1980s blazer (Gross "Gideon"; Gross, *Up*; Peele; Russo; Seidman; Tropiano; Walters). As Gay Liberation was slowly garnering visibility through the 1960s and 1970s, homosexuals were constructed as a corruptive and infectious force, which threatened to contaminate "the good of society" through recruiting, perverting, and distorting the natural order. To analyze the rhetorical motive of these representations, Burke begins with the primary assumption that rules this story, a fictive social perfection prior to the corrupting influence of homosexuality.

Perfection, according to Burke, is both the driving motive and the effect of symbolic systems. Through symbolic systems, humans have the capacity to extend beyond their natural world and envision, articulate, and imagine themselves elsewhere and otherwise (*Language* 3–4). Language is the vehicle where the human symbol user has the ability to name experiences, but also to differentiate and moralize experiences through the negative (9). As Warner asserts in his foundational queer text, there is serious trouble in the concept of the normal, as normativity, in itself, is a social production that gains its coherence through marking or designating itself through the not normal, or the constructed deviant. Perfection and/or normativity are always symbolic constructions, as well as sites of discipline, that separate humans from their worlds through the process of negativity. Only through language is the notion of perfection possible, and this capacity is coupled with the unique ability to "not be" something. Whereas in nature, a tree is always but a tree, in human language there is always the potential for you to not be pretty, young, straight, blond, republican, baptized, or George Clooney. The point is not to moralize or evaluate the human potential for conceiving perfection, as that would be futile and rather ironic, but to understand the ways perfection provides a primary motive in human behavior. As psychologist Daniel Gilbert's bestselling *Stumbling on Happiness* claims, "The human being is the only animal that thinks about the future" (4). Humans have the distinct blessing and curse of imagining themselves otherwise, and whereas Gilbert claims we do a pretty crappy job of anticipating what will make us happy in the future, we continue to idealize certain visions of our future selves. In addition, our symbolic systems allow us the capacity to construct altogether skewed perceptions of our past experiences, reframing, if not completely rewriting, how we felt in a particular memory or location. As multiple sentimental ballads attest to, "you don't know what you got til it's gone," because only when it is gone can you construct what you once had as ideal.

Symbolic perfection is more complicated than simply our ability to create a vision of the future or rewrite a remembered past. As humans are driven by or, as Burke claims, "rotten with perfection" (*Language* 16), failure to achieve our perfected longings and our inability to maintain our now perfected pasts produces the second primary motive. Whereas some wonderfully sentimental ballads claim that it is love that makes the world go round, Burke argues that "guilt" should replace the word "love" in those lyrics. Sitting at your designated table at any given wedding, many of us can recall the familiar sight of a hopeful couple dancing to that ever-so touching assertion, "What the world needs now is love, sweet love." Love may be "the only thing that there is just too little of," but when the romantic promises of this newly married couple fail to achieve their perfected aspirations, there will continue to be a shortage of "love, sweet love" and an abundance of guilt. Whereas God, the groom's best pal Jimmy, or fate might have brought this promising couple together, the more important question becomes, who or what tore them apart? Who is to blame for the erosion of this marriage, or the systemic downfall of this sacred institution?

When figuring out where and how blame should be assigned, there are multitudes of options at one's disposal with a few governing rules to the game. Just as Columbine was the fault of Marilyn Manson, Falwell blamed 9–11 on homosexuals, and the Jews were responsible for the economic troubles of pre–World War II Germany, social scapegoating is less reliant on logic than the principle of hierarchy (Burke, *Language* 15). Socially embraced scapegoating procedures are contingent upon who has the social influence to blame and who lacks the social influence to defend. This is why marginalized populations have historically taken the brunt for failed economies, social tragedies, crime, gun-toting teenagers, and failed marriages throughout history. As heteronormativity is the governing orientation of sexuality, the institution of marriage remains the uncontested and invisible center of the discussion, which shall never be to blame. Its assumed correctness exempts the institution from critique. As patriarchy marks an additional orientation of assumed correctness, the cultural production of violent hegemonic masculinity resists its own interrogation in situations such as Columbine or the brutal murder of Matthew Shepard (Ott and Aoki). Social hierarchy refuses such a possibility, and insists that Pearl Jam videos and homosexual panic provide more acceptable explanations. Returning to the failed marriage that did not have enough "love, sweet love," Dan Quayle might argue that if it were not for *Murphy Brown*, the domestic bliss of our once happy couple would not be another divorce statistic.

1960s Hollywood discovered a new factional scapegoat[11] to project across the nation, offering up symbolic punishment for the social imperfections of the day. Gay issues were not "big box office" (Russo 186), but the "intrinsically pathological and destructive nature of homosexuality" (Porfido 60) became the foundation for the new Hollywood "bad guy" (Russo 186). The media constructed gays and lesbians as "predatory twilight creatures" (48), fatally flawed monsters who were inescapably doomed (167). Furthermore, these representations perpetuated a logic that homosexuals recruit one another selfishly into their condemned life of misery, likened to "modern vampires who must create new victims in order to survive" (236). The homosexual was cast as predator, lurking in the shadows, secretly and ruthlessly scheming to corrupt innocent children, erode social decency, and viciously tear apart—assumed to be once perfect—marriages in hopes of dragging society into their self-created pit of despair. Visibility came with a price, and America's understanding of homosexuality was greatly determined by media representation (189). While once in "the closet" (248), gay and lesbian visibility assisted in bringing on a wave of violent backlash[12] (249), both on the streets and in the media.

The demonizing of homosexuals perpetuates the tragic motive, casting simplified binaries where righteousness and goodness is threatened by an absolute evil, ending with the punishment of the villain. Society is purged of its ills. This is, of course, until inevitable perfection fails to be achieved once again, and so the cycle repeats itself infinitely. After all, there are a lot of failed marriages, economic problems, and less-than-perfect children out there. Homosexuality is not only demonized in these representations, but heterosexuality is further championed as "the preferred way of life" (Seidman 30). Constructing a psychopathic transvestite serial killer, such as in 1974's *Freebie and the Bean*, provides the tragic satisfaction of a queer body being splattered across bathroom walls in the finale, reifying the correctness and goodness of heterosexuality. As with all binary configurations, goodness and rightness are fully reliant on conceptions and designations of the evil for their coherence. "Homosexuality was portrayed at best as unhappiness, sickness, and marginality, and at worst perversion and an evil to be destroyed" (Fejes and Petrich 398). By introducing homosexuality onto the Hollywood screen, heterosexuality never looked so good.

Because all members of our society are socialized to buy into the perfection of the heteronormative orientation, homosexual victimage turns hegemonic. It is not only the heterosexual heroes in popular films and television that are killing off the "evil" homosexual for the good of society. "Once homosexuality became literally speakable in the early 1960s, gays dropped like flies, usually by their own hand" (Russo 52). Whereas vilifying and killing off homosexuals works to perpetuate their demonization, heteronormative perfection is most convincing when homosexuals, themselves, take their own lives for the "good of society." This second form of symbolic purging is the process of mortification (*Religion* 207), where punishment is inflicted on one's self, substantiating the correctness of heteronormativity through the actions of the very populations it seeks to exclude. The construction that "homosexuality was clearly only for villains" (Russo 135) was playing out on both sides of the tragic frame, as homosexuals in film were openly legitimizing the brutality inflicted upon them. In *Midnight Cowboy*, Joe Buck, the street hustler played by Jon Voight, picks up a "john," and the events turn violent as Joe begins beating up the older man. During this attack, the older man, played by Barnard Hughes, mutters, "I deserve this. I brought this about myself, I know I did. Oh! How I loathe life!" (80). Russo reports that from 1961 to 1976, there were thirty-two films offering "major homosexual characters," from which thirteen commit suicide, eighteen are murdered, and one is castrated (qtd. in Fejes and Petrich 413). Through the frame of heteronormative perfection, mortification became a prominent representation in film, as the only noble approach for these "doomed people" (167) with the "fatal flaw" of homosexuality was to take their own lives.

This symbolic sacrifice in the service of heteronormative society is built upon limited myths of gayness that have a strong hold in popular representations. "The movies made gay self-hatred an inherent part of the species" (Russo 194–5), and the identifications of homosexuality with loneliness, bitterness, perversion, isolation, rejection, self-hatred, shame, guilt, a life of misery, and a doomed future perpetuate the logic of "show me a happy homosexual and I will show you a gay corpse." This line from Crowley's *Boys in the Band* solidifies homosexual misery, perpetuating the "harder path" narrative that shapes gay future. In addition, it justifies the actions of homosexual sacrifice, as the homosexual is better off dead. Not only is homosexual murder or suicide a justified action for social good, but the homosexual is also likened to a terminally ill creature who should be put down and liberated from an inescapable misery. Furthermore, those committing the act of suicide or murder are deemed more righteous for their actions, doing the only thing left to be done.

HISTORY PART 2: THAT WAS THEN AND THIS IS . . . NORMAL?

> Normalization is an ongoing and circular movement. Normalization is the process of constructing, establishing, producing, and reproducing a taken-for-granted and all-encompassing standard used to measure goodness, desirability, morality, rationality, superiority, and a host of other dominant cultural values. (Yep 18)

Pioneer scholars in gay representation, such as Russo and Dyer,[13] have meticulously detailed these early images of gays and lesbians, reminding us of a history many would rather try to forget. After all, now we have *Will & Grace* and *Ellen*, gay characters have become more commonplace in popular media, and many of these characters are still breathing when the closing credits appear. In the film adaptation of *Celluloid Closet*, the documentary ends with a strong theme of progress, marking the ways gays and lesbians in Hollywood have "come out of the closet," passed through the shadows, and have achieved a promising and progressive visibility in mainstream film. This detailing of Hollywood's triumph in breaking free from the "celluloid closet" is enough to make anyone stand up and cheer. It is a great story, an epic tale of an underdog hero who faces adversity and walks through the flames a better person. However, this triumphant final sequence in the documentary, based on Russo's research, has a slightly more upbeat tone than the original text. In the final chapter of Russo's text, titled "Taking the Game Away from Hollywood: Finding a Voice and Facing a Backlash," he is far more critical of Hollywood in the 1980s, praising several independent films, but openly skeptical about the potential for Hollywood to move past old models and storylines that ensure box office success.[14] As the revised version of the text was printed in the 1980s, and the film *Celluloid Closet* was produced in the mid-1990s, much of the Hollywood representation from that decade, such as *Philadelphia*, are simply lauded as part of the ongoing narrative of progress. This coming-out story places historical representations safely into the past, casting *Philadelphia* as our sign of a brighter future, implying that there is a great deal of distance that separates these discussions of "that was then" from the "this is now." Queer media critics have continually challenged the logic that blindly equates visibility, or even "positive" representation, with progress.

The emergence of queer theory in the late 1980s and 1990s sought to develop a conceptual body of thought to problematize and articulate the limitations of gay and lesbian assimilation. Resisting the equation of normalization with progress, queer theory posed a challenge to normalizing strategies for garnering social acceptance, which sought acceptance on reductive and exclusionary terms. Foundational to queer critique is the interrogation of heteronormativity as the central organizing system of relationship and social formation (Warner, *Trouble*; Yep), the essentialist assumptions of the hetero/homo binary (Sedgwick), and the complex intersections of race, class, gender, and sexuality (Cohen; Johnson; Muñoz, "Disident"). In a historical moment when the film version of *Celluloid Closet* was championing Hollywood's "coming-out party," queer theorists voiced skepticism for the terms and limitations of this "celebration." After all, how great is a party that is set in the world of heterosexuality where everyone is on their best behavior and sex or sexual expression for gay characters is outlawed in exchange for fancy clothes, apolitical stances, and a lot of white, yet tanned, faces?

By situating queer critiques within a Burkean discussion of tragic framing, the progress narrative is problematized by rethinking the temporal relationship between then and now. Rather than mapping a linear trajectory of "in the closet" to "out of the closet," Burke's iron law of history suggests a circular model fueled by perpetual repetition. Thus far in our discussion, tragedy has provided a productive frame for discussing the narrative logic of historical gay and lesbian representation, depicting symbolic sacrifice in the service of heteronormative reification. However, the underlying critiques of queer theory offer further insight into the ways tragedy continues to be deployed as a governing framework for offering representations of nonnormative sexualities. Considering the queer interrogation of the essentialized hetero/homo binary, tragedy is fueled by carefully guarding coherent binary formations, as the right or good must be clearly delineated from the wrong or the evil. The rigidity of the homosexual/heterosexual divide ensures a tragic clarity that preserves the privileging of heterosexuality, as well as foreclosing the potential for alternative, multiple, and shifting sexual desires. Gay rights movements are firmly committed to this gay identity politic, refusing more fluid discussions of sexuality. For example, in the popular 1980s primetime soap opera *Dynasty*, Steven Carrington presented a uniquely queer, yet frustrating, character, as his sexual object choice was constantly in fluctuation. Steven's refusal to definitively mark his sexuality could easily be read as (and likely was) the show's producers "playing it safe," playing upon the notion that Steven's same-sex attraction was confused and perpetuating the antiquated logic of homosexuality as a defective psychological condition. For this reason, many gay audiences criticized Steven for refusing to claim a definitive gay self and promote the normalization of gay identity. From a queer perspective, however, Steven occupied a liminal space of sexual expression, resisting the "either/or" confines of sexual identity. Although Steven's sexuality remained shifting and undefined throughout the majority of the show, audiences were less willing to sit within the ambiguous space of undefined sexuality, and so Steven's sexual relations with men positioned him, in the minds of many audience members, as "gay," but afraid to accept himself. Neither gay nor straight audiences seemed willing to let him occupy a fluid sexual identity. This discussion is not claiming that Steven Carrington was a fully queer character, or that his representation was without critical concern. What is articulated around this contested representation is the linkage between essential gay identity representation and progress, in the service of a rigidly defined hetero/homo binary.

As argued earlier in this chapter, tragedy is constructed through a heteronormative orientation, operating under strict allegiance to specific and closely guarded relationship formations. More specifically, these formations include heterosexual pairing, monogamy, government and religiously sanctioned unions, and procreation. This governing orientation of sexual tragedy marks a trained incapacity that forecloses and disciplines the potential for multiple sexual expressions and kinship formations, as heteronormativity presents and defines the primary sexual motive. Returning to the example of *Dynasty*, Steven's sexual uncertainty was not represented as a neutral playing field where he simply ought to select one or the other. Not only was the "either/or" mandate for Steven to pick a singular sexual identity an ongoing theme in (and around) the show, but heterosexuality was also repeatedly presented as the desirable, correct, and healthy path. If a gay man appeared in Steven's life, you could safely bet a hefty wager that a fatal accident would kill him off before too long. Steven's same-sex relationships were consistently cursed, whereas Sammy Jo and Claudia—Steven's two female love interests—were viewed as sympathetic, desirable, "correct" pathways for Steven to pursue. What was fascinating about watching Steven's ongoing sexual crisis was his awkwardness in either type of relationship. His straight performance was as queer as his gay performance, never quite fitting in and always drawing attention to the flimsiness of the conventions.

From a gay assimilationist perspective, the idealized representation for Steven Carrington would have Steven "come out" as definitively gay, find a suitable gay partner, have a Carrington-style wedding gala, settle down to raise Steven's son Danny, and present a "normal" marriage that rivaled Fallon and Jeff as the show's "favorite couple." This normalized vision, while radical at the time of *Dynasty*, is becoming more and more common in contemporary media. However, this effort to achieve "normal" status carries with it a long and complicated set of mismatched luggage that queer theorists have worked to unpack and sort through.

Normalizing Steven Carrington presents a narrative of progress only when sexuality is theorized as a singular axis of oppression. A normalized Steven Carrington becomes Blake Carrington, a masculine, white, upper-class, able-bodied male with one minor and potentially forgivable deviation, his sexuality. This poses two primary oversights that articulate the basis for the majority of queer media criticism. One, the normalizing of Steven Carrington perpetuates a logic that further restricts gayness to the white, male, middle- to upper-class body, refusing to account for how issues of race, gender, and class do not exist on "mutually exclusive terrains" (Crenshaw 357). In the grand scheme of media representation, Steven was *already* a normalized representation. By claiming sexuality as the sole and specific object choice of gay and lesbian concerns (Butler, "Against"), normative constructions of race, class, and gender remain privileged, perpetuating the exclusionary practice of denying the intersections of multiple forms of privilege and oppression. This leads to the dangerous assumption that has historically plagued identity-based movements for decades. A single oppression framework for gay representation is rightfully subject to the same critiques launched against NOW from women of color, the criticisms of women within the civil rights movements, and the marginalized voices of people of color, women, and transgender populations within the Gay Liberation movement. Discourses of sexuality *are raced, classed, and gendered* (Cohen; Ferguson "Of Our"), and the refusal to address these complex intersections—claiming a transparent sexual subject—is to "reap the dividends of whiteness" (Perez 171) and further perpetuate the "bullying" (Villarejo 69) and "color-blind" (Manalansan 143) insistence of normativity.

Fighting for recognition and acceptance within socially constructed norms results in complicity with the governing heteronormative orientation. This quest for normative acceptance defines an uninterrogated allegiance to the tragic sexual frame, as it remains reliant upon a normal/deviant binary formation. Vying for normative status of gayness does not break the tragic cycle, as the norm will always produce its exterior deviance. Deviance of the norm is what provides the norm with definitional coherence. The symbolically constructed "not" works to keep the norm discrete, as well as "correct." Normalizing Steven Carrington's gayness would serve to grant social acceptance to a limited conception of sexual expression, specifically masculine, white, gay men who pledge allegiance to heteronormative systems, avoid politics, and never have sex. Welcome to the 1990s.

The 1990s brought in a wave of "positive" gay and lesbian representations in both film and television, such as *Will & Grace*, *In and Out*, *Ellen*, *My Best Friend's Wedding*, *Object of My Affection*, *Party of Five*, *The Next Best Thing*, and numerous others. Brookey and Westerfelhaus posed the question, amidst this flurry of "positive" representations, is there still a role for the queer media critic (142)? Queer media criticism[15] has developed a strong body of work that interrogates the limitations of normalized representation (Battles and Hilton-Morrow; Brookey; Brookey and Westerfelhaus; Dow; Seidman; Walters) echoing the claim that positive representation "is not the same as political progress" (Dow 136). Hart argues that several of the newly positive gay storylines on television shows were continually met with negative consequences for the character (606), where "romantic happiness is not to be found" (605) and homosexuality remains a problem that other characters must deal with (603).

The "normal gay" of the 1990s provided a "heterosexual view of homosexuality" (Fejes and Petrich 401) where gay men (as women were commonly absent) adopt a few stereotypical traits, but otherwise were "heterosexual in every other sense" (401). "Much of the era's gay-themed programming was fundamentally about being straight in an era when increased gay visibility and gay rights battles highlighted and challenged heterosexuality's ex-nominated privilege" (Becker 212). The heightened visibility of gay men due to AIDS was accompanied by "well-meaning approaches that plead for tolerance by representing gays as no different from heterosexuals, a 'liberal' strategy that dictates complete asexuality" (Gross, "What" 152). "Network television does not present gays and lesbians in the context of their own identity, desire, community, culture, history, or concerns, but rather woven into the dominant heterosexual metanarrative" (Fejes and Petrich 402). Battles and Hilton-Morrow suggest that *Will & Grace* makes homosexuality "palatable to a large mainstream television audience by situating it within safe and familiar popular culture conventions" (89). Rather than seriously tackling the experiences facing queer characters, the texts emphasize the obstacles and processes of straight characters dealing with queers, and are "largely geared towards the comfort of heterosexuals" (Dow 129).

Gayness becomes the obstacle, the problem to be dealt with, divorced from any political reality of gays or lesbians (Battles and Hilton-Morrow 99). This apolitical posture is demonstrated through the heterosexual female/gay male friendship, which became a common theme in numerous films and TV shows of the 1990s. Shugart argues that these texts "do patriarchy one better" (80), by using the claim of "positive representation" to perpetuate multiple systems of oppression. Herein, the gay male is regularly overseeing the sexuality of the heterosexual women who, in turn, are positioned as weak, needy, and always sexually available to gay men. Primarily white, middle class, and traditionally masculine, these gay men occupy a paternal role in the lives of their straight female friends (86), performing the role of the ideal partner, and reinscribing heterosexist and misogynist scripts. However, as these are gay men, they manage to escape the charge of sexism inherent in the text, while still performing traditional patriarchal dominance (88).

Another trait of the "normal gay" is their insistent good behavior and absence of sexual expression. *Will & Grace* relies on traditional (and traditionally oppressive) heterosexual relationship models (Battles and Hilton-Morrow 91), where Will's sexual desire for men is downplayed to resemble "male bonding" (94), whereas the intimate relationship between the straight white female and the middle-class, masculine, white male (who happens to be gay) is placed center stage, coded as a traditional heterosexual couple (94). Brookey and Westerfelhaus assert that contemporary media both promote positive gay images and "simultaneously tames and contains gays and gay experience" (142). Using the film *To Wong Foo, Thanks for Everything! Julie Newmar*, Brookey and Westerfelhaus argue the drag queens in the film are deified, exhibiting "almost supernatural power" (150), serving the heterosexuals in the film, always on their best behavior, and constantly self-policing from posing any threat to the heterosexuality of the straight men (151). Their privileging of heterosexuality further curbed the threat of the "normal gay," as the "good gay's" job, much like the men of *Queer Eye*, was to facilitate and preserve heterosexual relationships (Bateman 13). Labeling this the "down-side to the positive representation" (Brookey and Westerfelhaus 153), these sanitized versions of queer sexualities function to reify heteronormative systems, while divorcing themselves from a sense of community, identity, desire, personal struggle, or oppression.[16]

The preservation of heteronormative comfort offers an entry point into theorizing how assimilationist gay representations, or what Duggan refers to as "homonormativity," achieve normative status through perpetuating the tragedy of sexuality. Burke defines "casuistic stretching" as the method of introducing new ideas or principles "while theoretically remaining faithful to old principles" (*Attitudes* 229). Herein, an orientation is stretched to "coach" (230) in ideas from one set of associations to another. The key component of casuistic stretching is that the orientation, in this case heteronormativity, is not ruptured, but safely expanded, while preserving its coherence. Assimilationist strategies seek to stretch heteronormative orientations for the purposes of claiming the inclusion of "normal" gays who are just like everyone else (everyone assumed to be heterosexual, married, and invested in systems of capitalism and procreation). Again, operating on a single oppression framework, normative systems of whiteness, masculinity, and economic status become "bridging devices" (*Attitudes* 224). The bridging device is a "symbolic merger" to "transcend conflict" (224), which allows the potential for extending the inclusivity of an orientation's domain.

Stretching or attempting to bridge dominant orientations requires complicity with the core belief systems that construct and maintain dominant ideologies. In other words, to construct a symbolic merger with heteronormative systems requires an element of sacrifice, where the "normal gay" is permitted inclusion, but only through the presentation of a desexualized and depoliticized identity. Those who fail to honor the heteronormative mandate of desexualization fail to be counted as "good sexual citizens" within "the circle of citizenship and social respectability" (Seidman 15) and are, by default, cast as the "bad gays" or "bad citizens" (17). The closeting of queer sexuality performs a symbolic merger. The depoliticized mandate performs additional mergers with symbols of whiteness, class privilege, and patriarchy, "creating those 'areas of ambiguity' from which one can transform meaning" (Carlson, "You" 122). Through symbolic bridging with additional categories of social privilege, the "normal gay" is both silenced and complicit in perpetuating these systems of oppression. While white gay male representations are increasingly normalized, this is executed through the marginalization of queers who can not perform, or do not want to perform, the "tamed and constrained" construction of the "normal" and "deified" white, middle-class, gay male construction. Tragedy is not transcended through these representations, as the "bad gays" remain deviant and punishable,[17] further disciplined and demonized by the presence of "respectable," "decent," and "sensible" gays (Duggan). Gays are split into a tragic binary of "heterosexual look-alikes or deviant outsiders" (Walters 127). Tragedy, as the process of normalization (Yep 18), continues to circulate and heteronormativity is further strengthened as correct and finite. Queer sexualities are sacrificed, as well as intersecting axes of gender, race, and class for a seat at the heteronormative luncheon, where gay identity can be claimed, but gay or queered sexual expression is forbidden.

A Burkean framework rejects the linear progression of the closet metaphor in favor of discussing the tragic cycle that has been bridged and stretched for the purposes of upholding heteronormative systems. The villainous representations of "then" mark a tragic cycle that continues to circulate in the normative exclusions of "now." As the "then" and the "now" are instrumental in shaping the potentials of "to be," this project shifts the focus of queer media criticism to the future in search of a comic corrective to this ongoing tragedy.

ONGOING CRITICISM AND THE PROJECT OF THE FUTURE

The culturally distinct aging patterns of gay men offer media critics a new perspective to approach contemporary images of gay men, gay aging, and queer futures. The lonely, bitter, miserable "older" gay male myth is present throughout some of the current literature, but with little attention to the limitations and particular problems it presents. The televised representations of gay men in the late 1960s included psychiatric accounts that claimed being a homosexual male "automatically rules out the possibility that he will remain happy for long" (Hart 599). Russo claims that the primary message that comes out of the film *The Staircase* (1969) is, "Nobody loves you when you're old and gay—not even yourself" (192). How the aging myth was perpetuated in these early films requires little explanation, as death and misery were the only options awaiting the queer character frame after frame.

The 1990s "normal gay" bridges a symbolic merger with existing systems of oppression, tacitly agreeing to present a desexualized, white, apolitical, middle-class, consumer-driven construction of gayness. Stretching heteronormativity models for the inclusion of some gays perpetuates exclusionary practices, but also confines the "normal gay" within restrictive and violent heteronormative frames, which serve to discipline heterosexuals, gays, and queers alike (Yep). The rhetorical strategy of "heterosexuality with a twist" (Walters 24) may offer some gays a "virtual" (Vaid) place at the table, while casting the "bad gay" to the tragic "harder road," but the normal gays are marked in temporal terms, usually falling between their late teens and mid thirties. Adding to the multiple problems presented by the "normal gay" model is the ambiguous promise it holds for the future, as visibility in mainstreamed representations is wasted on the "young."

Gay and lesbian representation is always rhetorical, and the fear-inducing narratives of monstrous homosexuals and acceptance-pleading narratives of "normal gays" are not as opposed as they first appear. Both representations privilege and reify heteronormativity, rhetorically constructing and supporting its perpetual rightness, its correctness, and its dominion over the future. Heteronormative models of future remain idealized, logical, and desirable, continually casting out the potential of queered future models through "symbolic annihilation" (Gross, *What* 143). A happy, productive, or satisfying future is wedded to monogamy, procreation, government-sanctioned unions, and proper sexual citizenship. Our understanding of future marks a trained incapacity. Here the importance of continual criticism is mandated, as the illusions of progress, acceptance, or social equality in popular representation become very deceptive.

How do we escape this trained incapacity of heteronormativity and its stronghold upon the future? Queer theorists set their focus of potential at the margins of discourse, the unforeseeable fantasy and potentialities that linger outside the frame in the "space-off" (De Lauretis 26). Still, these margins of discourse, these unintelligible futures, are carefully guarded with bright yellow "do not enter" warnings, using cautionary tales of developmental failure, misery, and the "harder road" to discourage queered visions of future. Happiness or queerness are constructed as an either/or proposition, either acceptable or unacceptable (Peele 2), where straying from the heteronormative path is always a punishable offense, carefully policed to ensure the correctness of the heteronormative tragedy.

Burke's remedy for breaking a tragic cycle is achieved through perspective by incongruity in the advancement of comic correctives. Perspective by incongruity articulates a strategic pairing of ideas, similar to an oxymoron, where symbolic concepts from one orientation are remoralized and reconstituted through their connection to concepts excluded from a specific orientation. This process mirrors what Walters refers to as a "conscious integration" of gays and lesbian into dominant culture; "an opening up, a breaking through the tightly drawn wagons of heterosexual assumptions that could, potentially, challenge and expand our conceptions of family, gender, love, intimacy, sexuality" (24). For example, as this discussion has thus far isolated the heteronormative orientation as the focus of inquiry, heteronormativity is strongly invested in preserving strictly defined gender categories. The concept of metrosexuality came into being as a way of marking and accounting for the performance of more feminine traits in straight-identified men, such as grooming and shopping, while still working to keep gender and sexuality distinctions under close surveillance. In this sense, the orientation was stretched to allow for the phenomenon of the metrosexual, while still remaining true to the orientation. Gender/sexuality distinctions are not violated here, but the metrosexual is permitted inclusion through the bridging devices of homophobia and dominant heterosexuality. The very term "metrosexual" is synonymous with the declaration, "I'm *not* gay." It functions to allow a stretching of gender roles without loosening the rigidity of the hetero/homo binary. The only use of the term is to create a space for feminine (and consumer) performances that honor the preservation of hetero-dominance. "Visibility alone does not threaten heterosexual privilege" (Seidman 7) nor threaten the dominance of the heteronormative orientation. Symbolic mergers that perpetuate multiple systems of oppression under the tacit agreement of being "normal" fail to disrupt the heteronormative tragedy. Perspective by incongruity, on the other hand, goes further than merely stretching an orientation, but seeks to remoralize, disrupt, and ultimately recreate the restrictive orientation.

One example of this type of symbolic rupture would be "the metrosexual strap-on." Dominant thought would have many scratching their heads at the idea of a man and a woman using a strap-on in the bedroom (or the kitchen?). After clarifying that the couple's sexual organs are fully functional, and all of the potential orifices are considered, the realization that some men prefer to have sex with women who will penetrate them anally creates a rupture. Herein the heteronormative logic of heterosexual sexual activity is challenged. Through perspective by incongruity, the orientation is queered, as a man receiving anal penetration is unthinkable within current constitutions of heterosexual masculinity. Straight men do not do that! Well, actually they do, just as queers can live fulfilling lives and preachers masturbate, but these ideas rupture the trained incapacities of heteronormative orientations. Perspective by incongruity, according to Burke, provides a tool for introducing this comic corrective. Whereas tragic tales are stories of evil being punished and guilt being purged, forever repeating into infinity, the comic frame operates under an ethic of mistakenness and education.

("Oh, I was wrong, perhaps preachers do masturbate.") In comedy, there is no ultimate evil to be sacrificed, for the comedy is a story of mishaps and corrections. Comedy, in this sense, should not be conflated with humorous (Carlson, "Witty" 319), but should be considered as a framework that operates under the ethic of fallibility[18] (Cornell).

Perspective by incongruity performs a queering function (Goltz, "Perspective"), as it exposes the limitations of tragic and binary formations. Tragedy operates by marking an either/or distinction, which is then embedded with hierarchies of better or worse. Comedy exposes the false dichotomy of tragedy, the false opposites that keep anal stimulation and the heterosexual male rigidly at odds with one another. The negative, as well as binary formations, are symbolic constructs. Perspective by incongruity exposes the underlying substance (Burke, *Grammar* 29) that tragic opposites share, thus dismantling or remoralizing the rigidity of exclusionary symbolic systems into a comic corrective of fallibility.

This comic ethic of fallibility places education, rather than sacrifice, at the center of the poetic frame. While similar to tragedy in its circularity, comedy embraces the notions of perpetual criticism, education, and fallibility at its core. This tie to education and perpetual criticism places Burke alongside more contemporary rhetorical theorists working from ideological orientations (Wander) and critical paradigms (McKerrow). Brummett suggests the primary contribution and aim of rhetorical theory and rhetorical criticism are their pedagogical utility as heuristic devices. As "a set of 'how to' instructions, they are guides to symbolic action in the world" (103). Rhetorical criticism is not a systematic social science about asserting laws of behavior. The work is driven by its potential to educate and, for more critical approaches to rhetoric, offer emancipatory knowledges (McKerrow; Wander).

Forefronting a telos of permanent criticism (Ono and Sloop), McKerrow's critical rhetoric asserts the dual perspectives of the critique of domination and the critique of freedom (442). The critique of domination perspective defines a commitment to interrogating how taken-for-granted and hegemonic ideologies are rhetorically constructed, legitimated, and perpetuated within discourse (443). The critique of freedom mandates a "never-ending skepticism" (446), where perpetual criticism of discourses of power is embraced as a core perspective, although "not towards a freedom for something predetermined" (446). Rather than privileging prescribed outcomes or claims to progress, a critical rhetoric places education and fallibility as its center—a comic approach—embracing the need for an ongoing orientation of critical commitment for an undetermined future.

The yet-to-be determined future or aim of critical rhetoric suggests the importance of musement to a comic corrective. The concept of musement[19] creates a space for potential that is not yet seen, indicating "a stance of amazement before the mysteries and marvels of life" (Cornell 78). Through perspective by incongruity, orientations are broken down and reconstituted in ways that can never be determined in advance. Musement places an emphasis on potentiality and futurity. Muñoz marks the distinction between potentiality and possibility, suggesting potentiality is present, but not existing in present things ("Stages" 11). Musement becomes a governing ethic for queer theory, as queer theory locates its sight of potential away from the promises of heteronormative perfection, working to explore the unmarked territory of deviant potentiality, that "future horizon" (Butler, *Bodies* 53) that exists in the "space-off," running "alongside the represented space" (De Lauretis 26). Erni emphasizes the discussion of "becoming" to queer criticism, referring to "the practice of in-betweenness that can evoke progressive possibilities in the partiality, noncoherance, and ambivalence of identity" (163). The project of queer theory has been defined by its orientation towards the future, "a source rather than a destination" (Sedgwick, qtd. in Jagose 5), as the attempt to solidify its meaning runs the risk of stopping it in its tracks (Butler, "Against" 21). The project of queer world-making (Muñoz "Stages"), queer potentiality (Butler, *Undoing*), and queer's "unimaginable future" (Jagose 132) insists that queer theory continue to interrogate the margins of discourse, exploring and examining multiple ways of becoming, of being, and of existing inside the world beyond the confines of heteronormative mandates. This calls for queer media criticism to broaden its focus beyond the ways that gays and lesbians are represented in popular culture, to examine how futures are constructed, negotiated, and limited by the representations that exist via assimilationist approaches and heteronormative systems.

Comic criticism, grounded in the ethics of fallibilism and musement, provides a framework to critique and interrogate tragic heteronormativity without solidifying or foreclosing potential outcomes or futures. To answer the question, "What does a queer future look like?" is a dangerous question, as attempting to answer this inquiry sets another determined course in motion. Much like the early resistance to defining the term "queer" in queer theory, its definition would be an indication of its failure. Perspective by incongruity queers the limitations of heteronormative trained incapacity without determined outcomes. Burke's concept articulates a radical break from limited orientations, creating the generative potential for unforeseen shifts in thinking. Through mistakenness and education, a comic corrective ruptures the tragic cycle, but also points to yet-to-be determined possibility.

CONCLUSION: BEYOND THE STRAIGHT AND NARROW

> Rhetorical theory is creative insofar as it gives people the conceptual means by which to experience in the future. (Brummett 104)

In recent decades, the issue of gay aging has received little to no attention by media critics. Yoakam, from a social work perspective, selected two of the very rare representations of older gay men in film, discussing how the older gay male characters in *Love and Death on Long Island* and *Gods and Monsters* "ultimately result in frustrated and unrequited love" (79). Older gay male attraction to younger men is represented as a vulnerability—a weakness to the power of youthfulness—where intergenerational sexual expression is "neither desirable sexually nor appropriate socially" (68), constructing older gay male sexual attractions to younger men as exploitive (66) and abusive (70). Yoakam asserts that these images continue to perpetuate homophobic attitudes towards older gay men and calls out the absence of films that explore the dimensions of gay intergenerational relationships of any kind (79). Age, much like representations of race and class, is limited to normative-pandering models of queerness, specifically white middle-class males in their twenties and thirties that erase the existence of gay men forty and above. Through this erasure of differing ages of gay men, the media offers a limited perspective on gay lives, gay aging, gay futures, as well as potential gay futures. In short, the queer project of seeking out new ways of being in the world is undercut by the perpetuation of aging myths, fears, and absences, leaving heteronormativity intact as the only feasible and desirable alternative.

While visibility has increased over the last decades, eliciting heavily criticized claims of "progress," how does futurity figure into this newly visible gay construction? Burke provides an alternative framework to analyze contemporary representation and how it works to construct the meanings of future through analytics of the constraints of heteronormative orientations, symbolic punishment of vilified queer dissidents, tragic compliance of gay assimilation strategies, and queered potentials of rupturing and reconstituting future through comic correctives. How does the media shape the boundaries, structures, and expectations of queer futures? What does future mean? How are gay and lesbian futures constructed differently (or similarly) to heteronormative notions of future? Are the futures constructed in popular culture offering queers equipment for living out their own lives, or do the queers situated in these texts simply present a counter-narrative to reinscribe the presumed comforts of heteronormative systems?

As the mass media now contains and tames the seemingly positive representations on "Must See TV," confining the available scripts of gay and lesbian identity to heteronormative approval and comfort, much queer experience continues to linger outside the dominant audience's viewing. To understand the multiple ways that age and future are constructed in contemporary popular culture requires queer media critics to continue seeking out the silences, the absences, the oddities, and the ruptures that speak to queer audiences in unique ways. The long tradition of queering popular culture is still an important component of the queer project, even as an array of gay and lesbian characters is being splashed across television and film. There remains a plethora of queers lives, identities, experiences, and potentialities that are still kept in the shadows, away from hetero-dominant popular consumption, lingering in the "space-off" (De Lauretis 26) of explicit representation. Queerness still lingers in the subtext, the resistant read, and the plethora of images out there ought not construct the illusion that our potential futures are reflected on the screen. There remains a need to continue asking, where is the queer potential of "becoming" in contemporary queer media?

As of yet, queer media criticism has primarily focused on the exclusionary and marginalizing practices of normalized representation. This study places issues of age and futurity within this ongoing discussion, marking additional sites of exclusion and foreclosure through the perpetuation of the heteronormative tragedy. Using a broad sample of texts produced since the turn of the millennium, this study seeks to understand how the rhetorical construction of gay representation constructs meanings around the themes of gay aging and future. Additionally, this application of queer theory uses grounded textual analysis, as rhetorical criticism provides a productive site for analyzing how the "high level of social abstraction" of queer theory is "expressed in specific discursive practices" (Brookey 45). Thus, this project is both a critique of contemporary constructions of gay male future in popular discourse and a creative investigation for theoretical and lived potentials for future-making that cannot be predetermined.

The film version of the *Celluloid Closet* ends by declaring Hollywood "the maker of dreams." I would extend this claim to argue that popular culture is not only the maker of dreams, but also the maker of futures. Whenever we audience popular media, we see variations of futures projected onto our lives, creating both hopes and fears. At the end of the text, what meanings are we left with in the dark? John Hurt, in *Love and Death in Long Island*, stands alone on a pier, with a broken heart, in agony. Will Truman gets married, adopts a child, and lives a life that seems to identically parallel the heterosexual Grace. Brian and Michael on *Queer is Folk* do not know what is coming next, so they just keep on dancing as the final credits appear. What do these representations of futures offer? Who are they serving and supporting? We need to continue looking to the margins of discourse, "this necessary 'outside' as a future horizon" (Butler, *Bodies* 53), to locate the potentiality of futures beyond the tragic cycle of heteronormativity. Perhaps then, the future will become a site of play, potentiality, and possibility, freed from the tragic linear certainty guided by cautionary warnings. Perhaps then, the future might seem a little more queered.

3 Victims in/of Time
Gay Aging as Ritualized Horror

> Luck has nothing to do with it. Everything is preordained. Manifest destiny. You can't stop time from happening no more than you can will the oceans to overwhelm the world, to cause the moon to drop from the outer sphere. (Paul, *Rules of Attraction*)

> There are no words for taking away the one thing every kid is entitled to . . . their invincibility. (Ben, *Queer as Folk*)[1]

A purified vision of heteronormativity is substantiated through the kill, the tragic nightmare of punishment that is perpetuated through the sacrifice of gay male representations in cultural discourse. The cultural production of gay male identities—spanning genres of drama, comedy, teen drama, parody, dark comedy, sitcom, the buddy film, and the slasher film—adopts the literary frame of tragedy as its governing strategy for solidifying heteronormative correctness. In *The Philosophy of Literary Form*, Burke discusses how poetic frames, such as tragedy, are "treated as *equipments for living*, that size up situations in various ways and in keeping with correspondingly various attitudes" (304). Arguing a "sociological criticism of literature" (293), literary forms offer social critics a series of classifications, strategies, and poetic categories to understand how orientations are organized. Each poetic form "stresses its own peculiar way of building the mental equipment (meanings, attitudes, character) by which one handles the significant factors of his [or her] time" (*Attitudes* 34). As poetic frames provide "equipment for living," by offering differing social strategies for navigating and rectifying imperfections, the social critic is offered a body of concepts to help name social processes, uncover attitudes driving social ritual, and interrogate how governing attitudes might shape the treatment of others (34–7).

From a Burkean perspective, Hollywood's master narrative of gay male identity and gay male aging reiterates a tragic tale of sacrifice for the redemption and purification of heteronormative systems of relation, conceptions of future, and engagements with time. The specifics of the Hollywood tale have shifted, as the gay male is less commonly painted as the ruthless and bloodthirsty monster discussed in Chapter 2. The "essence" (Burke, *Philosophy* 301) of the heteronormative tragedy—however ironic, popular, or seemingly more positive—remains intact, as the cultural narrative perpetuates a tale of gayness as a punishable evil. The gay male future is framed as a ritualized sacrifice, a tragic punishment for the sanctification of "straight time" (Boellstorff), cautioning those who deviant from the heteronormative path that misery is insured. Regardless of genre, gay male lives, gay male aging, and gay male futures remain tales of horror.

Enlisting the horror genre as a metaphor to discuss the representation of gay male futures, few slasher film characters in contemporary media have captured the popular imagination as vividly as Freddy Krueger from the Nightmare on Elm Street series. Following in the tradition of *Frankenstein*, *Dracula*, and multiple horror film characters that have been read through a queer lens (Benshoff), Krueger provides a governing metaphor for this chapter by bridging the earlier models of the vilified gay male predator with discourses of gay male aging, heteronormative time, and future. More myth than man, Freddy Krueger embodies and articulates the tragic narrative of the aging gay male.

Freddy Krueger lives in the boiler rooms, basements, and dark alleyways of dreams. His face is hideous, scarred, and burned, as many years ago he was set on fire by the good parents of Elm Street for the protection of their community and their children. Freddy Krueger blurs the lines between the unconscious and the waking life, forcing his victims to remain awake, avoiding sleep at all costs, for his believers understand that the nightmare is deadly. He lives through the fear of others, the perfected suburbanites with white picket fences and impressionable children. His strength is maintained through the passing on of his story, the conjuring up of his terrifying image, and the narrative of the evil man who mercilessly preys upon the young innocents. He wears a glove of knives, where any touch is both sexual and violent. Lonely, isolated, bitter, and vengeful, Freddy is no longer a man, but a cautionary social tale. He is the sadistic extreme of the aged homosexual predator constructed in the rhetoric of Anita Bryant and early Hollywood tragedy. His threat endures, never fully dying. He is both present and absent. He *is* real, as long as others believe in him.

Hollywood is the maker of futures, and Hollywood is the creator of nightmares, as brutalized, beaten, and doomed queer lives remain recurrent themes across multiple genres of film and television. This chapter explores mainstream gay representation as a fragmented horror story, a never-ending dance with death that situates gay lives in constant relation to dying, loss, and looming mortality. Against this tragic backdrop, the cautionary tale of the "harder path" (Goltz, "Investigating") is located within seemingly progressive, if not well-intentioned, representations that perpetuate the devaluation of the gay male future through heteronormative temporal allegiance. Within this gay tragedy, the aging process emerges as a recurrent and ritualized nightmare, as the omnipresence of negative mythologies of the aging gay male continue to circulate in cultural discourse. The predator, the fool, and the invisible man hover in the dark corners of gay futures, further demonizing the older gay man while forever worshipping the young. The young do not escape the nightmare, however, for just like Freddy Krueger, the vilified and miserable mythologies of the older gay man haunt their dreams, closing in on them with each tick of the clock. The Krueger mythology of inevitable exclusion and repulsion defines the tragic punishment of straight time, for the now young—but soon to be older and grotesque—gay male perpetuates a mentality of "live fast, die young, and make a beautiful corpse."

The heteronormative tragedy of 1960s representation continues to play itself out, as the gay life and the gay future are represented through "tragic ambiguity, surrounding it with the connotations of crime" (Burke, *Attitudes* 39). Happiness, successful aging, or personal fulfillment for the gay male remains a punishable offense in the heteronormative tragedy—good fortunes that ought be feared—as they mock the heteronormative orientation and indicate "the first sign of punishment" (39). The concept of future within straight temporal logic is not only a *sight* of sacrifice, but aging and future are constructed *as* the punishment, *the* sacrifice that awaits the gay male. Dreaming of potential futures becomes complicated, if not terrifying, with the overshadowing awareness that "Freddy is coming for you."[2]

A NIGHTMARE ON GAY STREET: FOREVER DANCING WITH DEATH

> The only thing that's possible is that I can get beat up one too many times. (Michael, *Camp*)
>
> I could have come out to every mother in the world and I'd still be dead. (Marcus, *Six Feet Under*)[3]
>
> Maybe than kill yourself, maybe just stop being gay. (Clara, *Drawn Together*)[4]

In a recent editorial on AfterElton.com, Ficera suggests that minimal coverage of gay-targeted hate crimes in the news media has created the illusion for the American public that Matthew Shepard was the first and last victim of homophobic violence ("Don't Quote Me"). Contemporary film and television shows tell a different tale, where the bruised and bloodied queer body is commonplace, if not normalized, in the cultural imagination. Logics that assume "violence comes with the territory" (Russo 91) of gayness have not disappeared in the wake of increased visibility. Tony Soprano comments with disgust, "Every TV show, they rub our noses in it [homosexuality]."[5] The image of rubbing one's nose in queer visibility fails to address that it is often the queer body whose nose is bloodied, if not rubbed into the pavement in a pool of gore. On HBO's police drama *The Wire*, Brandon's body is brutally slaughtered like an animal and proudly displayed on the hood of a car, with his eyes yanked out, a body covered in cigarette burns, and the traces of a "torture fest" from which he "must have been killed five times."[6]

Marcus, on HBO's dark family dramedy *Six Feet Under*, is fatally stomped and whipped, left in a pile of gore that "looks like something Chef-Boy R Dee makes." Marcus's father comments, "We know why this happened. If he wasn't . . . [Cannot say the word] he'd still be alive."[7] After Vito is outed on *The Sopranos*, he is beaten to death and found with a pool cue forced up his anus.[8] Justin, on Showtime's gay drama *Queer as Folk*, takes a baseball bat to the head;[9] Michael, in the feel-good musical theater comedy *Camp*, is bashed in the hallways of his high school dance. On the teen soap opera *Dawson's Creek*, Toby is attacked at the bus stop;[10] Noah, the leading character on Logo's gay dramedy *Noah's Arc*, is beaten at a gas station.[11] *Mysterious Skin* offers a violent climax where Neil, the young street hustler, is raped in a bloodied bathtub. From police dramas like *The Shield* to the teen program *Degrassi: The Next Generation*, gayness remains a punishable offense. Unlike *The Laramie Project*, where homophobia and hate crimes are central to the film's discourse, many of these violent acts are enacted with little-to-no discussion or commentary, reifying the cautionary tale that homophobic violence is both unexceptional and just a part of being gay.

Normalizing violence against gay men enacts a tragic ritual where dominant audiences are temporally permitted to identify with nonnormative sexual desires—through a gay character—and then redeem themselves and heteronormative perfection through symbolically sacrificing the gay representation. Ott and Aoki identify tragic framing within the mediated discourse of Matthew Shepard's murder, wherein dominant audiences were permitted identification with Shepard—a white, middle-class "innocent" (489)—only to ritualistically purge their own iniquities through his slaughter. Foundational to the tragic ritual is the ability of the dominant audience to locate themselves and their own sinfulness within the sacrificial victim (490). Where the Shepard discourse shifted from a short-lived acknowledgment of broader systems of homophobia to the vilification of two uniquely evil killers—thus constructing symbolic distance between the defendants and the homophobic public (492)—dominant audiences are permitted brief pleasure in exploring queer desire through gay male representation prior to symbolic punishment. To permit gay male representation in the dominant cultural production, and thus allow dominant identification with homosexual desire, offers up a sacrifice for all sexual urges and iniquities that stray from pristine definitions of "correct" sexual expression. In short, gay male representation offers a scapegoat to sexual deviance, which explains why the gay male body in contemporary media is subjected to repeated violence.

Film and television define gay living, gay relationships, and meaningful gay interaction through tragedy and violence, enmeshed within a narrative of horror. Gay romance in the 1980s was scripted in hospitals, where devoted lovers cared for their dying partners/AIDS victims. Still, in several texts, gay love in the millennium remains tied to the settings of funerals, hospitals, and bloodied bodies. *Noah's Arc*, *Dawson's Creek*, and *Queer as Folk* each utilize gay bashing plotlines to initiate or reunite a romantic relationship for the victim. Moments before Justin's attack on *Queer as Folk*, he and Brian dance at the prom, dressed in tuxedos, drenched in soft light and romantic, if not clichéd, music. Crisp white tux shirts are soon soaked in Justin's blood, bringing signifiers of romance and horror into sharp juxtaposition.[12] Throughout Justin's recovery, Brian's deep devotion for Justin is never spoken, only symbolized by the white scarf from prom night that is caked with Justin's dried blood. Brian wears this spotted scarf, hidden under his clothes, for months. Homophobic violence becomes integral to their romance, just as a hate-driven bombing of Babylon, their staple dance club, rekindles their relationship in Season 5. The merging of gay romance with gay violence normalizes the violent homophobic act, but also encodes homophobic scapegoating with romanticized purpose.

Tragic mortification is also woven into the gay romance script, as seen in the film *Brokeback Mountain*. The disappointment Jack and Ennis feel in parting with one another, both love and shame for that love, is expressed through a fistfight. Their bloodied noses are simultaneously self-hating and romantic gestures, where Jack's blood-caked shirt is marked as the most significant symbol left of Jack and Ennis's relationship. Hanging in Ennis's closet at the close of the film, Jack's bloodied shirt is both a symbol of devotion and a document of violence, mirroring Brian's scarf on *Queer as Folk*. The conflation of gay romance and gay sacrifice creates a troubling complicity with homophobic tragedy, as violence becomes dangerously enmeshed in gay romantic scripts.

Bruised and swollen bodies account for just one of the many ways the representation of gay life is articulated through sacrifice. Rofes's 1983 publication on gay and lesbian suicide, titled *I Thought People Like That Killed Themselves*, names a cultural narrative that continues to circulate into the millennium. Just as Maureen in Hornsby's recent novel *The Long Way Down* reasons, "I didn't know anything about gays, so I just presumed they were all unhappy and wanted to kill themselves" (37), the suicidal gay remains a staple character in dominant vocabularies. *Little Miss Sunshine* opens with Frank in a hospital, following a failed suicide attempt. His sister says to him, "I'm so glad you're still here." Frank, stone-faced, utters his first line of the film, "That makes one of us." The easiest way to murder Yitzak (a.k.a. "The Fairy") in *Lucky Number Slevin* is simply to stage a suicide pact, referenced in the film as the standard "You do me—I do you—We're both Gay—the world doesn't understand" scenario. The "standard" scenario is demonstrated in these high grossing films,[13] as well as gay independents like *Latter Days* and *Shortbus*, perpetuating the tragic tale that "when the knife has fallen, Giovanni, if he feels anything will feel relief" (Baldwin 112).

The greatest testament to the sedimentation of the standard gay suicide scenario is its reoccurring appearance in cultural parody. In an episode of

52 *Queer Temporalities in Gay Male Representation*

South Park, set in a gay rehabilitation facility, young gay men kill themselves off by the handful. The discovery of gay corpses is played off like a "clean up on aisle seven" announcement in the grocery store.[14] Similarly, in the animated series *Drawn Together*, Xandir decides he must kill himself once he accepts he is gay. Melodramatically, he declares, "Goodbye cruel world," and stabs himself. However, as Xandir is a video game character, he has forty-nine lives left to terminate until "game over." Repeating his suicide over and over, he humorously confesses in exhaustion, "This could take a while." In an effort to cheer Xandir up, his animated friends throw him a "Gay Bash" to show Xandir how fun being gay can be.[15] The saturation of gay suicide and gay violence in popular culture has become comical, or, as Paul in *Rules of Attraction* moans, "so typical." As Paul dresses for a date, he is notified that his friend attempted suicide. Annoyed and disinterested, Paul resumes surveying his wardrobe, suggesting, "Call security, they'll be here in an hour." On the way to the hospital, with the suicidal friend *in* the car, Paul gripes about the inconvenience to his evening and a bad song on the radio. The other gay men in the car are screaming in dramatics as Paul sarcastically jokes, "He's not OD-ing. He's a freshman. Freshman don't OD." Gay suicide has become "so typical," a cliché, and a joke, that Paul's overly emotional friends come across as silly drama queens with nothing better to do.

As *South Park* and *Rules of Attraction* clearly exemplify the use of parody, offering a playful commentary of gay sacrifice in popular media, they usher in a discussion of potential resistance to the heteronormative tragedy. This study is focusing on mainstream articulations of gay male identity, aging, and future within dominant discourses, rather than marginalized or individualized audiencing practices. As argued by Sloop in his study of the cultural production of the Brandon Teena narrative, "mainstream discourses illustrate the rhetorically material ways that those who do challenge dominant ideology are ideologically disciplined" ("Disciplining" 169), marking how dominant systems of heteronormativity are upheld. In addition, this study—following Sloop's argument—is not claiming to explore gayness or queerness as a subjectivity (169), nor is it excluding the potential for queer strategies in audiencing. The intention is to look at how contemporary discourses define and constrain what it means to be an aging gay male approaching the future, and parody—while attempting to resist or mock the limitations of the discourse—fails to provide alternative articulations beyond the cultural narrative.[16]

This parody of the "over it" and "so typical" attitude surrounding gay corpses extends beyond animated series and dark comedies to seemingly more politically minded shows, such as *Queer as Folk*. When the body of a gay hustler is pulled from a dumpster, Brian calls the murder a "fashion statement," mocking the dead boy's wardrobe, and questions whether he, personally, fucked the killer at some point. "That would be hot," he smirks.[17] At club Babylon, the body of a gay man overdosing on the floor of the bathroom is no cause for alarm, but merely an obstacle, as dozens of men literally step over the body to rinse their hands and exit.[18] In a later episode, a series of corpses are pulled from the club due to a "bad batch" of drugs going around. Still, the music never stops, the club keeps going, and few even take notice of the bodies being removed from the premises.[19] In these representations, self-destruction is further normalized within gay culture and gay identity, and much like violence and suicide, it comes with the territory. This is exemplified on the erotic soap opera *Dante's Cove*, where an accidental cut on Kevin's hand is simply assumed to be a suicide attempt that was somehow "meth" related.[20] Kevin's friends and boyfriend all leaped to this assumption immediately, without question, even though Kevin had never used meth on the show, nor expressed any indication of suicidal ideation. Drugs[21] and suicide are simply the default narrative and the assumption is never questioned or interrogated.

Tragedy requires punishment, a purging of a symbolically constructed evil to redeem and reify the symbolic construct of goodness. Popular representations of gay male life are consistently engaged with flirtations with death to the point that death becomes an absent character, which is always present. Life and death move in close proximity to one another, where homophobic violence, suicide, and self-destruction are constantly waiting in the shadows, the alleyways, and the basements of gay male dreams. Tragedy subsumes the subplots that drive gay narratives, making them interesting, exciting, and problematically sexy and meaningful. In Dennis Cooper's novel *Closer*, several of his younger queer characters explore this flirtation with death, articulating its lure, its attraction.

> I saw this movie on TV tonight that made me think a lot. It was about a boy's death. He was like me. He took drugs and all that. The way he acted when he smoked a joint was a joke, but it wasn't too bad when he started to think death was great. The best part was when he took acid and thought he was dead. He saw these neat-looking skeletons who said, "We're you." And pointed down at their bodies. It scared him, but I would have stayed with them. It looked more fun than his life. (476)

Similar to the linkage of romance and violence, glamour and self-destruction share an uncomfortable relationship in these texts. In the opening sequence of *L.I.E.* Howie paces back and forth on the handrail of a Long Island Expressway overpass. Hands out to the sides, he tempts fate. Facing the freeway below him, he lifts one foot off the rail, exploring the line between risk and destruction. Jack, of *Dawson's Creek*, is flunking out of school and drinking like he "has a death wish."[22] He stands on top of a house, drunk and alone. Dawson yells at him to come down, but Jack throws his arms open and allows his limp body to fall off the roof, barely reaching the pool.[23] In the pilot episode of *Queer as Folk*, Brian and Michael stand on the roof of a hospital, discussing the birth of Brian's son. Brian questions the joy of "having some wrinkled little time clock to remind you you're getting older by the minute, by the second?" Stepping on the open ledge, Brian gazes down dozens of stories to the street below. "There is always one solution. I could end it all right now." Brian pulls Michael out onto the ledge with him, hugging him, in a romantic yet dangerous embrace, heightened by the awareness that death is an inch away.[24] Their flirtation with death is the final image of the pilot episode, an image suspended for several moments, which defines the relationship of Brian and Michael, the centerpiece of the entire series. Death is "always one solution," and whether or not these characters give into it, we repeatedly see images of them looking it in the face, acknowledging its presence, and negotiating—if not teasing—its possibility.

On *The Shield*, Julien chooses not to wear a bulletproof vest during a bust, in hopes that his life might be taken from him.[25] Rather than killing himself, leaving himself unprotected provides a way of opening himself up the promises of death. Julien's active refusal to take self-preserving measures provides a strong metaphor for unsafe sex and the risk of HIV/AIDS infection, the final recurrent theme that defines gay men's lives through complex relations with death. On *Queer as Folk*, Ben is marked as HIV-positive and is asked by his student if Ben will "give me the gift," referring to HIV infection. The student wants to "be liberated, free," assuming his contraction of HIV is not a matter of "if," but "when."[26] Michael, Ben's boyfriend, also flirts with the idea of consciously infecting himself with HIV to bring himself closer to Ben.[27] In *Mysterious Skin*, a teenage street hustler works for several years before he, with much confusion, is forced by a "john" to wear a condom. In *Queer as Folk*, Hunter is a teenage street hustler who offers sex without a condom for an increased price. When he finds out he has contracted HIV, he responds, "It's not a big deal, most guys out here have it."[28]

The narrative of the gay male body that is ritualistically sacrificed through HIV/AIDS is so deeply embedded in cultural vocabularies that the narrative no longer needs to be explicit. When TC comes out to his father in the romantic comedy *The Groomsmen*, a story of childhood friends reuniting for a wedding, his father's only response is a disgusted "Be safe." The economical scripting of these two simple words, "Be safe," and their ability to easily communicate complex meanings articulates the ever-presence of cultural narratives of threat, violence, and disease assigned to the gay male body. In *Happy Endings*, despite the fact that the gay male teen was a virgin, June's friend chastises, "How stupid are you? You screwed a gay guy without a condom?" In *The Next Best Thing*, there is a funeral scene early in the film, for Joe—whom we never meet. The cause of Joe's death is never explicitly stated, although Joe's disapproving family, a collection of queer mourners, his early death at forty-one, and the presence of red ribbons provide cultural signifiers to shorthand the sedimented "gay man who died of AIDS" narrative. Joe's partner David is also understood to be positive, based on brief shots of him facing a pile of bills and a collection of pills in his medicine cabinet. Their story needs no exposition, only a handful of signifiers for the audience to fill in the blanks to a familiar narrative. A similar device is used in *A Home at the End of The World*, where Jonathon's lesion is discovered late in the film, and we are to rely on cultural scripts to fill in this outcome. The issue is not the representation and discussion of HIV/AIDS, as popular media should continue to be discussing these issues. Rather than complicating the narratives and specifying these experiences, the stories rely heavily on clichéd narratives of tragedy to shorthand these experiences, efficiently coupling gay sex and the gay body with HIV/AIDS in the service of keeping the plot moving forward.

Unprotected sex and the dreaded AIDS test are familiar plotlines in several shows, such as *Six Feet Under*, *Noah's Arc*, and *Queer as Folk*. For leading characters, the outcome is usually HIV-negative, but the script functions to provide a short-term punishment for unsafe casual sex. Referred to in the Generation X slacker comedy *Reality Bites* as "the gay man's right of passage," the AIDS test subplot depicts a terrifying testing experience, an episode of deep depression where the character is certain he is positive because he deserves to be, and the redemptive second chance from a negative test result. These plotlines, while once again presenting gay lives primarily in terms of death, tend to over simplify the death sentence mentality of people living with HIV, but also promote the dangerous myths of "I deserve it" and "I know I have it." Awaiting the test results marks a liminal period of panic, shame, fear, and self-condemnation, where the characters metaphorically stand on the ledge of a building, flirt with the great distance they might fall, and negotiate with the absent/present character of death.

In the horror film, death lingers upon every frame, and we watch to see who will die next and how the next victim will be killed off. Homophobic violence, suicide, and HIV/AIDS provide strong recurrent themes that construct representations of gay lives through an ongoing dialogue with death, a fragmented tale of horror. The present and absent character of death continually dances in the shadows, the corners, and the alleys of the gay male narrative, as tragic sacrifice continues its circulation. On *Queer as Folk*, following a brief episode where Ted falls into a coma after a GHB overdose, Brian learns that Ted has left him in charge of whether or not to "pull the plug." Ted wakes from his coma to the sight of Brian fucking a man in the next hospital bed, and Brian is relieved of his decision-making obligations. To celebrate, Michael and Brian hit the dance floor of Babylon. With a giant smile, looking directly into Brian's eyes, Michael announces, "I want it to be you." Brian, with a smirk, replies, "I want it to be you too. You pull my plug." A smile is held between the two of them, their bodies rub up against one another, and they continue dancing as the episode ends.[29] The moment is tender in its depiction of a deeply committed friendship, but disturbing in the ways death is blurred with sex, glamour, and gay affection, each supporting the other in a construction of gay culture as a sexualized, cautionary, and thrilling dance on the ledge. Gay living is, once again, articulated in terms of looming tragedy and death rather than life. The heteronormative tragedy ensures that the gay male experience is constructed within narratives of death and punishment—reaffirming the misery attached to heteronormative deviance—and constituting life, progress, health, and future within the path of heterosexuality.

The previous section provided a foundation for the entire project, demonstrating how violent representations of gay punishment are not a thing of the past, as they continue to circulate in dominant media in the new millennium. Perhaps these discussions strike the reader as familiar, seeming to present nothing but a sequel to previous discourses on gay representation, best labeled *The Celluloid Closet 2: Freddy Lives* (and then dies, and dies, and dies again). Now that the notion of "progress" is thrown into question, generalized discussions of gay tragedy can begin moving into discourses of age, aging, and temporality, where time—specifically heteronormative systems of time—present a tragic temporal script that claims that gay lives are doomed to misery. The next section analyzes how gay male futures are constructed within discourse, establishing the concept of gay future as a cultural production of heteronormative temporal violence.

THE HARDER PATH: PARADISE LOST

> A lot of shit of being gay is grim. (Justin, *Queer as Folk*)[30]

> Patrick, when you came out you said that you didn't want to live the rest of your life in misery and I've never seen you more miserable. (Anne, *Broken Hearts Club*)

> It's a nasty world out there, so if Emmett doesn't have the guts to be gay, then fuck him. (Vic, *Queer as Folk*)[31]

> There's nothing we can do. I'm stuck with what I got here. (Ennis, *Brokeback Mountain*)

Isherwood's George asserts, "Damn the future. Let Kenny and the kids have it" (182), mirroring Edelman's claim that the future is perpetually hijacked from queers in the name of the sacred Child. Living a gay life in a violently homophobic and ageist society is constructed as "merely enduring and committing the longer and lesser and more perpetual murder" (Baldwin 118), as the gay future is constructed as sacrifice and punishment. Popular representation offers a strong counter argument to defining the term "gay" with its earlier connotation of happiness and joy. Text after text, representations equate gayness with a hard and miserable existence, a future of guaranteed doom and sadness, ensuring all audiences that punishment is served and the evil is purged (Burke, *Religion* 5). For those gay men who manage to live through the cloud of violence surrounding queer representations, symbolic punishment still awaits them in the end.

The seemingly "positive" depictions of gay teenagers in *Degrassi: The Next Generation* and *Dawson's Creek* restrict Marco's and Jack's representation to a non-stop avalanche of gay problems and turmoil. When Marco's life moves to the center of the *Degrassi* narrative, his gayness is constructed as his never-ending cross to bear. Marco's storylines consists of shameful coming-out sequences,[32] a gay bashing,[33] fear of being outed when running for student government,[34] the rejection of his blood at the school blood drive,[35] criticism for not being "out enough,"[36] and the never-ending task of educating heterosexuals one breeder at a time.[37] Marco's gayness is less an identity than a stream of situational obstacles that define his entire character. *Dawson's Creek*'s Jack McPhee endures a similar litany of hurdles; the familiar coming-out and heterosexual-education scenes, being targeted by the opposing football team for being gay,[38] losing the kids on his soccer team because of parental fear of a gay coach,[39] rejection from his high school prom,[40] and the ongoing struggle of always being "gay Jack" and nothing more.[41] Given the shortage of gay teen representation (Fejes and Petrich), characters like Jack and Marco are confined to delivering well-intentioned educational sound bites on behalf of gay cultural oppression. While important, what is sacrificed in these representations of daily gay hurdles is any sense of happiness, fulfillment, or existence outside of gay struggle. They do not live lives, but rather forever tackle issues. Jack says to Jen, "Why does my entire life have to be a fight? Why is something that's normal for someone else have to be political for me?"[42] Although Jack is written with a self-awareness of his own thinly drawn tragedy, as he explicitly marks this limitation, Jack never moves past the reductive plotlines of "gay Jack," spokesperson and tragic martyr.

The much-celebrated *Brokeback Mountain*—with respect to future and age—is simply the ongoing tragedy of two extremely miserable people. "Because of you Jack, I'm nothing. I'm nowhere." Ennis argues, "We're around each other and this grabs hold of us again, in the wrong place and the wrong time, we're dead." Jack fights back, yelling, "You wanna live your miserable life, you go ahead!" Of course, Jack's effort to live outside of Ennis's shame is met with a violent and fatal punishment. On *Six Feet Under*, David's straight brother Nate argues, "My life is a waste; at least I enjoy it!" David's only response is "Lucky you!"[43] In another episode, where David is told he needs to lighten up, he responds, "I'm a serious guy. I bury people for a living."[44] As a dedicated mortician, David symbolizes the tragic relationship between gay males and death in popular media, forever confined to an existence of negotiating and navigating the ever-presence of dying within daily life.

Gay culture, which is commonly reduced to bar culture—and more specifically young club culture—is often portrayed as shallow, empty, self-destructive, and self-loathing. This limited portrayal becomes the justification for several characters to seek heterosexual conversion. In *Shock to the System*, gay detective Donald Strachey investigates a gay murder by going undercover in a reparative therapy facility. Donald pretends to be one of the guilt-ridden gay men who desperately "wants their life back," "wants something better for themselves," and wishes to "choose a life, not a lifestyle." His undercover performance, however, leads to a personal breakdown as the out and proud "gay detective" quickly spirals into self-hating depression. Being gay, rather than the investigation, is the center of Donald's struggle, as he continually reflects on his ex-boyfriend who shot himself on the day he was discharged from the military and the "career, friends, and dreams" Donald gave up when he came out. "I'm cool being gay, you know that, but it's ridiculous to say it doesn't change things, doesn't affect your options." The film is about Donald's struggle of feeling "trapped" by his gayness, articulating the gay male life as tragic punishment.

The binary and tragic assumption that heterosexuality opens doors that being gay automatically closes is also reified in *Queer as Folk*'s gay rehabilitation plotline. During Emmett's struggle to "see the light," he is quick to dismiss his gay friends and community because it is not the life he wants for himself. Gayness is labeled as the road to misery, whereas heterosexuality is assumed to be the path towards happiness. The majority of this "rehab" subplot is played for laughs, with butch lesbians and flaming queens attempting to "breakthrough" via forced and awkward hetero-intimate experimentation.[45] Still, Emmett's "see the light" quest is treated seriously, as the audience is led to believe that he desperately wishes for another life, one that is not gay. Although Emmett eventually rejects "see the light," seemingly fueled by a "God loves you for who you are speech" from Ted, there are some problems that never seem to get resolved in the narrative. First, Emmett opts to leave the group only after a miserably awkward sexual encounter with a female, and we are left with the impression that he would have left "see the light" with or without Ted's inspirational speech. He did not stop wanting to be heterosexual, he just realized he could not be.[46] Second, Emmett's rationale for leaving the group, mirroring Ted's speech, is that God loves him just as he is. What remains uncontested in this subplot is heterosexuality's sole claim to happiness and a satisfying life. Emmett steps back into the club and picks up right where he left off, without any shift or desired change from his previous experiences, the very life he condemned as lonely, shallow, and unsatisfying. Although Emmett decides he is not heterosexual, the heterosexual ownership of "the happy life" remains intact, whereas the gay life remains the shallow and meaningless default option Emmett wished to flee.

Living as a gay man comes with no guarantees for happiness, as living the dream of white-picket heterosexual perfection lacks similar promises, but several films perpetuate the assumption that gay lives are inherently miserable lives. Michael from *Camp* exclaims, "My life is shit, " and gay characters on *Six Feet Under*, *Dawson's Creek*, and *Will & Grace* routinely lament that being gay is "just too hard." In *Running with Scissors*, the fourteen-year-old Augusten is fucked by the thirty-five-year-old Neil, laying in a confused and uncomfortable daze afterwards. Augusten asks, "What just happened?" Neil, in numbed indifference, replies, "You think you're gay? That's what gay men do. I wanted you to know the truth." Although this encounter is actually an isolated instance where an older schizophrenic and self-hating gay male introduces a young gay male to gay *sex*—and awkward and unsatisfying sex at that—the script generalizes the encounter to a totalizing statement of what it means to *be* a gay male. It may come as no surprise that gay lives are regularly demonized by the voices of heterosexist judgment in these texts, such as conservative parents, gay bashers, and the yet-to-be enlightened heterosexual friends. Even sympathetic voices, such as a cop on *Dawson's Creek*, will suggest, "The odds are stacked against you" without hesitation.[47] What is more troubling is the constant reification of gay misery, loneliness, and desperation from the gay characters themselves, supporting and embodying—rather than complicating—these myths. They testify to their own tragic existence, offering first person accounts of the seemingly factual linkage between gayness and punishment.

Tied to the "harder path" narrative is the deep-seated mythology of gay men's failure to achieve normal psychological and sexual development. Rooted in the more oppressive excerpts of Freudian theories of sexual development, the gay male exists in a state of stunted progression (12–3). This theorizing of sexuality fuels the construction of same-sex attraction as infantile and inverted, and is most clearly drawn in the film *Chuck and Buck*. Chuck is a twenty-seven-year-old man who has spent his entire life taking care of his recently deceased mother. Obsessively fixated on childhood games, sweet candy, and boyhood toys, Chuck seeks out his childhood playmate, Buck, in hopes of being "best friends" again. Chuck wants to play games with Buck, like they did when they were young boys, specifically "Chuck and Buck fuck and suck." Chuck stalks Buck, makes him juvenile collages of their childhood photos, and comes over to play. At twenty-seven, with a mouth of rotted teeth from sweets, and a haunting soundtrack of childhood music everywhere he goes, Chuck is constructed as the perverted invert who simply has "got to grow up." Themes of arrested development appear in multiple incarnations throughout culturally mediated representations. In *Sex and the City*, Stanford has a brief relationship with a man obsessed with his doll collection. "I was willing to look over the receding hairline, but the dollies?"[48] These narratives play of the cultural stereotypes that situate gayness as a developmental flaw, a deviation from the natural cycle of human socio-sexual development that unifies "normal" sexualities and demonizes its detractors.

Extending from themes of arrested development is the cultural production of gay men as developmentally stagnant. The suicidal James of *Shortbus*, a film about an underground New York sex club, confesses, "I look

60   *Queer Temporalities in Gay Male Representation*

back to things I wrote when I was twelve years old and I'm still looking for the same things now." In the political sitcom *Spin City*, Carter's ex-boyfriend decides he is now straight and plans on marrying his girlfriend. Carter is shaken by the news, exclaiming, "He's moving on and I'm standing still."[49] Determinations of "moving on" and "growing up" are defined by heteronormative models of marriage and children, while positioning the aging and single gay man as stagnant and developmentally failing. "Here we have a misfit, debarred forever from the best things of life, to be pitied, not blamed" (Isherwood 28). Brian on *Queer as Folk* is continually mocked for his "Peter Pan complex." In *Rules of Attraction*, Paul's first line in the film, after being kicked and spit upon, is, "I just get this feeling my life lacks forward momentum, you know?"

Forward momentum is defined through socially sanctioned models of progression, "the light" that promises heterosexual bliss, identifying the governing logic of "straight time" within these texts. Halberstam defines this temporal engagement as fueled by the systems of procreation, conservative definitions of family, heterosexuality, and normative conceptions of maturation (*Queer* 1). As noted by Boellstorff, straight time literally approaches time as a straight and linear sequence of heteronormative milestones (*Queer* 228). As these texts embrace straight time in condemning and criticizing nonnormative maturation and stagnation (under a heteronormative criteria of what constitutes movement), straight time is reified as the only model for conceiving of temporality. As gay lives, as well as many differing queer lives, do not fit or follow the prescribed trajectory of straight time, these lives are coded as failures. Halberstam calls for a queered consideration of time that moves away from limiting and heteronormative conceptions of "youth," "adolescent," and "adult," which are contested terms that seek to mark and stabilize straight time's authority.

The temporal regime of straight time constructs gay futures as dreaded, harder, and miserable, as the temporal map used to locate this tragic conception of future is drawn from a heteronormative model. The notion of "looking forward" implies the actual act of looking, as well as the assumed logic that our futures are somehow foreseeable in the present, fully contradicting the queer objective of exploring the unseen, the "not now," and the "not here" that lingers at margins of discourse (Muñoz, "Stages"). "Future," as constructed in popular media, is radically different than the quest for a queer futurity, as "future" is confined and determined by violently heteronormative discourses, and "futurity" seeks to look outside of these discourses to the margins of intelligible, yet potential, articulations.

The expression of "looking forward" becomes a contradiction in the ways gay futures are currently constructed, as optimism and forward-thinking are defined through heterosexuality, whereas stagnation and failure remain the defining models of gay futures. Heteronormative discourses define the future through the sacred Child, thus positioning queers as antithetical to dominant conceptions of future (Edelman). The dread, fear, and negative expectation have little to do with the world becoming a meaner or uglier place, but a tragic and sacrificial temporal regime. As the limitations attached to dominant conceptions of the gay male future have been presented, this chapter moves to explore the cultural production of gay male aging. Constructed as a distinct—as well as a tragic—process, the mediated articulation of gay male aging positions the gay male body in a ritualized sacrifice to the purification of straight time. It is the aging gay male body that is constructed as ugly, the aging gay male presented as the punished, and the ongoing tick of the clock that reminds all gay males that Freddy forever waits in the shadows of their futures.

DEAD MEN WALKING: MONSTERS AT THIRTY

> Faggot, faggots everywhere, and not a drop to drink. I can honestly say I don't want to have sex with any of these people. (Emmett, *Queer as Folk* at an over-thirty mixer)[50]

> Because you have the most marvelous youth, and youth is the only thing worth having . . . You have only a few years in which to live really, perfectly, and fully. (Wilde, *Dorian Gray* 24)

Bergling suggests that over forty in gay culture is old, and below thirty is young, and the thirties are a liminal space between the two (198). However, just as the camera adds fifteen pounds, it also seems to subtract ten years. Only one thing on *Queer as Folk* is more depressing than a gay bashing or an HIV scare—the dreaded birthday, and turning thirty is the age of doom. Brian warns, "Strange things happen at your thirtieth. You look great the night before but when you wake up your ass is on the floor." Ted responds, "I'm thirty-three, what does that make me?" Ignoring Ted, Michael jokes, "Did you guys just hear something?" Brian responds, "A voice from the dead."[51]

Ted, being the only main character over the age of thirty at the beginning of the show, is referred to as "dead man walking,"[52] constructed as the least sexually desirable of the four, constantly jealous of Brian's sexual conquests, secretly pining over youthful men, and living his life in a self-effacing state of rejection. Emmett consoles Ted, asking, "Why don't you try to go for someone like you, not—" "Young and cute," Ted quickly interjects.[53] His first line in the series is, "Talk about feeling ancient" as he stands at the bar, watching the beautiful boys of Babylon dance shirtless.[54] Later in the show, Ted attempts to do the unthinkable and date someone close to his age. Unable to be turned on by this "older" man—who looks mid-thirties and is supposed to signify "old" through thinning hair and an average build—Ted calls it off. His date furiously indicts Ted for "still hanging around younger guys who don't want you and never will!" Ted's flustered response to the "old" man is to go to the gym and get on a treadmill. Ted returns to Babylon, embracing his tragic fate as the invisible old guy, by declaring, "I was rejected by everybody [in the club]. It's good to be back."[55]

Ted is introduced as "the old one" at the beginning of the series, although Brian and Michael each pass the dreaded thirtieth in the first season. On the cusp of Michael's thirtieth, Brian says, "Hey, see that guy Mikey? He just turned thirty. That's what you're going to look like in a couple of days!" Brian points to a man on the street, near-seventies, wearing all leather, with vacant and buggy eyes. The boys laugh at the man as he passes them on the street. The older man defines the tragic punishment of gay aging, a sacrifice in the reification of youth dominance and a ghostly reminder—who wanders aimlessly in the streets—of the punishment that awaits the boys in the future. For the remainder of the birthday episode, Michael laments this "tragic event," which guarantees that "I'll never be young and cute again," that "I'm turning into a geezer," and that "my life is over." Brian throws him a giant surprise party, and for a fleeting moment the birthday is happy until an ugly fight ensues and guests run for the door.

The repeated lesson of *Queer as Folk* is that birthdays, and particularly birthday parties, are a recipe for catastrophe. When Ben walks into his surprise birthday party in Season 2, he responds by chewing Michael out in front of all the guests. He yells, "I told you I didn't want a party! I don't want to celebrate my goddamn birthday!" Off to the side, Brian quips, "Finally, a man with the right attitude!"[56] Ben had just returned from the doctor to find out his HIV was detectable again, and the birthday "celebration" is, once again, tied to sickness, illness, and deterioration. Still, in a show where age fear, age mockery, and youth worship are foundational to most episodes, few events solidify *Queer as Folk*'s "thirty equals death" mantra more succinctly than Brian Kinney's thirtieth birthday funeral. Complete with a coffin, a tombstone cake, and an official membership to the "Dead Faggots Society," Emmett announces to Brian, "It's the last day of the rest of your life." Melanie offers some "death-day cake." Brian is told to make a wish, to which a funeral participant interjects, "He already has and he's still thirty." Later in the episode, Brian, home alone, celebrates his "deathday" with a "very special gift" for himself, "the greatest orgasm of my life." He hangs himself with a silk scarf from the rafters of his loft, and masturbates while suffocating, nearly killing himself. After Michael saves him, Brian comments that death "wouldn't be the worst thing that could happen. To go out in a blaze of glory, like Cobain and James Dean, Hendricks. They're all legends. They'll always be young and they'll always be beautiful."[57]

The entire episode surrounds Brian carrying on "like it's the end of his life," to which Brian insists, "It is." He makes it very clear that "I don't want gray hairs and wrinkles. I don't want to be a grandfather, and I definitely don't want to grow old with . . . anyone else." When Lindsay asks him what he does want, as they are shopping in the store, Brian holds up the silk scarf he hangs himself with and says, "This." This is notably the same silk scarf Brian wears to the Prom on the night of Justin's attack, which is soon to be soaked in Justin's blood.

Brian is constructed as the most queer character, fully rejecting child, marriage, and future in favor of an unapologetic commitment to casual, public, and experimental sexual expression. This construction of Kinney helps to explain why his battle with aging fear and denial is an ongoing theme throughout the series, presenting age—itself—as Kinney's Achilles heal. His individualism, hubris, and unapologetic rejection of heteronormativity mark him as the ideal sexual criminal (Burke, *Attitudes* 39). Tragedy emerged as the punishment for the crime of personal ambition and pride, violating the pious and conservative propriety of the great tragic playwrights (39). In *Queer as Folk*, Brian's unwavering rejection of heteronormativity, while pious to a queered orientation of sexual expression, presents a modern-day representation of a classic tragic figure. Whereas attractive to dominant audiences for his steadfast commitment to fulfilling sexual desire, such pride demands a tragic sacrifice. Aging and future are Kinney's punishment, redeeming heteronormative temporal dominance and reifying the social order of heteronormative temporal correctness through his slow and painful deterioration of youth.

The primary characters on *Queer as Folk* all live to see the series ending, and for that, there is some testament to life after thirty in gay Pittsburgh. Still, age remains an ongoing joke and a deep-seated fear throughout the entire series, intensifying in the final season. Through multiple plotlines, the series depicts a perpetual battle between gay men and the ticking clock, always negotiating a lingering awareness that time is catching up with them. Brian routinely shaves years off his age, obsesses over his body's maturation, fights to hold onto his Peter Pan image, and proudly claims, "I plan on being dead by the time I'm thirty-nine."[58] While actively engaging in the fears and scripts of gay male aging, the series demonstrates the gay aging tragedy without complicating it, thus adhering to the heteronormative claim to future and the authority of straight time.

The "accelerated aging"[59] model is present in multiple representations, such as the popular sitcom *Will & Grace*. Jack is celebrating his twenty-ninth birthday, happily singing and performing in his usual narcissistic style, until Karen points out Jack's age miscalculation. As Jack is actually thirty, he is stunned for a moment, and then passes out cold on the floor. In a panicked frenzy, he calls Will on the phone, having a complete meltdown. Will comments to Grace, "He's talking crazy, using words like 'irritable bowel' and 'steady job.'"[60] In another episode, a fight between Jack and Will is quickly resolved after Jack informs Will that his anger is giving him unsightly age lines on his face.[61] Although conforming to the one-shot banter of the television sitcom model, signs of aging on *Will & Grace* are demonized and used as material for insult and diminished value. The question, as stated in the gay drama *Boy Culture*, remains, "Why is it that gay guys feel forty at eighteen?" The film poses the question but fails to provide a specific answer. Why does gay aging become a topic of discussion at seemingly "younger" ages, and why is it so feared?

Isherwood's *Single Man* finds himself as an older gay male playing the role of "a mean old storybook monster" (21) to the imaginations of the neighborhood children. He is "That Man" (21), that thing of childhood ghost stories and community tall tales. In literature, the older gay male has often been cast in these monstrous and predatory roles, such as Guillaume, the "filthy," "evil," "disgusting old fairy," who is "ugly, ugly" with "a body just like sour milk!" (Baldwin 106–7) and always subject to the humiliation of young boys (106). Younger gays have almost nothing positive to say about growing older, as it represents little beyond fear and loss (Bergling 162; Kooden and Flowers). One participant reported that "living to be old is '*probably* better than dying young'" (162), and Bergling is right to point out the serious problems with the term "probably," as if there was uncertainty to whether death might be a better option. Looking solely at the cultural production of aging gay males, the use of "probably" begins to make more sense, as the older gay male remains somewhat of a mystery and a question mark beyond limited stereotypes. The older gay male has not moved too far from the tragedy of Baldwin's Guillaume, Isherwood's monster, and the haunting nightmare of Freddy Krueger.

The television series *Dante's Cove* is a soft-core, sex-filled celebration of young muscular gay men living in a haunted resort hotel, filled with witches, supernatural powers, chiseled abs, and bed-tanned asses. The show begins in 1840, when Grace, a powerful witch, finds her fiancé Ambrosius having sex with another man. Grace murders her fiancé's lover and locks the thirty-year-old Ambrosius in the cellar, cursed to remain in chains for an eternity, where only "the kiss of a young man" can break the spell. With a wicked grin, she says to Ambrosius, "I've forgotten how you so love your own reflection," and instantly turns the hunky Ambrosius to an old man with stringy white hair and sagging muscles.[62] Rather than an eternity in the cellar, it is the curse of age that makes Ambrosius moan and wail in misery. With his youth stolen from him, he is seen as disgusting and worthless, never to win the attention of a young man's kiss.

One hundred and fifty years later, Ambrosius has finally mastered witchcraft and manages to lure a hunky young blond boy into the seller. He uses his powers to create the illusion that he is still young, luring the entranced young boy into a kiss. Once they have kissed, the boy sees Ambrosius as his older self and instantly vomits. The curse is broken, however, and Ambrosius is quickly restored to his cherished youth and beauty. The breaking of the spell marks the last time we see an older gay man in the young and muscular world of *Dante's Cove*. The aging gay male is constructed as cursed and doomed, a monster locked away in the basement, whose only aim or salvation is the hard-won attention of young boys.

Considering the long history of representing gays as vicious killers and bloodied victims (Russo), as well as this increased ageism present in recent gay popular media, it was only a matter of time before every negative mythology found itself playing out in a singular text. *Hellbent* marks the first explicitly gay slasher film, where a masked killer massacres a group of West Hollywood gay boys on the night of Halloween. Slasher films traditionally offer gross stereotypes, objectified bodies, and thinly drawn motivations of mass killings, and *Hellbent* remains somewhat true to the genre, delivering stereotypes and objectified bodies galore. What is missing from this gay slasher flick is any verified explanation for the killer's motives. Early in the film, one of the soon-to-be victims theorizes, "[The killer is] probably some forty-year-old gay guy who just came out of the closet." He argues the killer must pissed off because he is old and ugly, a motive he says he "couldn't blame." With that ridiculous stereotype out of the way in the first twenty minutes of the film, one might be hopeful that a better motive was waiting to be revealed in the third act. This expectation, however, is never met, and the only thing we ever find out about the killer is that he collects human heads, targets gay men, and only kills attractive guys in their early twenties. The latter is made clear, as the killer outright rejects the advances of a boy whose costume is full female drag. The soon-to-be-victim, costumed in drag, chases the killer down a dark alley, pleading that he is really an underwear model who is actually extremely hot. The killer stops and walks back to the boy in drag, who offers his drivers license as proof of his beauty under the make-up. The killer seductively wipes some makeup off the victim's face with his thumb to verify his "hotness," and then chops his head off. The killer is coded as gay in the film, based on several sexualized cruising scenes and the erotic smearing of the drag queen's makeup. The killer is muscular, has facial hair, and appears at least mid-thirties, although the certainty of his age remains unverified. At the end of the film, there is a passing comment that his face, which is always obscured by a mask, is hideous. The viewer is left to assume one of two scenarios. First, the angry, older, ugly gay killer theory was correct, as the ageist discourse, the critique of his face, and his lecherous cruising allude to this conclusion. The other alternative is that the film simply fails to provide a motive, deviating all together from the slasher film genre, yet reifying a precedent followed in Hollywood for decades: gays bodies are slaughtered, gay people are monsters, and this requires no context, explanation, or additional motive. *Hellbent* pieces together the fragmented horror story of tortured gay bodies, the literal flirtation with death, and the monster myth of gay aging into a tidy hour and a half, a triple feature of tragic punishment and purging.

The lecherous older gay male stereotype (Brown et al. 8) has many villainous masks, but none is more deeply rooted in the popular imagination than the monstrous pedophile. The older gay male body is coded with sexual predation, trolling the streets for young boys to cruise and abuse. These images play on a long and oppressive history of marking older gay men as "trolls" who seek to consume younger "chickens" (Fox). The stereotypical troll is worked into the basic plotline of several films, such as *Mysterious Skin*, *Bad Education*, and *L.I.E*, but also is enlisted in very subtle ways to signify fear, caution, and anxiety. Younger male bodies are used to signify a welcoming or nonthreatening gay bar, club, or location. To signify the connotation of a gay setting or encounter as creepy, threatening, and/or humorous, the older gay body suddenly becomes visible. For example, in *Boat Trip*—a film about two heterosexual men who accidentally board a gay cruise—Roger Moore plays an older gay man who continually hits on the accidental passengers. Moore's advances become the tip-off moment for the straight men to realize they landed on the wrong cruise. Moore's sexual innuendos and persistent come-ons are played for laughs, with silly lines like "care for a bite of my sausage" at the breakfast buffet. The older male body, here coded as gay, solicits a humorous response because he is the dirty old predator who scares the straight guys. Simultaneously, the heterosexuality of the two men is reaffirmed, as the predatory and desperate older gay male is merely a sight gag, posing no real threat of possible sexual relations or mutual attraction to the straight men. Place Will Truman in the exact same scene and the humor would not work, as the older gay body functions in unique ways. In their analysis of the discourse surrounding the Shepard murder, Ott and Aoki specify that Shepard was able to construct audience sympathy because he was "coded as unthreatening" (495). While marking Shepard as white and middle-class, and speculating that he would have been less likely to garner the popular attention he did had he been a person of color, Ott and Aoki continually mark his youth as an additional factor in his constructed innocent and unthreatening depiction. Furthering their line of analysis, this study argues that Shepard's murder would have been far less likely to receive national attention if he had been an older gay male, whose body is coded with an absence of innocence and imminent threat.

The casting of Roger Moore as the older gay seducer in *Boat Trip* is particularly interesting, as Moore is most commonly associated with his roles in several James Bond films. In *Boat Trip*, Moore has the same accent, has not aged substantially since his Bond days, and maintains the same suave and sophisticated presence that made him famous, yet once he is coded as gay he becomes both ridiculous and predatory. Whereas popular media continually points to the Bond men as exemplars of sexy (and assumed to be heterosexual) older men, Moore's body, when marked as gay, is no longer sexually desirable. Instantly, he becomes a creepy, unattractive, and silly old troll.

The use of older gay bodies to signify "look how scary this place is" has become a standard device in the Hollywood master narrative. The first time Jack walks into a gay bar on *Dawson's Creek*, the encounter is about Jack's fear and his own internalized homophobia. He is greeted by an old man, seemingly alone, who says, "You're adorable" in a manner that makes Jack all the more anxious.[63] As Jack goes to bars later in the series, more accepting of himself, the bars become younger, and thus less scary. Similarly, in *Trick*, Gabe's first club encounter at the beginning of the film is with an older man with a deep voice who stares Gabe down, making Gabe uneasy. The man then offers the line, "You're cute as shit," to which Gabe nervously shies away. On *Queer as Folk*, Woody's is a bar that is shown nearly every episode, commonly filled with guys in their twenties and thirties. Yet, when Jennifer nervously enters, looking for her teenage son, the camera makes a series of cuts to people in the bar, showing a close-up on a man well above fifty.[64] The same effect is used when Jennifer attends Justin's art show at the gay community center.[65] She stands at the entrance, nervously, while an older man with overstyled white hair and a shiny gold shirt passes her by. In these moments, older gay men make a rare appearance to signify embedded fears and mythologies attached to older gay bodies. Much like in *Boat Trip*, the substitution of a younger man in these situations would produce a radically different read.

Older heterosexuals are often thought to be asexual, whereas older gay male sexuality is constructed as excessive and insatiable, and thus humorous. The film *Nine Dead Gay Guys* stretches this device out for the entire film, where two young Irish hustlers try to make a living by selling their bodies to a cast of older, gay, and horny stereotypes. *Best in Show* and *The Producers* present flamboyant older queens in supporting roles, who drape themselves in kimonos, screech when they talk, and live and die by the sexual double entendre. The TV Series *Reno 911!* offers the pink-bandana and cut-offs-wearing Jim Dangle, a character that keeps the Blue Oyster Bar gag from *The Police Academy* series running twenty years later. In *Police Academy*, when someone took the wrong turn in an alleyway, they always ended up at the Blue Oyster, a gay bar filled with leather daddies dancing cheek to cheek to the same tired rhythm. The older gay man, much like the Blue Oyster Bar, is a cautionary signifier, a sight gag, that someone has made a wrong turn, violated the laws of temporality, stepped onto the wrong boat, or somehow has been lead down the wrong path. Once inside, however, the older gay male is not likely to be seen again.

THE INVISIBLE MEN: NOW YOU SEE ME, NOW I'M DEAD

> You look better this way. You should die more often. (Brian, *Queer as Folk*)[66]

> There would be the wrinkled throat, the cold, blue-veined hands, the twisted body, that he remembered in the grandfather who had been so stern to him in his boyhood. The picture had to be concealed. There was no help for it (Wilde, *Dorian Gray* 126).

> Do you think I'm ridiculous? (Louis, *The Hours*)

The description of the film seemed promising: an aging gay man who reflects on the life he has led and "where he's ended up—alone but not necessarily lonely." This was the synopsis on Netflix for the 1990 release of *An Empty Bed*, a film about a gay retiree in New York. The film opens with the ticking of the clock, as Bill wakes to a deep and sickly smokers cough. An empty wine bottle and TV dinner box sit in his trash, from the previous evening. Bill spends his day reflecting on past relationships that went sour, watching young boys play basketball, and remembering brief encounters with faces from long ago. His girlfriend from his youth, who since has been married and raised children, asks him, "Are you satisfied with your life?" Bill replies, "For the most part. Believe me, there was no other way." The sixty-minute film is generously paced, with time allotted for Bill's slow and pained climbing of stairs, his longing gazing upon younger bodies, and a flood of memories from when he was once a younger man. He moves through his neighborhood like a ghost, mostly ignored and invisible to the bodies around him. The film ends with Bill talking to a past lover on the phone—James, who ended up settling down and having children. Bill says, "I'm really glad you are happy," and hangs up the phone, once again alone in his cold and depressing apartment. Bill watches TV in the dark, smoking, and the credits roll. *An Empty Bed* offers yet another tragic tale of regret, isolation, invisibility, aloneness, *and* loneliness—reaffirming heteronormativity's discursive hijacking of the future and the correctness of straight temporalities.

Not limited to independent short films, the model of the invisible and miserable older gay male appeared in Wolfgang Peterson's 2006 summer blockbuster *Poseidon*, a disaster film set on a cruise ship. As action films are quick to rely on cultural stereotypes and signifiers to economically establish a character, the brief set-up of Nelson, played by Richard Dreyfuss, warrants attention. Nelson first appears on his cell phone, almost in tears, desperately pleading for his younger ex-boyfriend to return his call. In his next scene, Nelson sits at a table with several older men and orders a $5K bottle of wine, which he insists on purchasing. When the men at his table question this lavish expense, Nelson replies, "Carpe diem," and then quickly breaks down to explain that his partner has left him. He recounts how "he met someone" and "he didn't mean to hurt me." Speaking directly to an older—assumed to be gay—man at his table, Nelson states, "You know the old song so I don't have to sing it for you." The men share a knowing look, and Nelson steps out onto a deck of the cruise ship. He checks his phone, which has no new messages, and then tosses it into the ocean. He climbs on the railing of the cruise ship and is about to commit suicide, when he notices the giant tidal wave approaching the ship—which fuels the disaster plot for the next hour. In a manner of ninety seconds, the stereotype of the suicidal, miserable, older gay male is easily constructed with minimal information or exposition. Just as the young lovers with the overbearing father, or the renegade Navy man who wishes to work by himself, Nelson articulates a cultural character, an "old song and dance," whose narrative is easily pieced together through his age, his sexuality, and his breakup. In the catastrophe, thousands die, and less than ten people survive the horror of a cruise shift flipping upside-down in the middle of the ocean. Nelson ends up the ironic survivor, the man who has lost interest in life and was moments away from suicide before the disaster hit.

Living life as a gay man and a hit man for hire, Winston (a.k.a. Leroy) has not cried in over twelve years. In *The Mexican*, the character of Winston is played by James Gandolfini and describes himself as "somebody I don't like very much." This changes when he meets Frank, a mid-forties gay postal worker who is hitchhiking his way to Las Vegas. After spending a transformative evening with Frank in the hotel room, Winston recounts the evening's events to Samantha over breakfast. For a fleeting moment, Winston's life of misery and sadness seems to be turning around. Quoting Frank from the night before, he says, "The past doesn't matter. It's the future that counts." In a swift and tragic punishment for turning an optimistic eye towards the future, Frank is literally tossed out a high-rise hotel window as Winston finishes his eggs. Victimage and redemption quickly reify heteronormativity's claim to future, as Winston's happy life is violently ripped away from him within minutes of allowing himself to consider the concept. Twenty minutes later in the film, Winston is shot dead, leaving the remainder of the film to explore the reconciliation and future of the heterosexual protagonists.

Angry and bitter representations, like the jaded and sarcastic private detective "Gay Perry" in *Kiss Kiss Bang Bang*, are allowed to survive his gunshot wounds—as their misery provides symbolic punishment and upholds heteronormative correctness—but happiness or redemption for the older gay man comes with a price. As Burke's discussion of tragedy is grounded in Greek tales of crime and punishment (*Attitudes* 38), the representation of a happy or redeemed older gay man is punishable offense to the heteronormative orientation. The solidification of older gay misery is needed to retain the illusionary promises and correctness of heteronormative systems. Much like pride, good fortune, and hubris were actively feared in earlier tragedies, as they warranted punishment from the gods (38), the happy older gay men becomes a boastful challenge to heteronormativity—not unlike Brian Kinney—which demands sacrificial punishment. Happiness tempts fate, mocks the structure, much like a soon-to-be victim in a horror film uttering damning lines like "It's all over now" or "We're safe here."

In *L.I.E.*, Big John is set up as the dirtiest and most self-loathing of men. He drives around town in his teenage-boy-magnet car, sniffing the torn pocket of fifteen-year-old Howie's jeans. In his house is a pile of Polaroids of young boys that he has taken home at various times. John gets stellar dialogue like, "Five inches is a lot of snow, and a lot of rain, but not a lot of dick. You got more than five inches?" His much younger houseboy tells him he should be ashamed of himself. He calmly replies, "Oh I am. I am. I always am." Yet, once John develops a nonsexual friendship and respectful mentorship with Howie and begins to question his past relationships with boys, he is shot to death. Gordon Dietrich plays the goodhearted talk show host in *V for Vendetta*, who is forced to keep his homosexuality a secret under the oppressive and conservative regime. He is kind and respectful, accepting of his sexuality and constantly joking in the face of adversity. Ten minutes after we find out he is gay, he is beaten, a sack is thrown over his head, and he is counted among the deceased. Gordon is taunted as he is beaten down, "Not so funny now, is it funny man?" On *Queer as Folk*, Emmett has a short-lived relationship with George Shickle, a graying millionaire over twice his age. Although George is first disciplined with a flood of age jokes, calling him the "crypt keeper"[67] with the "three-hundred-year-old pickle,"[68] George and Emmett develop a caring and respectful relationship that ends right after it gets started. While leaving on an extended vacation to Europe to kick off their life happy together, George dies on the airplane before the flight ever reaches foreign soil.[65] Perhaps the happiest representation of an older gay man in film is *Broken Hearts Club*'s Jack, played by John Mahoney. Jack is upbeat, fun, educated, energetic, and always providing guidance to his cohort of twenty-something employees. Not surprisingly, Jack has a heart attack and dies, for no other reason than to provide the younger characters a chance to reflect on their own mortality for a fleeting moment. As in *The Hours*, Virginia Woolf discusses her decision to not kill her character Mrs. Dalloway, yet is convinced she must find another life to sacrifice. Woolf's young niece asks, "Why does someone have to die?" She replies, "So the rest of us should value life more." Enlisting a Burkean critique, the symbolic sacrifice of older gay men operates to support the value of heterosexual lives and straight temporal engagements, reifying their illusionary perfection through the purging of alternative visions of time, aging, and future. For those who fall outside of the rigid confines of heteronormative systems, however, rejecting the kill and allowing someone to *live* might provide a similar effect of valuing life more.

Jack's partner in *Broken Heart's Club* is known as "Purple Guy" because he always wears purple and none of the other characters in the film ever bothered to learn his real name. We are supposed to believe that the deceased Jack was one of the most significant figures in their lives, whom they worked with, played softball with, and deeply cherished, yet no one has a clue what his partner of twenty years is named (Walters 145). Older gay men are often shuffled to the periphery of gay culture, as well as representations of gay culture, whereas the trials and tribulations of younger characters are forever in the spotlight. There is no instance where this is more apparent than poor Uncle Vic, the older HIV-positive set piece on *Queer as Folk*. Vic spends the majority of Seasons 1–3 in a flannel robe, popping medications and offering one-liners from the far end of the dinner table. Like Richard in *The Hours*, he seems "to have fallen out of time," watching the world go on around him. In Episode 3, he gives his club ID to Justin, saying, "You can take it. I'm through with it," as his days in gay bars are over. One would think he might want his ID at some point, but Vic is only shown going out by himself once in Seasons 1 and 2. In that singular outing, he was framed and arrested for indecent behavior in a public men's restroom.[70] Vic is the saddest of representations, yet he is vocal about his invisibility. In one episode, Emmett simply asks Vic how he is doing. Vic suspiciously answers, "Why are you so interested in me all of a sudden?" Emmett claims he was just being friendly. Vic responds, "Bullshit, you boys never talk to anyone over forty unless you have it."[71]

Vic was correct in his indictment, as Emmett only spoke to Vic because of his current HIV scare. Several episodes later, when Brian asks Debbie how Vic is doing, she freaks out, assuming Brian must have AIDS.[72] To notice Vic means somebody must be sick. Vic exists on the show to feed the storylines of other characters. During gay pride, Vic makes an unexpected appearance at Babylon, to which Michael bitches, "What are you doing here?" Emmett corrects Michael, saying that even old men can celebrate pride. However, Vic was not there to celebrate. He had come from the hospice to tell Emmett that Godiva had passed.[73] Godiva, although we never see her or hear of her before her death, is an older drag queen who, while unreferenced in the show before or after this episode, seems to be Emmett's best friend for about thirty minutes of mourning. Leave it to Vic to be the bearer of bad news, as Vic, throughout the show, is always available to explain why friends should not sleep together, why partners should not move in together, and multiple narratives from his life of things that have not worked out. Vic attempts to go back to work at the diner, only to fail miserably and yell, "I'm useless, I'm worthless. I'm more than useless, I'm ridiculous!"[74] After being arrested in the public restroom, Vic is given a monologue that has more words than he usually speaks in multiple episodes:

> At my age, and with what I've got, to think someone could find me desirable? Talk about pathetic! . . . When I look in the mirror I see someone I barely recognize. I still imagine I'm like Brian, able to walk into any bar and have anybody that I want and I've had plenty too. Now, instead I see this tired, somewhat faded older man who measures his life from a pill bottle and nobody wants. I can't even remember the last time somebody looked at me, touched me. It was probably that Filipino nurse who gave me the barium enema. That was a treat.[75]

In the end of Season 3, Vic starts dating Rodney, and while their relationship is never developed beyond passing reference, Vic finally emerges from his flannel-robed shell. He opens a catering business with Emmett, moves in with Rodney, and seems, for a fleeting moment, to not be the same guy who uttered the line, "As an older gay man in this world you might as well be invisible."[76] We hear from other characters that Vic and Rodney are having sex, that Vic is happy, and we even catch five seconds of a dinner party where Vic and Rodney invite six other older gay men to dinner. Vic's sister Deb asserts, "Love is possible no matter what age you are," referencing George and Emmett's relationship as proof.[77] Subscribing to the tragic ritual of gay aging and undercutting any hope or optimism, Deb's line is uttered a mere ten minutes before George dies of a heart attack on the airplane. The tragic ritual that older gay male happiness is short-lived and requires punishment is further reinforced, as Vic dies before he and Rodney ever finish unpacking. The happy gay men never seem to last long, as this marks a basic and punishable sin to the integrity of the heteronormative social system. As Vic has always lived on "borrowed time," as he believed he would have died several years earlier due to his health, his temporal engagement has always been "out of time," removed from the linear timelines embraced by the other characters. In this sense, Vic represents what Halberstam marks as a queered engagement with time, as he operates outside linear narratives of progress, maturation, and child. Whereas the existence of his character offers the potential for a queered engagement with time, it is foreclosed by the narratives emphasized in the program, constructing Vic as peripheral, often decentered from the major plot arcs, and perpetually miserable. For a fleeting moment, Vic is happy, expressing optimism about the future, until he is quickly killed off. The episode with Vic's funeral, however, offered Vic more attention, praise, affection, or airtime discussion than the previous three years combined. In true Vic fashion, his death was about the fears, anxieties, and personal dramas of the *other* characters.[78] Unlike Woolf's theory in *The Hours*, the value of life was not increased through Vic's death. Rather, their own mortality and sense of impending death became all the more urgent and condemning for the main characters. How might the entire discourse of age in *Queer as Folk* be challenged by permitting Vic or George to live in a state of happiness as older gay men, who are not punished for a smile on their faces? What if they too, like Mrs. Dalloway, were allowed to live?

The heteronormative tragedy plays out stories of horror, peripheral lives, and invisibility for the aging gay male. The older gay man is still used as a foil in crime dramas, such as *Lantana*, where the audience is supposed to entertain the possibility that the mentally unstable Patrick might have killed the wife of the man he is secretly sleeping with. *The Night Listener* sends Robin Williams, who was recently dumped by his much younger boyfriend, on an obsessive quest to find a fictitious teenage boy who brings purpose to his depressed existence. *The Next Best Thing* offers "two of the most evil queens in show business" on the periphery of the story, as well as a doting father who learns his devotion to his son holds no ground in a court of law. The hot young hustler X refers to his devoted older clientele as his twelve disciples in *Boy Culture*. Richard, locked in a dark and dreary apartment in *The Hours*, is cursed with having to face the hours that await him, as his body slowly deteriorates from AIDS. Staying alive only for his dear friend, he chooses to let his body fall out the window and escape the hours he faces. In *Mysterious Skin*, an older man takes a hustler home, having to pay someone to merely touch his body, which is covered in lesions. "Oh make me he happy, make me happy" he moans in sad desperation, asking Neil to simply rub his back and offer the simplest of physical contact, which he so desperately longs for.

According to popular media, *Queer as Folk* is quite accurate in labeling birthdays as tragic events. Gay aging is constructed as a tragic ritual of punishment, exclusion, and sacrifice, where the aging gay male is cast out of a youth-worshipping culture and disciplined in the service of supporting the correctness of heterosexual models of future and temporal engagement. Within this heteronormative tragedy, gay future, health, and longevity are devalued, offering limited promise in looking forward. In the rare appearance of older gay male characters, they tend to range on a scale from at best peripheral and humorous, and at worst monstrous. These invisible men who are absent, missing, and lingering in the outside of the frame become the most concrete models of what it means to be an aging gay male—the images of gay future. If *Sex and the City*'s Stanford is correct in arguing, "Even guys like me don't want guys like me,"[79] and *Queer as Folk*'s Brian believes older gay bars present yet "another reason to die young,"[80] what does it mean to be "young" gay man in contemporary popular representation?

LET'S HEAR IT FOR THE BOY: THE KING OF BABYLON

> When you're young like I am now, and you're fairly good looking and you know how to dress, it's like you're the "golden child." ("Will" qtd. in Bergling 43)

The forty-year-old David on *Queer as Folk* critiques the "the single most tragic flaw of gay culture," its "pathological obsession with youth, beauty, and smoother muscular bodies." Brian, in his usual dismissive sarcasm, responds, "I know, what a shame."[81] The setting for this dialogue is the annual King of Babylon competition, where men strip before a packed house of club-goers in hopes of being crowned the highest of honors. As David's age has been the ongoing joke for several episodes, with a never-ending list of one-liners about prostate massages and dentures, ageism becomes an explicit topic in this one episode. Brian dismisses David's critique, as well as my own, by reducing it to "an opinion put forth by a bunch of hypocritical, jealous, guilt-ridden, self-loathing, middle-aged, sexually frustrated, pseudo-intellectual fags who wish they were straight." While it is always a nice change to have characters in a text reverse the tables to analyze the critic, the episode reduces the ageist critique to the limited opinion Brian offers. In his usual crafty and conniving manner, Brian secretly signs David up for the King of Babylon competition, and David takes the challenge. Michael, David's younger boyfriend, is furious, telling David he will "make a fool out of yourself dancing around in your underwear at your age." Dancing on the pole and sliding down his Levi's, the crowd at Babylon cheers David on. The moral of this story is that David is, in fact, jealous of youth and secretly desires the attention he criticizes. Michael calls David a hypocrite for tossing all his politics out the window and abandoning his critique of youthism after receiving positive attention.

The "King of Babylon" story goes much further than the redemption of age and the exposed hypocrisy of gay cultural critique. First, David's critique of gay culture indicted the "obsession with youth, beauty, and smoother muscular bodies," a standard that David's body conforms to on several levels. As a series regular for most of Season 1, David's body has been on display for several sex scenes with Michael prior to its dramatic unveiling. His body is muscular, tight, and hairless, having been noted as extremely fit for his age in previous episodes. Second, his reception at Babylon is qualified by his age and his status as a doctor, which is considered "hot," but only "for an older guy." Finally, while David does not make a fool of himself, he does not—nor do any other of the buffed out gym regulars—earn the title of the King of Babylon. This honor is bestowed upon the golden boy of Babylon, Justin Taylor, who is a thin seventeen-year-old, who has yet to attend his high school prom.[82]

At the center of television and film constructions of gay culture sits the golden boy, the younger gay boy who shifts attention whenever he enters the room. He is the Kevin of *Dante's Cove*, the Justin of *Queer as Folk*, and the Kevin of *Broken Hearts Club*.[83] The golden boy is the underwear model that *Sex and the City*'s Stanford insists "travels with his own personal lighting director,"[84] and the "Wonder Boy" James Leer of *Wonder Boys*. Frank in *Little Miss Sunshine* attempts suicide because the young graduate student he fell in love with rejects Frank and chooses to be with Frank's scholarly rival. Frank's inability to gain the attentions of his young student is a mark of his failure—a possession lost to a competitor—much like the fellowship his competitor is awarded. The golden boy is a prize to be battled over, much like the boyish Kevin who sits at the center of a love triangle with Toby and Ambrosius in *Dante's Cove*. As the object of desire, he has the power to give himself, such as the character of Troy in *Queer as Folk* who offers Ted a "mercy fuck" during gay pride as his generous way of "giving back to the community."[85] Cooper's novel *Closer* articulates the power bestowed upon the golden boy in his description of George, whom Chuck refers to as "an incredibly beautiful boy" (42). George recounts afterwards in his diary, "I allowed this guy Chuck to have sex with me . . . I was like something he wanted to buy but couldn't really afford" (42).

Mirrored in the dance remixes of "Let's Hear It for the Boy,"[86] "Forever Young,"[87] and "Nothing Stands in Your Way When You're a Boy,"[88] when Justin Taylor steps onto the dance floor of Babylon, youthism is reified with every turned head. In need of extra cash, Justin offers, "I have a great ass and I'm blond. You have no idea how far that gets me."[89] Justin proudly announces, "I still have youth on my side,"[90] and "I'm cute. I could fuck anyone I wanted."[91] Justin enters the King of Babylon competition for the sole purpose of showing Brian he is not to be taken for granted. Although Brian never enters the contest, Brian is, in many ways, constructed as the unofficial King of Babylon. Although Brian is sexual royalty of Liberty Avenue and is supposed to be all-powerful in the land of fucking, age becomes the primary variable that knocks him off his thrown. Justin takes the stage of the King of Babylon contest and the crowd falls under his spell.[92] Lacking the qualified "for your age" support of David's dance, the entire club is obsessed on this boyish blond in his underwear. Brian is attempting to pick up Sean, his "lucky pick" of the night, but Sean stops kissing Brian repeatedly to gaze upon Justin's body. Justin approaches Brian and Sean after his stripping triumph and steals Sean from Brian with no effort. As Justin and Sean head off together, Sean says to Justin, "I guess we could have a three way, but he is kind of old." Justin has wielded the power of youth in Brian's face. Dethroned, Brian watches the boys screw each other with a desperate longing, now cast as the tragic voyeur who is punished for his age. Ted proudly narrates, "The cub stole the lion's prey."

In *Six Feet Under*, David plays a late-twenties to early-thirties man who has limited to no experience in gay bars, offering a fresh perspective on the unique ways age functions within gay cultural settings. When David goes on a date with a man in his mid-twenties, there is a great moment when his date confesses, "I've always liked older guys." Taken aback, and seemingly unaware, David half asks and half realizes at the same time, "I'm the *older* guy?" His date, who happens to be studying to work with the elderly, launches into a speech about hating the ways younger gay guys treat the older queers. "You know, 'tired old queen, fossil, troll,' as if we aren't going to end up there, ourselves, one day, if we're lucky."[93] As David is fairly removed from the "gay scene," he does not seem to follow this discussion with any interest, and provides a counter-perspective to the blind worship of youthism. In a later episode with the same date, David asks, "Is dating like an excuse to figure out who you wanna be when you grow up?" The date replies, "I don't know. Is dating like an excuse for you to see who you wished you would have been when you were my age?"[94] David's naïveté regarding the discourses of age in gay culture provides an interesting challenge to youthist ideologies but also points to the ways extreme youthism becomes somewhat foreign to those at the margins of gay cultural identification. The designations of "old" and "young" operate on a sliding scale within these texts, acknowledging that "older" and "younger" are always subjective and situational. In addition, as David marks an exemplar of the gay man who fully embraces straight temporality, he sees himself preparing to get married and settle down, rather than a cast-out member of gay cultural youthism. Firmly committed to systems of heteronormativity and locating his identity within them, David appears removed and unfamiliar with the tragic discourses of gay aging.[95]

In the first episode of Season 1 on *Queer as Folk*, Justin arrives on the scene and is repeatedly marked as "too young" by the gay regulars on the show. His youth does not exclude him from sexual propositions, however, as the first person he speaks to on the gay strip is a late-forties man who tries to take him home and gets pissed at his polite refusal. This same night Justin meets and has sex with Brian to the soundtrack, "You think you're a man, but you're only a boy. You think you're a man but you're only a toy." Justin occupies both roles of the dream boy to take home and the naïve newbie who is not to be taken seriously. As Michael's and Brian's descent into thirty is marked as the beginning of "old," *Queer as Folk* suggests that the limited window of sexual desirability falls between eighteen and twenty-nine. Although this limited age window is reified within bar culture, "old" is always dependant upon context. The much older George Shickle, Emmett's short-lived love interest, proclaims, "At my age, everyone is a boy."[96] Like David of *Six Feet Under*, George has lived outside the world of youthist gay clubs and offers a counter-perspective that draws attention to the limitations of youth worship. As Emmett is considering getting butt implants, George's perspective is that "plastic surgery is for foolish old men who refuse to grow up gracefully." Emmett kindly challenges George's statement, arguing, "In my world, if you don't look like you just stepped out of a Calvin Klein underwear ad, you're nothing."[97]

Tensions of insider and outsider familiarity with gay youthist norms help to identify the unique ways age is constructed differently in heterosexual contexts, removed from the unique ritual of tragic aging in gay cultural contexts. Although Roger Moore can be read as dashing and handsome as a distinguished-looking heterosexual male, as a gay male he is coded as silly and predatory. Articulated perfectly by Howie in *L.I.E.*, when he begins developing a friendship with Big John, "I'd say you're just like James Bond, but James Bond doesn't go around blowing boys." John Mahoney played the heterosexual father on *Frasier* for years, without the slightest consideration of sexual tension between his character and his nurse Daphne. Yet, as Jack in *Broken Hearts Club*, when he tells one of the younger men who works for him that he loves them, there is an awkward silence. Jack, to fill the awkwardness, disclaims, "Oh don't get nervous. Little kids and senior citizens don't say it so you'll say it back." The predator myth dominates the majority of the times an older gay man enters the frame, to the point that it needs to be addressed and dispelled before the dialogue between a younger man and an older gay man can proceed. It becomes the pink elephant in the living room, the Freddy Krueger phobia. When Justin runs off to New York to be a street hustler on *Queer as Folk*, the cast tries to figure out who should go after him. Vic removes himself from the discussion, suggesting, "If I go, it's a little Phagan in *Oliver Twist*."[98]

Age is positioned in the center of a gay cultural battle, where youth is granted power through worship and age is feared as predatory, if not vengeful. The "good" older man must be completely disarming, allowing the youth full agency in pursuing the older man, less he be branded a troll. In *Boy Culture*, the elderly Gregory announces to his paid hustler, "Our time will come, but not until you desire me as much as I desire you." Anything less than submission to the will of gay youth becomes demonized and subject to villainous stereotypes (Goltz, "Laughing"). George and Emmett's brief relationship is admissible only because Emmett remains completely in control of sexually initiating their encounters, and George is written as possibly the most saintly man who ever walked the earth. In Neil's earliest hustling encounters in *Mysterious Skin*, Neil enjoys having older men perform oral sex on him, but this does not compromise the ways the older, sometimes very friendly, customers are coded as carnivorous pedophiles. The battle of youth worship and predatory age plays out as the older man drops to his knees, declares, "You are such a beautiful boy," and drops his face into Neil's crotch like a pie-eating contest. Even in the land of animation, the same scenario plays out on *Drawn Together*, where the more-than-willing Elmer Fudd orally services the teenage Xandir.[99]

Queer as Folk's Brian is often marked as the "old one" in reference to his relationship with Justin, but Brian also claims the power of youth in his interactions with men his senior. In order to land the advertising account of Marvin's company, Marvin—mid-to-late forties and married with kids—wants Brian's body in return. Brian agrees to the terms, slowly stripping his clothes away, as Marvin sits in a chair, taking in the show. For a moment, Marvin seems in control, and Brian's usual authority is briefly compensated. Marvin lowers himself to the ground, kneeling before Brian's naked body when the phone rings. Upon Brian's request, Marvin, on his knees, crawls to answer the phone. Brian takes the seat in the hotel chair, naked, holding a champagne bottle, as Marvin remains kneeling on the floor. On the phone, Marvin lies to his daughter, who broke her arm, claiming to be too busy with work to come home. The roles switch, and the youthful and naked Brian informs Marvin that his "visit to queer world is over," standing up and walking out the door stark naked.[100] The initial placement of Marvin in the chair ordering Brian around, based on his financial power, was instantly usurped once Brian removed his clothes. Marvin was reduced, like so many older men before, to a cowering fool at the feet of "something he wanted to buy but couldn't really afford."

Youth wins this battle sometimes, but other times it ends violently. As discussed previously with *Hellbent*, or the violent beating of Neil's body in *Mysterious Skin*, the myth presents the older gay male as a marginalized monster seeking revenge on the youth that overpowers and excludes him. In Cooper's *Closer*, George's young thin body lays naked on the floor, numbed with Novocain, as Tom hacks away at his fleshy ass. George's blood covers the floor and the rug around him. Tom, who is described as "an older man" who "looked like a stork wearing glasses (88), slowly tears George's body apart. George listens to his own mutilation, hearing himself being "chopped down" (99). Tom's desire to mutilate and dissect the young male body is coupled with George's troubling ambivalence towards life.

The question is how the situation ought to be read. Is the glass half empty, arguing that age is demonized, or is the glass half full and youth is revered? Rather than an either/or discussion, the issue of ageism and youthism is better served as a discussion of both/and (Burke, *Counterstatement*). The metaphors of the chicken and the troll (Fox) work together in the ongoing tale of heteronormative tragedy, as one provides the other its definitional coherence. Youth worship needs the devout "chicken-hawk" for its power, just as the miserable troll's fate is secured by the ageist "chicken." Where this discussion is complicated beyond the simple dismantling of a false binary is the temporal evolution of the chicken into the troll. The worshipped becomes the worshipper, losing power within the hierarchy as time goes by. Whether thirty equals death, or David's forty-year-old body is impressive "for his age," the commodification of youth will always result in one common denominator: the tragic punishment of the gay male through age, devalued longevity, and a future constructed through deterioration and regret. Each day is one step further into the loss of value in a youthist/ageist economy of gay cultural construction.

The separation of ageism and youthism as isolated concepts or differing areas of study fails to interrogate their coextensive relationship. As a final example, *The Deep End* tells the story of a mother who is desperate to protect her son Beau from his relationship with an older gay man. When she finds Beau's boyfriend Darcy dead, she falsely assumes Beau was responsible and devises a scheme to hide the body and protect her family. Darcy is scripted as a lecherous, violent, dangerous gay man, who secretly videotapes Beau during sex and sells these tapes. For these reasons, Darcy's death, even though an accident, is presented as a welcomed and deserving punishment. Darcy represents the corrupting result of "gay culture," the doomed monster with his foreshadowing license plate "6 FT BLO." Beau, however, is the innocent child who does not understand the dangerous and corrupting life he is flirting with, this "harder path" that requires a tragic punishment. The film is viewed through the eyes of Beau's mother, where Beau and Darcy are not the "good guy" and the "bad guy," but more of a "before" and "after." The monstrous and rightfully sacrificed Darcy represents the thing she fears for her child, a future with no future.

The interworkings of youthism/ageism articulate the power of gay aging mythologies, still reliant on the vampire-like conversion stereotypes of earlier Hollywood representation. It is not a singular bite that turns the innocent into the monster, but time itself, a passed-down legacy of youthism/ageism that remains coded in pop cultural discourse. The future is crafted as an unwelcome place for the gay male, a sight of miserable, if not grotesque, transformation. Mantras such as *Rent's* "No Day

But Today" speak to the privileging of the now and the uncertainty of a tomorrow in the time of AIDS, but also to complicity with heteronormativity's claim to the future as its sole property. Hearing Jack on *Dawson's Creek* argue, "It's not my future I'm concerned about, but the present,"[101] reifies Richard's speech in *The Hours* that "no matter what you start out with, it ends up being so much less." These texts articulate and validate the heteronormative claim to the future, while simultaneously sentencing the gay future to tragedy. Much like Emmett's struggle to "see the light," happiness and future remain the sole property of the heteronormative orientation.

Old Hollywood models of sacrifice and heteronormative redemption cycles continue to circulate, as the texts in this chapter vilify and demonize the very concepts of gay aging and gay future. This chapter has demonstrated the fragmented horror story that constructs gay male lives as tragic sacrifices in the reification of heteronormative systems, imposing disciplinary order on the cultural narrative of gay male aging through tragic framing. Embedded in the gay horror story, death and suffering linger in the margins of gay lives. Homophobic violence, AIDS, suicide, and guarantees of a "harder life" offer the promises of sacrifice and misery—whether through scapegoating or mortification—for those who dare stray from the heteronormative script. This horror film is further complicated by the interworkings of gay male youthism/ageism, for just as the body count rises throughout the progression of a slasher film, the gay aging narrative is a progression of loss. Heteronormativity positions gay males in a tragic narrative of straight time, a violent and disciplinary temporality that shores up heteronormativity's assumed correctness by crafting time, aging, and future within a limited and oppressive framework. Time becomes a punishing force, a ravisher of youth, which guarantees that misery, isolation, and rejection await the aging gay male.

Freddy Krueger is not only the embodiment of the gay aging myth, the predatory and monstrous older gay man, but is also the embodiment of gay time and gay future. Gay aging is not just punishable; gay aging *is* the temporal punishment. Gay male aging is constructed as a tragic ritual, solidifying heteronormative order and its claim to the future. The future is an ever-approaching nightmare where gay health, longevity, and happiness are punishable crimes, yet dancing with death is romanticized. Research continually rejects these aging myths (Berger, *Realities*; Berger and Kelly 62; Brown et al.; Dorfman et al.), yet popular culture keeps them very much alive. Like Freddy, the nightmare is deadly as long as one believes it. Fear gives Freddy the power to diminish hopes, prevent dreams, and contain futures—foreclosing the space for potential futurity. Much like the tragic ritual of gay male aging, Freddy is powered through fear and powerless when he is no longer feared. Both of these horror stories, however, repeat themselves in film after film, sequel after sequel, keeping their power very much alive in the cultural imagination. Tragedy is a circular process, forever repeating itself until the frame is transcended, gaining power through its own momentum and its own self-securing correctness.

What would happen if Vic or George were allowed to be happy, healthy, and satisfied as the final credits roll? How is the tragic ritual of gay aging challenged or rearticulated in Hollywood's master narrative? If not the tragic temporal punishment of doom, gloom, misery, and exclusion, then what is next and how might it be actualized? What does it mean to *live* as a gay man and to *live* with age? These "innocent questions" are explored in Chapter 4, as normative gay defense strategies—a series of rhetorical negotiations, postures, and compromises to overturn the tragic sentence of misery and punishment—are interrogated. The normal gay male must remove all doubt that he poses any sexual threat to society, heteronormativity, or dominant systems of orientation, adopting and supporting the correctness of heteronormative temporal blueprints. In short, the older gay man must argue a plea of innocence, distancing himself from queer politics, queer temporal engagements, and queer sexuality to erect a child-loving, commitment-minded, family-oriented, and privilege-blind defense. Futurity is sacrificed for identification with the future.

4 Future Identification
Symbolic Mergers with Heteronormativity

> *JOEY:* [A year ago] all you can see is the pain and the loneliness that's making your life different from everyone else's.
>
> *JACK:* ... As opposed to now when all I can see is the pain and the loneliness that makes our lives the same. (Dawson's Creek)[1]

The mediated production of both gayness and dominant cultural values, and subsequently the mediated production of the differences and similarities between gayness and cultural values, are a matter of rhetorical construction—bridged and severed through processes of identification. According to Burke, identity is nothing more than a multitude of identifications, a series of systems, institutions, orientations, or corporations with which one identifies (*Attitudes* 263). Identification is primarily a "function of sociality" (267), which is inevitably tied to one's environment. Shared identifications result in the construction of a consubstantial "we," where the symbolic construction of a mutually shared substance can be created (*Grammar* 21). The concept of substance, according to Burke, draws attention to the very nature of symbolic language and its capacity to construct polarity, division, and the negative. "Substance differs from itself, for it moves between a sense that denotes what a thing intrinsically is," yet paradoxically defines its innateness through which it is not (Tomkins and Cheney 226). The paradox of substance suggests that all things—no matter how different—can be seen from an alternative perspective that identifies some common ground.

Thus far, this analysis has explored heteronormativity's construction of gay males within a tragic frame of punishment and the gay male aging process as a tragic ritual, which serves the purpose of redeeming and reasserting the illusions of heteronormativity's and straight time's perfection. Through the construction of the tragic binary of homosexuality and heterosexuality, gay male futures are articulated as substantially different, equated with ritualized punishment and sacrifice in a tragic tale of horror. This chapter explores the symbolic construction of the future within a heteronormative orientation, shifting the focus from gay male representations of tragic sacrifice to normalized gay male representations seeking identification and symbolic merger with heteronormative temporalities and futures.

"Future" is an abstract symbolic construct, one which differing identities may or may not identify. As argued, in the previous chapter, gay male future is articulated through punishment rather than reward. Through this framing, the gay male is denied identification with future, as the tragic framing of the gay male future lacks the inherent reasonableness of investing in the future. Burke discusses this relationship between future and identification through the example of gerontocracy, a society where age is rewarded and respected—permitting and inherent "'logic' of life" (*Attitudes* 221). "Even a young man can 'identify himself' with such a course of events, since it gives a logic to the inevitable biologic curve of his own development. It makes old age a promise rather than a threat" (221). As the tragic framing of gay male futures denies such "logic," casting the gay male within a system where the future is threatening, identification with the future is no longer desirable or reasonable. The following chapter examines this relationship, interrogating what it means to identify with the future, or more pointedly, how are identifications with the future constructed? To begin this discussion, it is important to first locate and name the primary scripts that erect the notion of "future" within dominant heteronormative systems.

In a classroom exercise, students are asked to fill in the following statements with whatever words or phrases come to mind.

1. In one year I will be _____.
2. In five years I will be _____.
3. In fifteen years I will be _____.
4. In thirty years I will be _____.

Following the exercise, answers are discussed with the entire class. After several semesters of utilizing this activity, students define (and confine) their futures through a handful of repeated trends and themes. In one to five years, the focus of student answers centers on themes of finishing their education and securing a stable job. The fifteen-year projection, however, presents near-unanimous attention to two major themes, marriage and children. Given the option of selecting only a word or phrase to define themselves in fifteen years—with an infinite number of potentials at their disposal—the overwhelming response from each class is identification with the roles of spouse and parent. Although many of these students may not get married, and statistically a good number of those who do will experience divorce, the heteronormative script is *the* primary cultural blueprint for planning lives, futures, and understandings of successful aging. The identities of spouse and parent define the dominant understandings of future, as well as the means by which students establish identification with the future.

The heteronormative tragedy constructs the future in terms of a false binary, a two-sided coin. Existing on one side are the false promises of heteronormative perfection and guaranteed happiness. These scripts, the promises of intelligible and satisfying futures, are what Hollywood dreams are made of. Heteronormative temporal perfection tells a story of happily ever after: love conquering all, the blessed gift of children, and a guaranteed slice of the American dream. Monogamous love, marriage, and procreation provide the keys to the kingdom, the honor of respectful sexual citizenship, and identification with a future worth embracing. On the other side, there is punishment and misery for those who fail to embrace and perform the assumed rightness of heterosexuality or fail to identify with heteronormative structures for future building. The future shifts from a site of identification to the experience of alienation. Burkean alienation explains the experience where one no longer identifies with their world or system, as it has become unreasonable (*Attitudes* 216). While the break from identification requires the creation of a new identification, in terms of the future, this becomes more complicated. As Edelman discusses, dominant discourses have positioned the Child as the symbol of the future and have thus positioned queers as rhetorically anti-future, and they are thus cast as aliens to the future. Where many queer theorists challenge the assumed fixity and correctness of heteronormative systems,[2] gay assimilation strategies seek normative inclusion through strategies of identification with heteronormativity. Brookey argues the presentation of the "good," the "sensible," and the "relatable" gay person is a rhetorical process of identification (46), where the "alienating aspects of deviant sexuality" (50) are downplayed and heteronormative values are placed front and center. The promises of the "harder road" nightmare of heteronormative violation are abandoned in the quest to win access to the socially sanctioned narratives of marriage, child, and happily ever after. As identification with heteronormative conceptions of future constructs a heteronormative identity—identity being the composite of multiple identifications—the focus of this section is placed on the rhetorical strategies of assimilationist representations. Through the construction and assertion of an identifiable gay male, normalized representations use dominant ideologies as bridging devices (Burke, *Attitudes* 224), building symbolic mergers with dominant systems to gain access to an identifiable future.

Constructing identification with heteronormative systems requires a reasoned and strategic negotiation similar to the court of law, from which the very notion of tragedy is derived (Burke, *Attitudes* 38–9). Enlisting the courtroom as a governing metaphor, the analysis examines heteronormative codes of conduct enacted to plead the case for gay inclusion into normative frameworks of intelligibility, identification, citizenship, family, and future. The jury sits in the chair of judgment, upholding dominant ideologies and values. Scripts are constructed to bridge identification with the jury. Posture, manner, and affect are carefully monitored. Normative violations are masked and denied. Within the court, heteronormativity is the irrefutable law of the land, a series of codes to which the proper gay citizen must pledge unwavering and fully convincing allegiance. Successful identification with the jury bridges a consubstantial (Burke, *Motives* 21) "we-ness" whereas failed attempts mark the defendant as other, deviant, and sentenced to tragic punishment.

The courtroom metaphor helps to articulate the important distinction between symbolic merger through bridging devices and perspective by incongruity, as bridging devices seek to transcend conflict without necessarily remoralizing or reconstituting the dominant orientations. In this sense, bridging devices perform a casuistic stretching, where new principles are asserted without challenging or violating previous principles (Burke, *Attitudes* 229), such as heteronormativity and race, age, class, and gender hierarchies. The rhetorical move of pleading normalcy to the heteronormative court seeks to claim access for some gay men within heteronormative temporal scripts, asserting a "good gay" model that continues the tragic punishment of those who fail, refuse, or cannot adopt normative and assimilationist performances. In short, bridging devices work to support and uphold heteronormative mandates, rather than problematize and interrogate heteronormativity's corrupt and oppressive authority.

The first section of this chapter examines how normalized representations of gay males define their futures through the sanctified institutions of marriage and child. Reaffirming the invisible authority of the identifiable heteronormative future, these representations perpetuate the tragic binary of future scripting, upholding the assumed correctness of child/spouse identifications and marginalizing the intelligibility of queered potentials for future. The second section breaks down the process of symbolic merger, marking the strategies and concessions that normalized gay representations must perform to construct identification within the heteronormative trial. The "identifiable gay male" is constructed as a safe, apolitical, everyday guy who happens to be gay. He pledges allegiance to the correctness of the status quo, adopting a nonpolitical homonormative (Duggan) position, in exchange for dominant identification and the promises of a viable and reasonable future. In the final section, the symbolic merger between heteronormative future models and the "identifiable gay male" is interrogated for its self-serving compliance with and exploitation of multiple forms of social oppression. In the process of reaffirming the oppressive reign of marriage and child as the sole determinations of positive futures—perpetuating the tragic future script—race, class, sexuality, and gender oppression become the primary vehicles for bridging dominant inclusion. The privileged merger between the identifiable gay male and dominant cultural values provides the foundation to discuss the potential strategies for extending beyond the assimilationist/queer binary to theorize a coalitional queer identification with future.

RUNNING TO THE ALTAR: SAYING, "I DO" TO THE FUTURE

> Every gay man I know is running off to Hawaii, putting on a kaftan, reciting vows, and feeling superior to me . . . I'm like an outcast of the outcasts. (Stanford, *Sex and the City*)[3]

The flowers will brown and the ice sculptures will melt, and then what? (Nuru, *Touch of Pink*)

When rumors started to spread that Vito was gay, Tony Soprano's first response to the allegations were hesitant, warning everyone that, "A man's reputation's at stake, a *married* man!"[4] In *Lucky Number Slevin*, before Slevin's father is murdered, he pleads for mercy on the grounds that he has a wife and child. Mr. B. in *The Groomsmen* argues, "The definition of an adult is a person that has a job, is married, has kids, and owns a home." Outside of hundreds of rights and privileges awarded by the government to legally recognized couples, the institution of marriage grants a socially sanctioned entitlement to the future. Beyond the arguable claims that marriage guarantees happiness and success, marriage is culturally marked as a sign of a meaningful life, a life that matters and/or mattered. Looking through obituaries, the cultural assumption is embedded in specific and limited forms of kinship.[5] "He is survived by his wife and children." "She spent her life devoted to her three children and loving husband." Although the patriarchal assumptions embedded in Tony Soprano's statement should not be ignored, the phrase "a married man" carries with it a deeply understood meaning that this is a man of significance with markers of success, relevance, and value bestowed upon him by the larger culture.

In negotiating potential futures, the privileged state of marriage is so deeply embedded in discourses of success, meaning, and value that the effort to articulate alternative forms of temporal meaning are instantly coded as failed compensations. Marriage—followed by procreation—defines heteronormativity's promise of satisfaction, fulfillment, and recognition, and this trained incapacity to envision alternative futures is the ruling logic of the heteronormative courtroom. "Happily ever after" is always preceded by a "they," a couple or a larger family that walks into a horizon of scripted bliss. Futures of marriage and limited articulations of "family values" work to foreclose the intelligibility of queering future scripts, the project of asking, "What else might the future look like?" Whether in the media or in the classroom, the notion of a happy, satisfied, and meaningful life for an aging person—without spouse or child—is abstract and nonexistent, if not paradoxical.

Marriage is the holy grail of gay assimilation, as "the ideal national citizen is married" (Seidman 182) and marriage is constructed in discourse as the only alternative to the "harder road" nightmare. Marriage offers an alternative to the youthist logic that thirty equals death, by way of the heteronormative logic that thirty equals "settling down." It answers the question, "In fifteen years, what will I be?" In *Chuck and Buck*, Buck's plan to marry his fiancée becomes the mark of Buck's progression and maturity, whereas Chuck is the developmental failure deteriorating at the periphery. The film sets up a binary of two choices, two narratives of development, perhaps more appropriately titled Chuck *or* Buck: future or no future.

There are two trends of heteronormative marriage worship that exist across the majority of the analyzed texts. The first is gay-identified men who reject or avoid gay relationships, believing that happiness is limited to heterosexual monogamy and marriage. On *Dawson's Creek*, Jack stands outside of a coffee house, seeing his male date waiting inside for him, but Jack cannot bring himself to enter. "I walk through that door and my entire life is going to be different." "I'm not telling the world I'm gay. I'm actually gay." Lingering outside the coffee shop, Jack notices a man and a woman sitting together. He recalls, "I didn't want to be me. I wanted to be them."[6] In Season 6, long after Jack has "accepted himself" as gay, he jumps at the chance to marry Emma to secure her citizenship, showing more interest in marrying Emma than he ever has in his boyfriend David. Similar critiques have been launched against *Will & Grace*, where the heterosexism is reinforced in the text through marking opposite sex relationships as the most desirable and successful (Battles and Hilton-Morrow 92), coding Will and Grace as a heterosexual couple (94), and perpetuating homosexuality as a problem to be addressed (99). In the film *Camp*, the openly gay Michael sleeps with Dee, explaining, "Maybe I didn't want a whole lifetime of feeling the way I have." These texts parallel the dynamic in *Queer Eye for the Straight Guy*, which "serves up the image of gay men looking longingly at the spectacle of heterosexual romance" (Bateman 17). The gay man is positioned as heterosexuality's and marriage's greatest champion and supporter, desperately wanting to gain access and celebrate the heterosexual union. In the Lifetime film *Wedding Wars*, Shel, a party planner, begins a nationwide strike of gay workers who shut down their businesses until gays are awarded the right to marry. As the majority of the gay businesses in the film are stereotypically related to party planning—hairstyling, flowers, catering, baking, formal wear—Shel's own brother's wedding quickly falls apart. However, on the day of the scheduled wedding, Shel delivers a public speech in the face of political defeat. He proclaims, "We are going to make marriage stronger and more beautiful than ever!" Passionately announcing that "everyone deserves a beautiful wedding," Shel solicits the help of the hundreds of gay protestors to "save" his brother's wedding, who quickly resurrect the entire event, redecorate the tacky decor with gay-approved sophistication, and track down the bride and groom just in time. The image of hundreds of gay men and women running in a mass frenzy to save the wedding of a homophobic speechwriter and the daughter of a homophobic politician defines the normative gay plea. Gay men fighting to preserve, and then emphatically applauding, heterosexual marriage is a common theme in multiple films, such as *Sweet Home Alabama*, *Boat Trip*, *Connie and Carla*, and *All Over the Guy*.

Although the Fab Five of *Queer Eye* appear content celebrating and accessorizing heterosexual marriage, the second trend represents gay characters eagerly planning their own slice of marital bliss. As David brushes his teeth, following a successful first date with a lawyer on *Six Feet Under*, a chipper Norman Rockwell narration of 1950s Americana plays in his imagination. "David Fisher and Benjamin Cooper invite you to a holiday open house. Merry Christmas from Ben and David!"[7] David smiles in giddy excitement, enjoying, without sarcasm, his possibility of enacting the Rockwell-esque performance. The reality series *Boy Meets Boy* openly espouses the "political" objective of showing the world "all gay men look for is love," and gay men are "normal," while privileging the "relationship-minded" gay male and vilifying the gay male looking for the "hook-up." The rhetorical strategy works to challenge the narratives that demonize gay men as sexually undisciplined, incapable of commitment, and anti-family, by constructing a "normal" gay who wants the same thing as "everyone else." Brookey's analysis of *Philadelphia* suggests that the gay community in the film creates identification through consubstantiation with dominant values, presenting a homosexual community that is deeply invested in monogamy, family values, and heterosexual relationship models. This rhetorical move works to build a symbolic merger with dominant values, constructing the gay community as deeply committed to heteronormative systems of relation. The gay male is as devoted as heterosexuals, if not more, to the institution of marriage. In the pilot episode of *Sex and the City*, Carrie and Stanford comment that the gay community is the only place where love and traditional romance are still in existence, suggesting that "the straight community is closeted."

On *Degrassi: The Next Generation*, Marco and Dylan are the first couple to move in with each other after high school, enacting a domestic and blissful performance the heterosexual characters fail to achieve. Films such as *The Family Stone, Kissing Jessica Stein, Rent,* and *Talladega Nights: The Ballad of Ricky Bobby* each position the gay male couple in a peripheral, deified (Brookey and Westerfelhaus), and uncomplicated performance of devoted couple-hood that beats the heterosexuals at their own game. In the animated parody *Drawn Together*, Xandir is the video game character that is on "a never-ending quest to save his girlfriend." His gayness seems to complicate this life mission, and following his suicidal bouts discussed in Chapter 3, he begs the magic genie to make him straight. The genie responds, "You can shove that wish up your gay-hating mangina," as the genie is an out-and-proud gay male. Within moments, Xandir falls in love with the genie, but "happily ever after" is cut short when the genie is immediately kidnapped. Suddenly Xandir is on a "never-ending quest to save his boyfriend."[8] Heterosexual relationships and gay relationships become interchangeable, a mere switch of partner, which, as *Boy Meets Boy* continually asserts, are no different. When Grace tells Will, "Someday you'll make a beautiful bride,"[9] Grace and Will bridge identification with themselves and their audience, testifying that they both simply want the same thing. In addition, gay male commitment to marriage bridges identification with the future itself, constructing gay identity through heteronormative identification. Marriage is reaffirmed in these texts as the primary site of future meaning, perpetuating a false binary that claims marriage and monogamous coupling are the only alternative of the "harder path."[10]

THE NEXT BEST THING: ALL RISE TO THE SACRED CHILD

> Fuck the social order and the Child in whose name we're collectively terrorized; fuck Annie; fuck the waif from *Les Mis*; fuck the poor, innocent kid on the net. (Edelman 29)

> I thought we didn't have to deal with kids. (Ricky, *Noah's Arc*)[11]

"Listen up, Michael. They are heterosexuals. They think all of us perverts are only after one thing—to get our hands on some sweet piece of little boy meat."[12] Following a false accusation of child molestation, Brian spews the cultural script that has demonized gay men for decades: the gay male is a pervert, a child molester, and a threat to innocent children everywhere. Edelman's discussion of the sacred Child[13] addresses these issues through the concept of reproductive futurism, arguing political discourse of the future is hijacked in the name of the Child (2), queers are constructed in cultural discourses as anti-child (3), and queers are discursively confined to the sacrificial position of anti-future (28). The Child signifies the future and the anti-child discourse attached to queerness, according to Edelman, foreclosing the "possibility of a queer resistance to this organizing principle of communal relations" (2). Situating Edelman's critique in a Burkean framework, identification with the Child defines identification with the heteronormative future. In turn, refusal to construct identification with the heteronormative definition of future—a queered resistance that rejects an identity via the Child—is forced into the tragic and demonized position of anti-future. "Queerness names the side of those not 'fighting for the children'" (3).

Instead of following Edelman's queer rejection of the sacred Child and boldly telling Annie to fuck herself, normative gay representations work to construct identification with heteronormative futures through the rhetorical strategy of Child-worship. The Child is held up high on the shoulders of normative gay men, who cheer in unison with heteronormative mantras, in hope that their voices will blend with dominant ideologies. In a heartfelt confession, David on *Six Feet Under* recounts watching a father and a child at church and feeling ashamed and disappointed for being gay. "I want to be that guy at church with the kid on his knee." Simultaneously, David is sympathetic, apologetic, religious, and ashamed, yet his only wish is to be a good dad and take his son to church. Keith replies, "You can have a kid on your knee, David."[14] David bridges dominant identifications through his own self-loathing of gayness and his loyalty to heteronormative procreation scripts. The child becomes central to David and Keith's romantic relationship as David's devotion and loyalty to Keith's niece is instrumental in Keith's realization that David is a "good guy" and the kind of man he longs to be with. On *Will & Grace*, Jack and Will arrive to an annual gay get together that is usually filled with sex, drinking, and partying. This year, however, all of their friends are coupled with infants, and the weekend of debauchery shifts to a plotline about babysitting. The couples explain to Will that there is a point where "parties, drinking, and casual sex stop doing it for you," reifying the future binary or either shallow dance clubs or domesticated suburbia.[15] Their friend Larry proudly announces, "I have what I've always dreamed of, a family." Will quickly affirms, "I can't wait to be a father." The rest of the episode explores Will's concerns about making a good father, stemming from his inability to calm a crying baby. Will pouts about his fears, and the audience is begged to sympathize with this upstanding gay man, much like David, who wants nothing more than to receive "the best dad in the world" coffee cups on Father's Day. Looking down at the sleeping baby, Will comments to Jack, "I want this. This is heaven."[16]

No film has worked harder to construct a noble and dedicated gay father character that gladly rejects his shallow gay existence for a crack at child rearing than the much-criticized *The Next Best Thing*. The title of the film is explained in a conversation between Robert, the devoted gay father, and Robert's mother. She states, "Having a child is the best thing in the world." Robert believes Sam is his biological son for the first five years of Sam's life, conceived accidentally on one drunken night with his best friend Abby, played by Madonna. Robert and Abby live together and raise Sam as their own. Robert refuses to bring his boyfriends around and honorably avoids serious involvement with other men, putting his "true" family first. He explains, "I don't want to be some gay uncle who lives on the other side of the tracks with his roommate Bruce." Robert pledges his distance from the gay community, arguing, "I'm bored of it all. I'm bored of the parties, drugs, bored of the body obsession." No matter how devoted a father, once Abby begins a serious relationship, tensions mount, lawsuits are filed, and it is revealed that Robert is not Sam's biological father. Perhaps the most blasphemous scene in the film takes place in the custody hearings, when gay-icon Madonna briefly allows her lawyer to attack and humiliate Robert on the stand for his "questionable" lifestyle. It was like hearing the Pope use the "f-word," watching Abby—inseparable from Madonna—violently condone the heteronormative punishment on her "best" friend. The title, *The Next Best Thing*, ends up referring to Robert's joint custody of Sam. Although he cannot access the wife and child script directly, Robert's dutiful fatherhood is rewarded with the *second* best thing in the world, joint custody in raising the Child.

The representation of gay men desperately fighting for "the best thing in the world" spans across multiple films and television shows. Trey and

Alex squeal in delight at the prospect of adopting a child on *Noah's Arc*. *Sex and the City*'s Carrie Bradshaw is ambushed on the street, in broad daylight, by a gay couple, Lou and Joe, who casually request the service of one of her "top notch eggs."[17] *Saved!* concludes with Dean, a gay male and accidental father, running around the hospital celebrating, "She's perfect!" Although Dean has been kicked out of his house, his school, and the Mercy House—a Christian gay rehabilitation center—the discovery that he will be a father offers him a "happy ending."[18]

The rhetorical strategy of bridging gay men into reproductive futurist ideologies is further supported through their investment in traditional family values. As Brookey points out, family values are another political device often used to demonize gays, where the creation of identification with family values and the gay community further works to bridge gay males into heteronormative systems (45). Films such as *Little Miss Sunshine* and *Mambo Italiano* remove gay characters from gay settings and situate their lives and devotions within the heterosexual family. Similar strategies are used in television shows such as *Brothers & Sisters*, where Kevin Walker is openly gay, but the narrative is centered on the biological heterosexual family—all other relationships remaining peripheral. In *The Night Listener*, Robin Williams plays Gabe, an older gay writer who has recently been left by his younger boyfriend. Lonely and lacking purpose in his work, he develops a phone relationship with a teenage boy he has never met. Gabe discovers Pete does not exist, as he is the creation of a lonely and mentally ill woman. Gabe questions, "How can I be missing someone who never existed? Am I that pathetic?" As parenthood and generativity are coded as the primary locations of future meaning, identification to heteronormative future scripts will always be contingent upon the Child. In short, identification with the future—without identification with a child—results in alienation and a sense of "missing someone who never existed."

Audience identification through the shared values of marriage and the Child create a sympathetic homosexual character that wants nothing more than a "normal life," which can be equated with inclusion to heteronormative modes of temporality. Vito on the *Sopranos* is not just any gay man, but a married gay man with children, providing him with access to dominant identifications/identity. Herein lies a tension, as the Child becomes a primary narrative of meaningful future and the justification for homophobia. Phil, the man who orchestrated Vito's murder, comments, "Maybe it's better for the kids not to have that role model."[19] The homosexual is a bad influence and threat to the Child, yet the normative gay male works to construct his identity by fully honoring and respecting the sanctity of the Child.

Constructing sympathetic gay male representation through mergers with marriage and child sets up the potential for the universal scapegoating function. Rather than a punishment of evil, the universal scapegoat is one who audiences are asked to identify with, even mourn, although their punishment is scripted as necessary or inevitable. For example, the mainstream success of *Brokeback Mountain* presents Jack Twist as a sympathetic gay male character who is punished at the end. Much like Andy, the lawyer in *Philadelphia*, audiences are permitted to mourn these deaths, feel bad for them, and even feel a sense of release in their feeling bad. In addition, the presentation of a normative gay male representation that preserves and upholds the sanctification of the Child marks the important distinction between symbolic merger and perspective by incongruity. Perspective by incongruity seeks to reconstitute and "transcend" the tragedy, ultimately remoralizing the tragic heteronormative orientation. Pledging allegiance to the Child and seeking identification by adhering to tragic definitions of normalcy and correctness constructs a merger with dominant frameworks, yet fails to interrogate or problematize the underlying tragedy and heteronormativity that circulate around the Child.

In one *Queer Eye* episode, the Fab Five performed makeovers for the Boston Red Sox as part of a charity event to give back to the community.[20] However, this community was not the queer community. The charity event was designed to help fix the lights and fencing of a suburban Florida Little League field that was damaged by a hurricane. Young, white, middle-class boys defined the community that was being assisted, as the *Queer Eye* fundraiser extended the Fab Five's deep investment of heterosexual romance to include the sacred Child. As the guys from *Queer Eye* pass out bundles of new equipment to the suburban children, Carson comments, "Not so bad hanging out with the gays, is it?"[21] By constructing suburban white middle-class boys as part of their community, the Fab Five rhetorically position themselves within the dominant frames of community, bridging themselves into heteronormative identity and values.

The marriage and the Child are the heteronormative future script, the road from which the "harder path" departs and is constructed as deviant. Marriage signifies success and happiness, as Ted's mother on *Queer as Folk* explains as she stands over her son in a coma. "I wish you had someone to love you. I mean, if you did, maybe this wouldn't have happened."[22] The disapproving mother of the gay male is often the character to stand in judgment of her son's "choices," presenting the double-edged statement of "not being able to imagine a life without children." The cliché both honors the child's influence in the parent's life, but also condemns the childless to an uncertain fate. In *Mambo Italiano*, Nino's mother passively asserts, "It's your life. If you want to flush it down the toilet, who am I to stop you?" "If you don't care about growing old without a wife, without children to look after you . . ." Marriage and Child are constructed as *the* future script, the central norm by which all other variations of meaning, life, and self-worth are marked and disciplined.

Will and Grace contemplate having a child through several episodes in Season 4, but the moment where the discussion first emerges warrants specific attention. After a photo shoot with a famous photographer—modeled after Annie Leibowitz—Grace and Will keep requesting reshoots, obsessing on their appearance. The photographer Franny grows angry, yelling, "Don't you two have anything better to do than obsess about looking perfect in a photo? Don't you have lives?" Grace replies, "Yes we have lives. I just got TiVo." In mounting anger, Franny yells, "How about getting something real to focus on, like a dog or a plant or an addiction—something! ... Just do something! Have a baby! I don't know. I don't care, just get out of my life!" Grace and Will stand together awkwardly, at first giggling at the thought of having a baby. Their expressions move from nervous laughter to seriousness, as the thought of having a baby together is contemplated. Franny snaps a photograph of their sober expressions, confidently stating, "That's the one." The episode ends with their faces, stilled by the camera, in a black and white image. Although they have been through two photo shoots already, the contemplation of having a baby together is what brought out their humanity and made them real.[23] Although Franny mentions having a baby within a dismissive list, which also includes addiction and plants, the episode claims that contemplating a baby suddenly gave them access to "a life" and showed their inner truth to the camera. It follows the logic stated by Lisa in *Six Feet Under*, who asserts, "Having a baby puts everything into perspective."[24]

Under heteronormative definition, the future is constructed through the logic of straight time and is mapped according to systems of marriage and the Child. Cultural discourses construct a tragic frame where identification with this, however limited, conception of future is required to construct identification with a future of happiness. In popular gay representation, neither the statistically high rate of divorce, nor the irony that child-raising reports *decreased* happiness (Gilbert 242–4) challenges the heteronormative claims to future. Identifiable futures remain cast in limited and exclusionary terms that work to support the absolute authority of straight time. Several gay representations are making rhetorical efforts to bridge themselves into heteronormative identification, and in turn they are rhetorically bridging themselves into identification with a future. Pledging allegiance to marriage and child, however, articulate only a portion of a far more complex rhetorical negotiation for constructing the identifiable gay. The analysis now shifts to the courtroom, as pleas for the identification with dominant value systems and the bridging of heteronormative scripts of future is a trial by jury, where queers remain guilty until proven innocent.

PLEADING FOR THE FUTURE: PERFORMING IDENTIFIABLE CITIZENSHIP

> We do live in a post *Will & Grace* world. Do you really think people still care who you sleep with? (Jack, *Dawson's Creek*)[25]

> Everyone is different, but everyone wants to be the same ... so eager to be part of a group that they'll betray their own nature. (Alfred, *Kinsey*)

Perhaps the most blatant critique of gay men pleading for acceptance in the court of heteronormativity comes from the television show "Gay as Blazes," a parody show-within-a-show on Showtime's *Queer as Folk*.[26] Mocking assimilationist representations of gayness—while simultaneously self-congratulating *Queer as Folk's* own version of "queerness"—"Gay as Blazes" portrays uptight, upper-class, elitist gay men who hypocritically turn their noses up at public or non-monogamous sex, while celebrating fidelity, domesticity, and socially-sanctioned respectability. In the same episode, a gay couple that emulates the lifestyle promoted on "Gay as Blazes" hires Emmett, and he is initially impressed by their sophisticated and "normal" lifestyle. The uppity gays deliver lines such as, "Such a shame he's a stereotype, rather than a role model" and proudly boast "ten years of fidelity." The fight for normative acceptance is mocked throughout, as they proudly declare, "We're not all sexual predators. In fact, the only thing we like bound in leather is a good novel."[27]

"Gay as Blazes" presents a parodied representation of what Duggan has coined the "new homonormativity." Arguing against the sexual "politics" of neo-liberalism, Duggan interrogates the creation of a "sensible" and "reasonable" gay mainstream, which casts queer objectives for social reform as radical and extremist. The non-politics of neo-liberal homonormativity pushes for a privatized gay culture defined through domesticity and consumption, and where equality is narrowly defined as the "formal access to a few conservatizing institutions" (190). This "political sedative" (189) that sets its goals on marriage and heteronormative inclusion embraces the argument that homosexuality is an involuntary way of being that poses no threat to heterosexual majorities. This "new world order," according to *Queer as Folk*, where "what's good for the heteros is good for the homos"[28] is the focus of this next section. Extending on Edelman's claim that queerness and future are positioned in opposition to one another, neo-liberal strategies of identification and the performance of good sexual citizenship (Seidman 189) are deployed as rhetorical strategies to gain favor within the heteronormative court. Rather than challenging the oppressive assumptions of heteronormativity, these gay representations are actively seeking entrance into narratives of heteronormative temporality, pleading their devotion to these normative scripts in an effort to gain access to normative identification. Centralizing heterosexuality in relation to homosexuality, these texts articulate gayness "through the eyes of confused heterosexuals, struggling with their own reactions and feelings" (Walters 104). This section outlines the gay defense script of the heteronormative court, a series of bridging devices (Burke, *Attitudes* 224) where gay representations adopt apolitical, sensible, safe, and nonthreatening postures to cater to the norms and comfort of dominant values. A model of gay male aging and future is presented that extends identification across the polemic of the heteronormative tragic frame, by turning a blind eye to the backs upon which these bridges are constructed.

DO YOU SWEAR YOU ARE GAY, COMPLETELY GAY, AND NOTHING BUT GAY?

> Not that I wasn't 100 percent gay; just that, it was important to me to be as-straight-as-the-next-guy gay. (Tobias 86)

> Trust me, there are only three ways a man can go. He can let the status quo defeat him—like Moritz. He can rock the boat—like Melchoir—and be expelled. Or he can bide his time, and let the System work for *him*—like me. Think of the future as a pail of whole milk. One man sweats and stirs—churning it into butter—like Otto, for example. Another man frets, and spills his milk, and cried all night. Like Georg. But, me, well, I'm like a pussycat, I just skim off the cream. (Hanschen, *Spring Awakening* 77)

The 2007 Tony Award winning musical *Spring Awakening* is an updated version of Frank Wedekind's controversial play from 1891. The story revolves around German adolescents coming of age and struggling to understand their sexuality within a highly repressed culture. The events are tragic for the heterosexual characters, as Melchoir, the leading male, loses his girlfriend and unborn child to a fatal abortion and his best friend to suicide. Dropped in the middle of this tragic tale are Ernst and Hanschen, two males coded as gay, who have a brief courtship scene towards the end of the play. Ernst sings, "O, I'm gonna be wounded. O, I'm gonna be your wound." In response, Hanschen sings, "O, I'm gonna bruise you. O, you're gonna be my bruise." In a dramatic flip from many of the texts discussed in Chapter 3, Hanschen and Ernst are not the tragic characters of this story, but rather peripheral and somewhat out of place in the narrative. Hanschen's metaphor of letting the system work for him by skimming the cream off of the top, without making waves, articulates his strategy for accessing a future for himself. Sidestepping the tragic fate of Melchoir, Moritz, and Wendla, Hanschen blends into the sexually repressed backdrop of the musical, nonthreatening and exempt from the sexual sanctioning that drives the play. Although the play is over a century old, the updated version of the play offers a useful exemplar for the construction of "normal" gay sexuality in contemporary entertainment.

Ironically, the first requirement in constructing an identifiable gay representation is a firm and absolute commitment to a fixed gay identity, thus reifying and supporting the coherence of a hetero/homo binary. Countering a foundational premise of queer theoretical work, the normative gay must pledge complete loyalty to a fixed and unwavering gayness that poses no threat or potential bleeding into the discrete category of heterosexuality. For the gay man to gain access into dominant narratives of citizenship and future, the foundational myth of heterosexuality must be respected, carefully protected, and never called into question. The Bravo reality show *Boy*

Meets Boy marks a contemporary example where the gay/straight divide is reified as a stable and discrete either/or formation, as coherent categories of sexuality are used to construct the show's premise. A thirty-two-year-old gay bachelor must choose from fifteen eligible men who he wants to go on an extended vacation with. The twist is that some of these men are "100 percent gay," whereas, according to the female host, some of the men are *absolutely straight*. The show prides itself on breaking down stereotypes of gay men, advertising a "world where gay is the norm" in an effort to show people "we are no different." Whereas it is interesting that the bachelor is thirty, and he dismisses any of the men who are older than him by the second elimination, selecting the boyish Wes as his final choice, the show reinforces the gay "norm" as identically aligned with heterosexual scripts of courtship and kinship. Marriage and fidelity are openly espoused as the desirable script, and sexuality is approached as a fixed, uncontested, and apparently quantifiable trait. As contestants are eliminated, there is a brief video montage of interview clips followed by the final and dramatic marking of sexuality. The words "gay" or "straight" appear over their picture, assuming the audiences at home will be shocked or validated in their own suspicions or hunches regarding a contestant's "true sexuality." While aiming to show how gays are just like everyone else, the show simply reifies a rigid sexual binary that quickly dispels any possibility of a sexual fluidity.

With the exception of overtly queer characters, such as in the films of Gregg Araki where sexual categorizations are actively and intentionally rendered incoherent, the either/or logic of sexuality plays out in the vast majority of cultural representations. The potential for a gray area of sexuality is left unintelligible in most texts. Mark on *Ugly Betty*, Kevin on *Brothers & Sisters*, Omar on *The Wire*, and Justin on *Desperate Housewives* are gay characters, and are openly labeled as such. On *Sex and the City*, when Charlotte is dating a man with "gay traits," she asks Stanford to meet him and determine if he is either gay or straight.[29] Although he claims to like woman, his "gay traits" are too much for Charlotte and she terminates the relationship. Characters who fail to abide by a clear hetero/homo binary are disciplined or vilified, as seen in texts where men who have engaged in homosexual relations attempt to form a relationship with members of the opposite sex. In the films *Touch of Pink* and *Mambo Italiano*, the men who are "really gay"—but opt to marry women—are demonized as liars and cowards, whereas the "out and proud" gay characters are respectable. The 100 percent gay character is privileged in these moments for permitting the coherence of heterosexuality to remain uncontested.[30]

This poses an interesting tension, as conservative logics invested in reparative therapy and the sinfulness of homosexuality may look upon the man who is "really gay," but chooses opposite sex marriage, as a noble effort. However, as gay representations move further into mainstream culture, the bisexual or queer representation is less tolerated, as it implicates the tolerant, open-minded, and multi-cultural "straight" audiences in the destabilization and interrogation of heterosexuality's coherence. In other words, the representation must adopt a minoritizing view of sexuality, as opposed to a universalizing perspective (Sedgwick 40–4), for identification with fluid sexualities calls into question all sexual identity.

I CALL TO THE STAND "THE BEST LITTLE (GAY) BOYS IN THE WORLD"

> Oh I know, I'm the strong one, the stable one, the dependable one cause that's what I do. (David, *Six Feet Under*)[31]

> Why not just let straight people be straight, gay people be gay, and judge people by the quality of their civic contribution? (Tobias 241)

The plea of "normal" in the heterosexual court is premised on the argument that, "Here you are looking at a fine, upstanding, kind, average guy who just happens to be gay." Access to straight temporality, heteronormative institutions, and the future mandate a nonthreatening construction of gayness. In their analysis of *To Wong Foo*, Brookey and Westerfelhaus identify the trend of presenting deified gay representations up for dominant consumption and acceptance. Seidman refers to this process as the assimilation of the "good sexual citizen," creating a "safe space of social tolerance" (137) for "normal" gays who leave heterosexual marriage and family ideals, as well as dominant gender divisions uncontested (137). Just as *Spring Awakening*'s Hanschen skims the cream off the top without disrupting the milk, the dutiful good gay man is the nicest, kindest, and most giving boy on the block who simply wants to be a part of an uncontested heteronormative system. The top-grossing box office film in this study[32] is the 2002 romantic comedy *Sweet Home Alabama*. Bobby Ray is Melanie's childhood buddy, a gay man who lives in Melanie's hometown and seems to spend all of his time working at a factory, taking care of his aging uncle, and drinking with the heterosexual boys from town. In a drunken scene, Melanie "outs" Bobby Ray to the entire town, only to offer an apology the next day that is completely focused on her life, her struggles, and her marriage predicament. As the kind and forgiving sidekick, however, Bobby Ray forgives her in an instant and leaps to Melanie's aid, dutifully performing the role of the loyal friend. In addition, the outing of Bobby Ray offers Jake, the straight love interest, an opportunity to demonstrate his own nobility, by welcoming Bobby Ray back to the friend group. Jack becomes the evolved and sensitive straight hero,[33] offering to buy his gay friend a drink. Bobby Ray jokes, "You're not really my type," to which a round of laughter follows. Bobby Ray exemplifies the concept of the "incidental queer," according to Walters, who is "located almost entirely in a world filled with heterosexual couples and their desires and longing. They are the 'gay friends' who have no friends of their own" (155). Kevin Walker on *Brothers & Sisters* makes this point in the third episode of Season 2, when he states, "The only gay friends I have are my sisters.'"

The good gay plea claims a distance from gay communities, arguing, as Angelo does in *Mambo Italiano*, "I have nothing in common with homos." Perhaps the most famous of these strategic removals comes from *Brokeback Mountain*. Ennis delivers the much quoted, "I ain't no queer," in a gruff, mumbled, deep voice that elicits laughs from gay and straight audiences. Mirroring the rehabilitation scripts from *Shock to the System* and *Queer as Folk* discussed in Chapter 3, good gays do "not fit in with the community" and "want something better" for themselves. Gay culture is reduced to a shallow and vacuous existence, reifying the authority and correctness of straight time and perpetuating the tragic demonization of non-straight lives, temporalities, and futures. Dennis, the leading character in *Broken Hearts Club*, experiences a crisis, stating, "I'm twenty-eight and all I'm good at is being gay." Wanting to progress and move forward in his life, he makes the choice to leave his gay community of friends to travel in Europe. Dennis's progress is defined through a departure from casual sex and partying into the only foreseeable alternative, preparation to enter a monogamous and committed relationship. Although "gay life films" (Walters 144) or "gay standpoint films" (Seidman 145) progressively represent a gay community not centered on heterosexuals in love or a community in crisis (Walters 145), Dennis's redemption comes through distancing himself from his gay community, friends, and lifestyle in a noble effort to be a better man. Growing up and breaking away from the gay community is marked as a desirable trait, one where the best little boys downplay gay identifications to claim affinity and construct identity through heteronormative systems.

The process of community vilification and self-distancing is closely tied to the most desirable of gay traits—gay shame and self-loathing. In Brookey's analysis of a *Newsweek* article about a lesbian couple adopting a suburban heterosexual lifestyle and raising a child, the lesbian parents explicitly state their hope that their child will not be gay. The couple explains, "'Because it's easier'" to be straight, and they also hope to have grandchildren (52). Brookey's analysis suggests, "Homosexuality is something they would not wish on their own children" (52). The good gay cannot plead normative inclusion without first confessing and forsaking their "crimes" in the heteronormative court. Gayness cannot be a choice, nor is it a something a "good gay" would ever choose. Throughout the cultural production, the "normal gays" seeking identification must first trudge through a pit of self-doubt, self-loathing, and intense shame. Season 1 of *Brothers & Sisters* begins with Kevin struggling with the shame of dating Scotty, an unapologetically flamboyant gay male who shows no fear or apprehension about loving other men.[34] Will Truman is positioned next to the campy and loud Jack McFarland, who constructs Will as the reasonable, contained, and not *too* gay male.[35] In a flashback episode to Will's initial coming out, Will offers the obligatory battle with self-hatred, the failed attempt at heterosexual relations, and the period of depression, bridging identification through his own homophobia and demonstrated efforts to "change."[36] *Dawson's Creek*, *Mambo Italiano*, *The Groomsmen*, *Happy Endings*, *Shortbus*, *Sopranos*, and dozens of other texts replay the much-expected narrative of shame as the foundation for normative identification.[37]

The extreme of identification through self-hatred is the act of suicide and self-destruction, or mortification; however, David's period of self-loathing in Season 1 of *Six Feet Under* provides a clear exemplar of identification through shame. A repeated narrative device in *Six Feet Under* places the living characters in dialogue with the recently deceased corpses, where the living character investigates their interiority through projected and imagined dialogue. Spoken through Marcus, a young gay boy who was brutally bashed, David navigates his religious guilt and self-shame through Marcus's brutalized and bloodied body: "I'm the one who was sick. So I liked men, I never should have given into it. I'm not what God intended. I could have had a family. I could have had a normal life . . . God challenges us so we choose good over evil . . . I'm still going to hell and you know it cause you're going there too."[38]

This rhetorical strategy acknowledges and speaks the normative judgment, forcing the gay character to perform a period of mortification, where dominant audiences bridge identification through homophobic vilification and heteronormative reification. Self-loathing is a mandatory component of the gay defense plea, as the hubris of "gay pride"—without shame—fails to uphold the assumed correctness of heteronormativity. The identifiable gay knows the routine, understands the laws of penance, and constructs a sympathetic and humble demeanor that audiences can safely build commonality with. Gamson discusses this process on daytime talk shows, where the presence of extremely homophobic attitudes tends to sway a studio audience to take pity on gay panelists and come to their defense ("Sitting" 562–4). On the flipside, the absence of a homophobic panelist pushes audience responses towards heterosexist judgment. The Burkean rule is that someone needs to be punished, and if the gay male takes that punishment upon himself, self-inflicting mortification and penance in acknowledgment of his own offense to the heteronormative order, the audience is redeemed and free to express compassion and sympathy. As a universal scapegoat—where the audience is asked to identify with the punished who engages in the tragic sacrifice of mortification—the gay male simultaneously redeems the dominant culture, reifies heteronormativity, and is permitted dominant identification with heteronormative temporal trajectories.

ALL POLITICS ARE STRICKEN FROM THE RECORD

> Tell me one thing you believe in . . . You are a walking talking marshmallow peep. (Aaron, *Latter Days*).

Out of the malls and into the streets! (the metrosexual pride slogan from *South Park*)[39]

This is not the time to be political. (David, *Six Feet Under*)[40]

On *Spin City*, Mike, the straight-identified lead of the series, pretends to be gay to help Carter save face with an ex-boyfriend. Following the scenario, which is centered on displaying Mike's discomfort and reasserting his unquestionable heterosexuality, Mike sarcastically quips, "So this is being gay?" Carter, equally sarcastic and dismissive, replies, "Yeah, this is what we're fighting for."[41] The presence of gay characters—as with all sexual, racial, economic, and gendered representation—is always political, yet the politics of normative representations often fall under the middle-class, white, heterosexist, and masculinist radar. When a gay character steps into the dominant media arena to plead for tolerance, identification, and inclusion, political discussions must be kept to a minimum. Obeying the fair-minded and apolitical posture of the "new homonormativity" (Duggan), the "good gay" model "creates a depoloticizing effect on queer communities as it rhetorically remaps and recodes freedom and liberation in terms of privacy, domesticity, and consumption" (Manalansan 142). In short, the equality sought by homonormative politics—a reasonable and depoliticized plea for inclusion—is narrowly drawn for obtaining "formal access to a few conservatizing institutions" (Duggan 190). Most relevant to this analysis is how homonormative politics seek access to straight conceptions of aging, time, and future by constructing mainstream identification for some gay men through the reification of normativity and the tragic exclusion of gendered, classed, raced, and politicized Others. Homonormative non-politics construct a "phantom mainstream public of 'conventional' gays who represent the responsible center," casting queer political agendas as irresponsible and extreme (179).

Within popular film and television, this "reasonable" non-politics is deployed through several rhetorical strategies. On *Dawson's Creek*, Jen escorts Jack to a gay meeting in hopes of getting Jack acquainted with gay friends and the gay community.[42] The meeting is a strategizing meeting for a gay/straight alliance, which the all-American Jack is quick to mock. He refers to the group's leader as a "fascist dictator" and dismissively comments that political homosexuals are always protesting something. Further belittling the meeting and marking his distance from the political group, he tells Jen the meeting "is getting a little gay for me" and leaves. The "fascist dictator" who led the meeting mocks Jack as "Captain America," making fun of his letterman jacket, yet quickly abandons all political agendas once he becomes a reoccurring guest role. On *Queer as Folk*, Justin joins a group calling themselves "The Pink Posse," who begin as a volunteer organization patrolling the streets to prevent hate crimes. Within two episodes, the leader of the "Pink Posse" is characterized as a dangerous vigilante, wanting to not only protect gays on the streets, but also taunt heterosexuals, solicit their anger, and then shove guns in their faces.[43] In both of these cases, the sensible center is marked through the demonized extreme of radical and irrational political groups.

On *Will & Grace*, political stances are either trivialized or sanctioned through heterosexual approval. When Will begins dating Matt, a network sports reporter, Will goes along with Matt's request that they have a closeted relationship. It is not Will's, but Grace's adamant protest of Will being closeted that inspires Will to end the relationship.[44] Grace, as a heterosexual with audience identification established, is granted greater leeway to adopt political positions, and through her approval, Will is shamed for not standing up for his rights. In this episode, it is Grace who is "more willing to stick to her guns" (Battles and Hilton-Morrow 100) and "the voice of social change" (99). Becker refers to this as a trope of the "helpful heterosexual," which "offers a reassuring image of empowered gay-friendly heterosexuality" (191). In most episodes of *Will & Grace*, however, politics are ignored, if not overtly trivialized, as the show tends to address homosexuality as a problem to be addressed (99). The emphasis on interpersonal relations fails "to acknowledge the social consequences of gay and lesbian persons living in a heterosexist culture" (Battles and Hilton-Morrow 99). In the episode "Star Spangled Banter," Will chooses to back the "gay candidate" for city government while Grace chooses to back the "Jewish female candidate."[45] Much to their surprise, after throwing a fundraiser for each, their candidates are unapologetically narrow-minded and openly prejudiced. They opt out of voting, feeling inadequate to participate in the process they know very little about, until they hear of a "black guy" running for office. In the final punch line of the episode, they jump off the sofa and race to the polls. The political dimension of gay representation is introduced in such a way that it becomes shallow, dismissible, and a source of humor rather than a serious discussion.

Shel, the man behind the nationwide protest in *Wedding Wars*, is called out by his partner—early in the film—as "not even political." Shel's political stand for marriage is more about brotherly competition than political issues. His politics are accidental, making Shel a prime candidate for the nonthreatening "good gay." After all, his only desire is to have his own pretty wedding, and he has respectfully remained closeted to his parents for years, keeping his gayness unobtrusive, until his conservative brother blackmails him into coming out in hopes of stopping his protest. The political comedy is not really about politics at all, but sibling rivalry, gays coming to terms with their own sexuality, the importance of biological family, and the message that everyone just wants to be as happy as a heterosexual couple on their wedding day.

Few scenarios are more effective in trivializing the politics of gay representation than the well-worn gag of a "straight guy" pretending to be gay. In these texts, gayness is further normalized and depoliticized through depicting gayness as easy, fun, and carefree. On *Degrassi*, J. T. claims to be gay so that Liberty will stop hitting on him.[46] He casually lisps, "It's not wrong, it's just the way I am" and struts away, constructing gayness as a haven of safety rather than an identity tied to violence, oppression, fear, and exclusion. The films *Boat Trip*, *I Now Pronounce You Chuck and Larry*, and *Three to Tango* stretch this scenario out for entire films, marking gayness with privilege, ease, and trivialized silliness. When the heterosexual lead in *Boat Trip* goes through a phase where he thinks he might be gay—due to a drunken night where he thinks he might have slept with a man but cannot remember—his crash course in "how to be gay" is a brief lesson on saying, "To die for," a few Bette Midler songs, and the lyrics to "I Will Survive." On *Dawson's Creek*, Pacey unknowingly goes with Jack to a gay bar, where he meets a famous food critic.[47] As a restaurant owner who wants to be reviewed, Pacey contemplates pretending he is gay in order to reap the seemingly numerous privileges of gay community membership. The subtext of these episodes is, "Look how good those gays got it," divorcing sexuality from any form of politicized discourse or oppression. *Queer Eye* chalks gay identity up to facials, pedicures, and good fashion sense. Batemen argues that *Queer Eye* "generates entertainment for heterosexuals," while solidifying heterosexual superiority and presenting gayness as superficial, stereotypical, and nonthreatening (15).

After T. C. comes out to Cousin Mike in *The Groomsmen*, Cousin Mike comments that being gay must make dating far simpler than heterosexuality. This argument mirrors Jen's on *Dawson's Creek*, who claims, "No hedging, no subtext. Gays have it so easy."[48] In a later scene of *The Groomsmen*, Cousin Mike drives T. C. over to see his long-estranged father. T. C. is terrified about seeing his father, who was extremely disapproving of T. C.'s sexuality when he left home eight years before. Cousin Mike, however, drops him off and screams "Gay Pride!" at the top of his lungs, as he playfully peels away. Much like Grace embodying the voice of social change, Cousin Mike demonstrates the ease of heterosexuals to speak, as well as joke, about "pride" and "coming out." This process places "the problem of homosexuality" back on the gay representation, making it seem as if their shame is really their own problem—all in their head—and the rest of the world is perfectly okay with gayness. In terms of building identification, these texts ask the audience to identify with the passivity of "liberal-minded, unprejudiced humanism; thus the arm chair quarterback is replaced by the armchair humanist" (Batemen 15). Politics are bypassed, constructing gayness as a personal problem facing the shamed gay individual, without implicating the larger culture.

Depoliticizing strategies have been the focus of much previous research, such as the silly and dismissible gay sidekick,[49] the gay character who exists to help mend the troubled heterosexual relationship, and the appropriation of gay culture through metrosexuality. In addition, many queer theorists have argued that normalized representation works to desexualize gay identity, divorcing gay representation from sexuality and sexual politics all together.[50] The taming, constraining, and privatization of queer sexuality (Warner, "Trouble") is foundational in the effort to claim proper sexual citizenship (Seidman 150–61), marking depoliticalization as a rhetorical tactic for constructing gay male identification with straight temporality.

Although Vic on *Queer as Folk* argues, "It's not drugs. It's not booze . . . It's just cock,"[51] gay sex remains a topic the "good gay" carefully sidesteps. In John Reid's autobiographical *The Best Little Boy in the World Grows Up*, he is careful to forewarn his readers of any sexual content, although he promises it will be "rated G" (91). As the quintessential "best little boy" he is also quick to assert that monogamy matters (98), and as "grown up" as he is, he still prefers the euphemism of "playing cowboys and Indians" to discuss his gay sexual fantasies (11). Jack on *Will & Grace* proclaims, "It's time to put the sex back in homosexual, Will,"[52] but gay male sexuality remains highly contested and deeply moralized, and is carefully monitored and disciplined within the heteronormative court of popular media.

The film *Boy Culture* opens with the lines, "If you're smart, you've guessed I'm a hustler. If you haven't, here are two clues. I'm gay and they have made a movie about me. Try to keep up." X is the main character who has been hustling for several years, yet X adopts a contradictory and moralizing attitude towards casual sex. In his mind, he is being paid for a job, yet he is quick to judge his roommates for engaging in casual sexual activity that is divorced from notions of romantic love. X's hypocritical position on casual sex is used to code him as a "good guy" deep down, espousing a politics of shame for casual sexual contact. Sex can be talked about, alluded to, joked about, and coded within playful euphemism, but mainstream representations of the normal gay is all talk and no action. In fact, there is a wealth of talk, innuendo, and fixation on the topic of sex, as mocked in the *Queer as Folk* parody "Gay as Blazes." The moralizing, dismissal, and vilification of sex lead to a discursive explosion of sexual talk. The parody captures the way sex is discussed throughout shows such as *Will & Grace* and *Queer Eye*, as well as the majority of films with central or peripheral gay representation. Conway argues that Will's sexuality is "neutered and tamed" (78), and his homosexuality is nothing but a harmless joke, "a quirky characteristic that lands him in humorous situations" (78). Jack sums it up when he states, "You are no fun. You're like a little Will-flower."[53] Jack, along with the guys of *Queer Eye*, are allowed to speak of sex regularly, as they embody the "carnival," already on the periphery and never posing a threat to established definitions of masculinity (79). What Bateman refers to as "homosexuality's fundamental principle: a love for and a desire to have sex with men" (13) is downplayed within the heteronormative court, emphasizing identifications with narratives of love, fidelity, and romance. The rhetorical strategy of bridging gay male identity into dominant heteronormative orientations

Future Identification 103

demands compliance with the neo-liberal agenda of marriage, child, and family, as well as the tactic understanding that sex is a private matter, best kept out of public view.

A BRIDGE ON THEIR BACKS: EVERY MAN FOR HIMSELF

> The narrative implies that it is only through the denigration of others that the 'gay conservative' identity can be formed. (Beirne 47)

> The gay citizen, it seems, can be tolerated only if a norm and an ideal of America is defended that asserts the good, right, and normal status of dichotomous gender roles, heterosexual love, marriage, and the family. (Seidman 140)

> Fuck! Aren't there any good old-fashioned queers left? (Brian, *Queer as Folk*)[54]

Seidman suggests that the rhetorical construction of the "good sexual citizen" erects an additional binary that demonizes a "bad sexual citizen" (150), which perpetuates a tragic framing of sexual expression through symbolic merger. Although heterosexuality "is the exclusive field of legitimate sexuality" (152), the "good sexual citizen" seeks identification with heteronormativity that explores the potential for some gay men "to become full American citizens" (157), through vilifying and moralizing the expression of nonnormative sexualities. In terms of aging and future, the "good sexual citizen" pledges a commitment to heteronormative temporality and a multitude of oppressive and exclusionary social systems in order to access a dominant mode of future. From a queer political position invested in a coalitional and intersectional theorizing of aging and future, this presents a series of concerns. Adopting a universalizing perspective, reifying the centrality and absolute truth of heteronormativity inflicts discursive violence upon all populations, as heteronormative systems discipline all sexual citizens (Yep).[55] Furthermore, the performance of "proper" sexual citizenship serves the politics of assimilationist positions, in turn demonizing queer subjects who may or may not be invested in enacting a limited performance of "good sexual citizen" or adhering to the mandate of straight time. Finally, the courtroom metaphor operates on an additional level to articulate how normative sexual citizenship, whether desirable or not, is not equally accessible to all queers, as "good sexual citizenship" cannot be divorced from systems of patriarchy, whiteness, and economic considerations. The ability for "proper citizens" to make their plea in court has always been impacted by a multitude of social systems of power, and the heteronormative court of sexual citizenship fails to provide an exception to this cultural script.

The next section of this chapter explores the inherent privileges assumed, but rarely marked, within normalized representations, as identification with heteronormative future is often bridged on the back of raced, gendered, aged, and economic oppression. The vast majority of normalized gay male representations in popular culture offer up the identifiable gay male as white, middle class, and "younger," whereas the existence of nonwhite, older, and lower class gays remains absent from the cultural production. This absence suggests that normative representations enlist dominant identification beyond marriage and future scripts, as the identifiable is complicit in their own reification of multiple privileges that are not marked, yet always present. Adopting and enlisting a queer position that is committed to an intersectional critique of social hierarchy and privilege, this study rejects the limited agenda of "white male queer theory" in favor of a coalitional politics that refuses to isolate sexuality as an autonomous axis of social oppression. The interrogation of narratives of future, aging, and queer potentiality require a coalitional approach to theorizing oppression, as discourses of sexuality are *always* raced, gendered, aged, and constructed through economic systems (Cohen; Ferguson, "Race").

The lines differentiating gay assimilation and queer resistance bend and bleed into one another across texts and characters. To situate sexuality as the sole focus of discussion might construct a spectrum of representation ranging from the prudish and monogamous Andrew Tobias (formally John Reid) model of the "best little (gay) boy" to the anti-marriage, anti-child, give me public gay sex or give me death attitude of *Queer as Folk*'s Brian Kinney. Marking sites of heteronormative resistance becomes a far more complex process, as the intersections of heteronormativity, neo-liberalism, homonormativity, and multiple forms of social privilege and oppression do not lend themselves to simplistic polarities. Although seemingly different when addressing sexual politics, Tobias and Kinney each rely upon a multitude of social hierarchies as bridging devices[56] for garnering normative inclusion of an identifiable gay male. Kinney[57] falls on the far end of the pro-sex and simplistically queer characters, such as *Noah's Arc*'s Ricky, *Will & Grace*'s Jack, and *Broken Hearts Club*'s Cole. He cringes at the sight of "watching two pathetic fags turn themselves into something even more pathetic, two happily married heterosexuals"[58] and mocks a "growing legion of dickless fags who think living like them will make us happy."[59] Brian's "holier than thou, I'm gay and if you don't like it you can suck my dick principles"[60] are a definite departure from the normative pleas of Will Truman and Jack McPhee, for Brian openly denounces *some* of the identifications gay assimilationists work to bridge. By downplaying how sexuality is raced, gendered, and classed, Kinney can comfortably adopt an oppositional politics, for sexuality is Brian's sole deviation from "proper" citizenship.

Brian rejects the heteronormative future script, adopting a queer counter-script of live fast and die young. He praises the departed Vic, saying, "He not only knew how to live, but he also knew when to die."[61] He embraces and performs resistance to traditional family values, adopting a openly self-serving mantra of "no apologies, no regrets."[62] The tacit identifications that fuel Brian's queerer-than-thou performance highlight the inherent privileges of "white male queer theory." As an early thirties, white, wealthy, educated, masculine, attractive, successful advertising executive, Brian performs queer resistance with glamorized ease and sophistication. Place Brian next to Will Truman or Kevin Walker in court, and their similarities—their reasoned manner, stoic posture, white skin, and Armani suits—begin to outweigh their differences. Brian's "queer" resistance to normalization sheds light on a multitude of additional bridging devices at work in normalizing representation, where "we-ness" extends beyond the heteronormative values of child and marriage to the homonormative systems of youthism, whiteness, consumerism, and patriarchy. While rejecting heteronormative futures, and failing to provide an alternative vision of future or potential in its absence, Brian Kinney demonstrates the limited potentials embedded within privileged white gay male queer articulations.

George Schickel, Emmett's short-lived and much older romantic partner, labels Brian as "the love child of James Dean and Ayn Rand."[63] The James Dean reference refers to Brian's queer rebellious spirit, his counter-politics, as well as Brian's continued obsession with living fast and dying beautiful. The Ayn Rand reference, however, offers greater insight into Brian's personal, self-interested, and unapologetic adoption of queer critique. Like Howard Roark in Rand's *The Fountainhead*, Brian is the untouchable and unwavering embodiment of a philosophy, one where he refuses to compromise his right to be screwing whomever, whenever, and however. Living out the promises that Henry Cameron makes to Howard Roark, Brian Kinney battles a world that hates him for his unshakable principles and his unwavering commitment to his own self-actualization. Championed in Rand's book and on the TV show, the stalwart integrity to a singular philosophical conviction is marked as admirable and inspired, not unlike the John Wayne/Dirty Harry performance of masculinity celebrated in American cinema. In *The Fountainhead*, Howard is perfect, as he is less a person than a philosophical commitment, where *The Fountainhead* characters of Gail Wynand, Dominique Francon, and Peter Keating are humanized by their own failure to live a rigid body of ideals. Michael, Justin, Lindsay, Emmett, and the remainder of the *Queer as Folk* cast adopt similar positions, sometimes afraid of Brain, sometimes in awe, sometimes angry, but always removed from Brian by their humanity and competing philosophies of right, wrong, fairness, and personal fears. Brian is the most complicated character in the script, just as Roark, because of his utter simplicity. Each action is motivated by a philosophical tenant rather than a human emotion or feeling.

What is complicated about Brian is how he performs a counter-normative queer position, while simultaneously bridging multiple identifications with audiences. Beyond normative pleas to the Child and marriage, Brian Kinney performs a symbolic merger with additional sites of dominant cultural values. He is a white, masculine, wealthy, queer male who embodies dominant values of individualism, patriarchal authority, and masculine rationality. These identifications complicate the theorizing of a discrete heteronormative tragedy or a heteronormative orientation. Dominant systems that govern race, class, and gender complicate orientations, marking simultaneous, alternative, and intersecting tragedies and identifications.

RACED, CLASSED, GENDERED, AND AGED AS FOLK

> Needless to say, the revolution wasn't for everybody. (Reinaldo, *Before Night Falls*)

> Two differences between gays and blacks are worth noting, too. Some people may not like blacks, but they can hardly argue that blackness is immoral, that blacks should be painted white . . . And, if you are black, everyone knows it. (Reid 212–3)

In *The Best Little Boy in the World*, Tobias (a.k.a. Reid) provides one of the hundreds of discussions that seem to forget that not all gay people are white. Foucault's theorizing of the homosexual body performs a similar assumption of the Anglo-Saxon subject, as the scripting of the total homosexual body presumes a body "not already marked as Negroid or Oriental" (Ross 167). In most circumstances, gay male representations fail to "address whiteness as an 'absent center' or privileged space" (Jackson 51). Whiteness is a concept to articulate the "everyday, invisible, subtle, cultural, and social practices, ideas, and codes that discursively secure the power and privilege of white people" (Shome 503). In her analysis of *City of Joy*, Shome marks three rhetorical enactments of white privilege within the film: whiteness articulated through civilization and progress, the relation between whiteness and the surveillance of nonwhite bodies, and the potentiality of whiteness to cross all cultural boundaries without sacrificing its own ideologies (506). Whiteness becomes one bridging device that operates to construct identification between dominant audiences and gay male representations, allowing the gay male identification with systems of the future through the tragic perpetuation of exclusionary racial systems.

Debbie on *Queer as Folk* wears politicized and humorous T-shirts as she waits tables at the Liberty Diner. In one episode, Debbie wears a shirt that reads, "Some people are too white,"[64] although there is no commentary or discussion. The T-shirt offers an interesting critique to the absence of nonwhite bodies in the world of *Queer as Folk*, as well as the privileged performances of whiteness that fuel its storylines. In the sexualized land of club Babylon, you will find nonwhite bodies scattered across the dance floor, as a barely dressed and muscular African American male is a common set piece in the background of numerous scenes. Sweaty and animalized, nonwhite bodies are on display, dancing on stage as go-go boys and shaking their nearly naked bodies among the masses of men. In terms of speaking characters, however, the five-year series only introduced a handful of one-episode characters signifying as nonwhite. In Season 1, Emmett is thrilled to have gained the attention of a young Asian boy who does not speak a word of English. The entire subplot surrounds the boy trying to explain to Emmett he is a hustler and needs to get paid for his services.[65] In Season 3, an African American flight attendant named Dijon, "like the mustard," seduces Emmett by performing the role of the sexualized servant. Emmett sits in a chair, as if an airplane passenger, and Dijon says he will "go to any length" to guarantee Emmett's satisfaction. Emmett, staring down at his crotch, replies, "I see what you mean by any length."[66] Arguing that the "cultural fixation on the black male penis needs to be understood as a legacy of lynching" (184), Perez argues; "the cosmopolitan gay male subject" assumes a communal ownership and objectification over "the brown body" (186). Marked as uncivilized, animalized, and eroticized, several scholars have argued that (white male) queer theory refuses to interrogate its own complicity with systems of whiteness, perpetuating the construction of brown bodies are spectacles for white consumption.

The eroticism and objectification of nonwhite bodies creates a space for gay male representation to construct identification through a tacit compliance with racist ideologies. On *Will & Grace*, Grace openly brags to everyone about her "hot black lover,"[67] and Will wins Jack's respect by hooking up with the "Slovaki vendor"[68] who does not speak any English. On *Reno 911!*, J. Dangle spends the entire series trying to bed Jones, the heterosexual and African American officer. After Jones gives up fighting and gives in to Dangle, we find out Dangle is in the hospital the next scene and can barely walk.[69] The unstated assumption is that Jones, as an African American, has such a large penis that he seriously injured Dangle.

The rhetorical linkage between whiteness and civilization spans the entire sample, bridging gay male representation with reasonableness, sophistication, and rationality. From *Queer Eye* and *Will & Grace*, to *The Producers* and *Sweet Home Alabama*, the cultural production of gayness asserts an urban and cosmopolitan identity linked with wealth, fashion, and consumerism. While Will Truman and Brian Kinney may differ in their sexual politics, they are united in their taste for Prada, Armani, and Gucci. As Carrie says about Stanford and his boyfriend on *Sex and the City*, "They worship the same God—style."[70] The cultural production of gayness as primarily white is directly tied into the cultural production of gayness as wealthy and middle- to upper-middle class. From *Rules of Attraction*, *Ugly Betty*, and *Happy Endings*, to *Boat Trip*, *Talladega Nights: The Legend of Ricky Bobby*, and *Best in Show*, gayness forms identification with whiteness through the plea of cultural sophistication. The very premise of *Queer Eye*, as well as the gay men in the films *Wedding Wars* and *Miss Congeniality*, is founded upon the cultural equation of gayness and cosmopolitanism. The relationship between systems of whiteness and the bridged identification of the gay male future presents a serious concern from a coalitional perspective, as gay identity and any gestures towards gay future are articulated in racially and economically exclusive terms. As gay male representation forges identification with mainstream audiences through the unstated perpetuation of whiteness, asserting gay identity as an urbane and exaggerated performance of cosmopolitanism, access to the straight temporal systems is achieved through reification of racism and classism.

Coupled with the sophisticated and consumer-driven identity is what Muñoz refers to as the performance of whiteness through an absence of affect ("Feeling" 68). Embracing a contained and reserved performance of whiteness, the performance of the cool, calm, and rational gay draws connections to dominant understandings of white performance. Placing Keith from *Six Feet Under* in dialogue with Carter from *Spin City* identifies a strong variation in how an African American gay male is constructed in popular media. Carter is portrayed as reasoned, fair-minded, upper class, and always keeping his emotions in check. In contrast, Keith is defined by his hot temper, violent family background, and tendency for aggression. Keith's partner David explains in couple's therapy, "I feel like I'm living in a mine field. Your anger is so random and so arbitrary"[71] Carter presents an African American representation linked to dominant identifications of whiteness, whereas Keith personifies the hotheaded, irrational, African American male from a violent home. Nero argues that as *Six Feet Under* progressed, Keith was made "blacker," and this blackness was positioned as somehow incompatible with gayness (239). Keith's unreasonableness and alienation from "gay sensibilities" (239) are used to demonstrate David's civility and calmness, bridging David into normative frameworks of whiteness, reasonableness, and identification. Furthermore, Keith's anger and aggression directly feed into David and Keith having hot and angry sex, further marking Keith as an uncivilized and sexualized "big black sex cop" while divorcing him from cultural institutions of blackness (Foster 110).

Supporting the invisible privileges attached to whiteness (McIntosh) is the lack of attention any of these texts, whether gay or "queer," offer to the interrogation or exploration of white privilege and how that shapes access to narratives of future. In one single episode of *Queer as Folk*, Brian is complaining to Melanie about being sued, and Melanie responds, "You'd still have it better than any woman or person of color because you're a white man, which still counts for something in this country."[72] Although this indictment is quickly dropped, never to be addressed again, it marks Kinney's race and gender as significant to his social standing. Brian Kinney's stoic and unemotional performance of queerness might challenge scripts of heteronormativity, but his performance strongly parallels dominant codes of civility, rationality, and reason, as well as a detached masculinity that mirrors Hollywood's independent and fair-minded cowboy model. In navigating these complex systems by which future is constructed and bridged through gay representation, gender politics present an additional area of concern for queer theorists.

The theme song to *Rick & Steve: The Happiest Gay Couple in the World* cheerfully sings, "Loving life, hating girls! They are the happiest gay couple in the world!" In the current wave of gay male representation, both heterosexual women and lesbians are routinely constructed in demeaning, subservient, and supportive roles. While texts such as *Noah's Arc* offer almost no female representation at all, there are numerous films and television shows that create audience identification through the reproduction of patriarchal systems. *Rick & Steve*, *Another Gay Movie*, *Queer as Folk*, *Broken Hearts Club*, and *Dante's Cove* exemplify a cultural trend of constructing lesbians as peripheral support systems to gay male storylines. The litany of objectified comments and "ewe gross!" commentaries on female sexuality run throughout many texts, asserting a gay male identity that is constructed in difference and disgust to lesbianism. Jack on *Will & Grace* refers to a lesbian couple as "Starsky and Butch, "moos" at them, refers to them in as "Mr. and Señor," and is reported to have serenaded them with "The Lumberjack Song."[73] Will corrects Jack for his behavior, yet Jack's actions provide the laugh lines and Will's efforts only serve to set up the next joke. In *Broken Hearts Club*, Patrick's sister Anne is cast as the nice lesbian, where her partner and Patrick play out the familiar script of gay man versus lesbian in a flurry of insults. The lesbian representation in these texts parallels the familiar model seen in the popular sitcom *Friends*, where Carol—Ross's ex-wife—and her partner Susan are repeatedly reduced to jokes about their sexuality, their relationship, and their intimate practices. Where *Friends* works to shore up the correctness and naturalness of heterosexuality, gay male texts make light of the "lesbians" (sigh) as an assertion of masculine power and patriarchal privilege.

Furthering gender concerns in the construction of Hollywood's identifiable gay male, the gay male best friend to the heterosexual female presents a relational dynamic that has received much criticism. Shugart asserts that *Will & Grace*, *Object of My Affection*, *The Next Best Thing*, and *My Best Friend's Wedding* construct heterosexual women within a paternal and patriarchal relationship with their gay male friends, as the female's sexuality is dictated by gay male approval. Shugart's analysis is useful in identifying this trend across additional texts, such as in *Six Feet Under*, where Robbie the flower arranger takes on Ruth as his project to fix, all the while referring to her as "cupcake."[74] The relationship between Jack and Jennifer on *Dawson's Creek* follows suit, casting Jen in the continual position of the disposable yet eternally loyal confidant. Upon leaving Jen's house to move in with his new fraternity, Jack comments, "Jen and I have been doing this 'Will and Grace' thing for too long."[75] The pattern is repeated throughout the series, showing Jack dumping Jen for boyfriends, football, and fraternity functions, yet always finding Jen waiting with open arms at his return. Jen counsels Jack that "best friends are nothing to sneeze at,"[76] yet Jack betrays his "soul mate" on multiple occasions, setting her up with his football buddies without her consent, violating her trust, and even trying to have sex with her when he grows depressed about being gay. The females in these relationships are cast as subservient and weak, subject to bodily criticism,[77] at the beck and call of the gay male, and always willing to chalk disrespect up to "that's just how he is." Reifying "male privilege predicated on control of female sexuality" (Shugart 80), gay men reinforce "patriarchal paternalism" (86) and bridge identification to traditional models of heterosexual male privilege.

The reliance upon oppressive social hierarchies to bridge identification with dominant values allows the civilized, reasonable, white, masculine, identifiable gay male points of connection with mainstream audiences, yet identification is bridged through an unmarked acceptance and reification of multiple social privileges. Access to heteronormative institutions is bargained for under a homonormative gag order, a complicit silence and agreement to embrace and endorse multiple social inequalities under the guise of normal, good, and identifiable citizenship. Bridging devices of race, gender, and class might be criticized as tangential to the primary concern of this analysis, which is the rhetorical construction of gay male future. Such a critique, however, fails to account for the importance of situating queer critique within a complicated intersection of multiple forms of social power, where the isolation of sexuality as the sole locus of study is an inescapable reification of a white male queer theory. Chapter 3 argued that discourses of sexuality are aged, yet sexuality and age do not exist in a vacuum. Discourses of sexuality are also raced (Ferguson, "Of Our" 86–8; Perez; Muñoz, *Disident*), gendered (Halberstam, "Shame"; Shugart), and embedded in economic systems (Duggan), and "those of us who fail to acknowledge our victimless status with respect to racism, sexism, and homophobia—are also perpetrators of discrimination" (Carbado 190). In terms of aging, and thus future, symbolic mergers with straight time and heteronormative temporal modes through homonormative assimilation is a privileged and oppressive strategy, failing to enact a queer intersectional interrogation. Articulating the future through the access of normalizing and oppressive systems of power demonstrates the limitations placed upon the concept of "future" through the framework of straight time. From a queer coalitional position, this notion of future is a bankrupt investment that demands allegiance to the heteronormative orientation and the multiple intersecting violences it reproduces.

The final chapter of this analysis locates and theorizes scenes, moments, and characters in the cultural production that gesture to an articulation of queer aging and future outside the tragic frame of heteronormativity and/or horror. Prior to leaving the heteronormative courtroom and the limitations of symbolic merger, however, it is important to offer specific attention to the final scenes, scripts, and images in the closing moments of several mainstream televised series. The final narration of these gay representations within the series' finales can offer assistance in locating the limitations of conceptualizing and articulating future within the cultural discourse. Perhaps the strongest gestures towards the future in these texts, series finales help to locate the limits of discursive intelligibility and the foreseeable gay future available within the cultural production. Marking the discursive margins of gay future in popular film and television, these texts locate the limitations heteronormative temporality places on queered notions of future and mark the starting point for imagining alternative models, meanings, and potentialities for queer temporalities and queer futures.

CLOSING ARGUMENTS: THE MARGINS OF INTELLIGIBLE FUTURE

The finale of *Will & Grace*[78] opens with a nightmare sequence, where Grace envisions raising her child with Will. Marked as a failure of progression, Will and Grace's banter has grown tired, as they resent one another for their compromised existence of regret, misery, hair loss, and weight gain. Grace wakes up from the nightmare, breaks her promise of raising the baby with Will, and moves to Italy to raise her child with the biological father. Will is furious for being deprived of his dream of fatherhood, and their relationship is severed. Jumping two years into the future, both Will and Grace are coupled with babies, living their long-espoused domestic dreams, which seem to perfectly mirror one another. At home, the now late-thirties Will tries to get his son to say, "My daddy is twenty-five," displaying his playful fathering abilities and the joy the Child has brought his life. Will and Grace are briefly reunited, only to confirm that separating and building traditional families was the best choice for both of them. Baby and spousal commitments occupy their lives, and it is another twenty years before they meet again, on opposite sides of a college dormitory, where both of their children are grown and leaving home to start school. The "fate" or "coincidence" of this meeting mirrors how they first met, as college roommates, living across the hall decades before. Their children, of course, fall in love, and plan the wedding and heterosexual life that was never an option for Will and Grace.

The *Dawson's Creek* finale also jumps into the future, where Jack is coupled with a local police officer. The episode is centered on the death of Jen, Jack's best friend and confidant. On her deathbed, he asks Jen if he can raise her baby, and she agrees before passing. In his final scene, Jack and Sheriff Doug kiss on the beach—stroller by their side—as an older woman passes by. Sheriff Doug, negotiating his own coming out fears, boldly announces to the older woman, "I'm just kissing my boyfriend." The lady replies, "That's nice dear,"[79] completely unphased by their affection.

112   *Queer Temporalities in Gay Male Representation*

In the final five minutes of *Six Feet Under*, we watch the lives of the main characters play out in a series of future flashes, where Keith—perhaps in his fifties—is shot during the robbery of an armored vehicle. David outlives him, suffering a heart attack in what seems like his seventies.[80] These closing arguments—however traditional, normative, and problematic—offer articulations of hope, future, and potential for gay male lives that were nonexistent in previous representations in mainstream culture. Gay lives are being lived after the credits roll, breaking away from the tragic endings that defined early Hollywood narratives. In these instances, alienation is remedied and identifications have been constructed with mainstream articulations of future, as the gay male future becomes intelligible through a heteronormative frame. Gay identity is built upon heteronormative identification, reaping its promises while complicit in its exclusions.

The queer future of Brian Kinney, however, fails to escape the cautionary penalties of the heteronormative tragedy. In the final episode,[81] Brian and Justin flirt with the idea of getting married and moving to a large mansion outside of the city. Brian undergoes a radical transformation, lovingly playing with his son Gus, passing up the opportunity to fuck a stripper at his stag party, and expressing desire for a quiet dinner at home. Melanie comments, "Better late than never, he finally grew a heart." In a conversation with Michael, both of them in suits having lunch and reflecting on the "good old days," Brian asks, "Pathetic, huh?" Michael responds, "Inevitable." The show leads us to think that Michael is correct in offering "a toast in the memory of Brain Kinney," yet Justin—Brian's queer protégé—calls Brian out and questions their marriage choice. Brian is afraid Justin is turning his back on his art career, and Justin fears he is turning Brian into something he should never be. Brian states, "I don't want to live with someone who sacrificed their life and called it love to be with me." In Brian's last queer stand, the wedding is cancelled at the rehearsal dinner. Justin leaves for New York with Brian's blessing after having "become the best homosexual you could possibly be." The series, through this exchange, is framed by Justin's arrival in Episode 1 and departure in the finale episode, learning queer politics from his mentor and lover.

True to Brian's character, his queer principles are placed before his feelings. In a discussion with Lindsay, he jokingly calls Justin a "selfish prick—thinks only of himself." Lindsay respectfully replies, "You taught him well." Rather than a triumph of queer politics, the episode depicts Brian in a conflicted depression. Lindsay tries to cheer him up, throwing out the first part of the Brian Kinney mantra, "No apologies." Brian finishes, "No regrets," but with a hesitant and pained discomfort that marks a shift, no longer performing the cool indifference he once personified. Determined to cheer him up, Michael drags Brian out to Babylon, now a deteriorating crime scene after a homophobic bombing. Michael pleads with Brian to dance with him in the demolished club space, claiming the music and magic are still present and the good old days are not over. Brian begins to say he is "too old," when

Michael furiously cuts him off. "You'll always be young and you'll always be beautiful! You're Brian Kinney for fuck sake!"[82] This repeated statement (see note) resituates Brian as a philosophical figure, likened to *Fountainhead's* Roark—more of a queer ideal than a person. Michael, Lindsay, and Justin need Brian to be true to Brian's politics, even if Brian feels their limitations. Battling the ticking clock of age for the entire series, and even more so in Season 5, Brian knows he cannot stay young and worshipped forever. He is stuck, trapped within a restrictive tragedy of selling out to marriage or fighting to remain the "hottest guy on Liberty Avenue."

The queer future of Brian Kinney, however, fails to escape the cautionary penalties of the heteronormative tragedy. In this final episode, Michael and Brian stand in the ruins of what was once the dance club Babylon, the sex-driven, base-thumping playground that provided the backdrop for the entire series. Together, in the vacant space, Michael coaxes him to begin dancing, somewhat awkwardly, devoid of music, in an effort to cheer up Brian. Slowly, music begins to play. The lights dim, a laser lightshow takes over, and shirtless men magically reappear, bringing Babylon back to its youthful utopian state. All their friends suddenly appear in the crowd, and Michael jumps off the platform to join Ben. Brian, elevated in the land of Babylon, cocks his head back and dances as the credits roll. Just as in so many scenes before, Brian returns to the club space of music, drugs, and sex, although each return is a little more strained, requiring more effort. The audience is left with Brian on top—for now—with his politics intact and age creeping up on him. The series stops here, rejecting any articulation of Brian's future and reaffirming the queer connection to the now, the present. While enacting a suspended adolescence and commitment to subcultural space (Halberstam, *Queer*), the show alludes to Brian's exhaustion and struggle to maintain his youthfulness, his sense that time is running out. Babylon begins to feel like something desperate for Brian to cling to, a space that will soon reject his aging self, rather than providing a refuge or departure from straight time.

Brian's last dance suggests that systems of whiteness, masculinity, and upper-class economic status—however powerful—fail to bridge identification with future, once the Child and marriage are rejected. Heteronormativity's sole claim to the future remains without contest, unchallenged by the queer resistance to the spouse/child system, as the youthist sacrificial ritual of gay male aging defines heteronormative departure. The tragic binary remains intact, and queerness is perpetuated as anti-future (Edelman), alienated from a future identification. Brian can either be married or alone, a doting father or an aging homo desperate for his fleeting youth. Given the reductive choice of death or settling down, Brian nobly chooses death.

Facing the statement, "In fifteen years, I will be_____" the gay male is locked into a binary of misery or heteronormativity. Although lingering at the margins of the cultural production, alternative futures have happened, are happening, and can happen—just as there have been, currently are, and will always be queers of all races, genders, and socioeconomic brackets. Mediated productions of the gay male cast these queer lives, pasts, and futures outside the cultural discourse, rendering them unintelligible to mainstream audiences. Where in contemporary queer media is the "fabulous resistance" (Erni 175) that queer academics have sought to theorize and embody? What are all the potential ways to define oneself in fifteen years from now? Where are all of the words and alternative systems of meaning from which we could potentially imagine and identify ourselves? Why is the "fifteen years" statement restricted to only a few terms of meaning and intelligibility? Extending from a tragic binary of the horror story or the heteronormative plea, how else might that sentence be completed, using creativity, alternative meanings, a coalitional consciousness, and a commitment to remoralizing a restrictive and violent system? How might we bridge alternative identifications with the future?

In fifteen years, I will be _____.
In twenty-five years, I will be _____.
In forty years, I will be _____.
Tomorrow, I will be _____.

5 The Dinner Party
Queer Gesturing to Time and Future

We got this far, Dad. I think you'd like it, I really do. Anyway Dad, it's our place, and it's yours too. (Jonathan, *A Home at the End of the World*)

In 20 years, he's [Otis is] happier than anyone else here, but that's another story. (Textual Epilogue, *Happy Endings*)

The dinner party device is so common in popular culture it has become a Hollywood cliché. Within the ongoing flow of events that propel the—usually heterosexual—protagonist of the story forward, the assistance of the "gay friend" is needed. Rushing to the "gay friend's" home, or calling his house in a narrative-driven panic, the protagonist interrupts a quaint gay dinner party, already in progress. Anonymous faces of men and women are obscured in the background, blurred in the distance, as the protagonist seeks help, guidance, or support for a heterosexual romance gone sour. Both present and absent, the camera remains focused on the protagonist, yet gestures to people, events, and lives at the margins of represented space. Demonstrating what de Lauretis refers to as the "space-off," marking an elsewhere at the blind spots of cinematic representation (25–6), this obscured event draws attention to the limitations of heteronormative narrative perspectives and the multitude of concurrent lives, people, and temporal engagements that exist alongside dominant representation.

The dinner party, the representational space-off, is a momentary perspective by incongruity, which can be thought of as "seeing from two angles at once" (Burke, *Attitudes* 269). The dominant narrative, which follows the protagonist through a progressive series of events, literally collides with an alternative temporal event, presenting the existence of additional stories occurring alongside the dominant script. An alternative existence of the "gay friend"—one who is primarily scripted within a dominant heterosexual narrative for the purpose of supporting and furthering the linear plot structure—is revealed in a fleeting moment, as anonymous faces, unheard conversations, and unfamiliar lives are thinly traced in the backdrop.[1]

The dinner party is a repeated motif throughout this final chapter, drawing attention to the unrepresented—yet present—queer space-offs at the margins of dominant narratives. Enlisting the dinner party as a metaphoric queer space conjures up layers of complexity, contestation, and history, as the notion of the dinner party carries multiple associations. Perhaps most obviously, the dinner party conjures up the highly celebrated and criticized art installation by Judy Chicago in the 1970s.[2] This landmark installation project sought to challenge and rewrite patriarchal narratives of history to include the important contributions of silenced and excluded females. The installation stages a ceremonial banquet to commemorate historical and mythic females, whose place in history is rightfully reclaimed. As the current project seeks to locate the absence of queer lives and queer spaces in the cultural narratives of future, Chicago's feminist "Dinner Party" productively informs the interrogation of narratives crafted in the favor of normative and oppressive ideologies.

Chicago's "Dinner Party" also conjures a telos for ongoing and perpetual criticism (Ono and Sloop; McKerrow), as this feminist installation marks a contested gesture. Paralleling many of the complications that face any social movement, the collaborative body of workers who spent years devoted to "The Dinner Party" are often obscured under the recognition of Chicago as "the artist" on record, thus reinforcing the patriarchal structures in place both within and outside the art world. In addition, Chicago's "Dinner Party" has been strongly critiqued for its representation of race and class, marking a contested gesture, one that seeks to reclaim feminist historical contribution, yet is performed in a manner that requires further interrogation. As the dinner party provides a guiding motif for this chapter, associations to Chicago's installation project offer productive and important dimensions to the notion of the queer space-off. Similar to Chicago's project, much queer theoretical work has been strongly critiqued for perpetuating systems of class, whiteness, and patriarchy under the simplified and privileged banner of queer resistance. The very notion of a queer dinner party, as represented in popular culture, is tied to white, "Queer Eye," cosmopolitan, and urbane associations. Purposefully selecting a metaphor that places these problems in the forefront, the dinner party cannot and should not be divorced from the reductive and limited ways that gayness has been represented primarily as a white, male, middle-class identity. Herein, while the dinner party motions to a "space-off" when it is placed at the forefront of representation, it too marginalizes multiple others, constructing additional blind spots to the limited perspective it affords. The intention is to draw attention to the space-off of the dinner party—the concurrent narrative that runs "alongside the represented space" (De Lauretis 26)—while never losing sight that the space-off is subject to further critical interrogation, always enacting additional narrative foreclosures and exclusions.

The conclusion of the film *Happy Endings* relies on the familiar cinematic device of textual epilogue to define the future of the film's characters. Of the three leading gay male characters in the film, Charley lives "almost happily ever after" with his new urologist boyfriend, and Gil, Charley's previous boyfriend, lives alone and spends Christmas with his lesbian friends and their infant. In both of these instances, the futures of these gay men are rendered intelligible through their affiliation with heteronormative narratives of couple and child. The final textual epilogue in *Happy Endings*, however, offers an alternative and optimistic nod towards the future for Otis, the younger gay male in the film who struggles to come out to his father and embrace a gay identity. Otis is both "happier than anyone else here" and this happiness presents "another story." Otis's future is something else—a mysterious question—that gestures to an alternative and queer mode of experiencing future unintelligible to the narrative conventions of Hollywood cinema. The textual epilogue comments that Otis and his new boyfriend Alvin are together for six years, yet it is in twenty years that Otis is marked as "happier than anyone else," distancing his happiness from the narrative conventions of coupling. Neither marked with a partner or a child, counter to the "anyone else here" in the ensemble narrative, Otis's queer future challenges heteronormativity's ownership of the "happy ending," offering an entry point to engage queer articulations of time and futurity.

The heteronormative tragedy of the Hollywood narrative operates under a temporal regime that Boellstorff refers to as "straight time" (229). Straight time, which adopts a linear—and so literally "straight"—approach to time, defines a temporal trajectory through heteronormative progression that relies upon the assumed naturalness, correctness, and inevitability of heteronormative time orientation. Central to the logics of straight time are cultural understandings of childhood, adulthood, marriage, procreation, and productive citizenship, which work to define and cultivate limited and linear engagements with time, and thus future. Otis's textual epilogue offers a subtle, yet productive, break from the logics of straight time through a queering of the Hollywood fairy tale. The text announces that "he's happier than anyone else," both situating his engagement with future in resistance and in difference to the other characters, while also marking him as a singular entity. Rather than the assumed heteronormative convention of "they" living "happily ever after," Otis—a gay male now in his late thirties—is "happier" by himself. This wink to queer futurity works "in opposition to the institutions of family, heterosexuality, and reproduction" (Halberstam, *Queer* 1), referencing the existence of a queered engagement with future.

Building from the heteronormative tragedy presented in Chapter 3, this final chapter shifts attention away from the temporal punishment of gay male aging—the disciplining of queers to straight time—to theorize the potential for a queer temporality gestured from within the cultural production. Rejecting the plea for homonormative acceptance as a productive avenue for queer politics or futurity, as argued in Chapter 4, this analysis interrogates the foundational heteronormative underpinnings of dominant narrative structures. As Hollywood narratives are subject to the limitations of genre, and genres determine the limitations of what is possible within the narrative world of a given popular text (Lacey 47), the cultural production offers subtle variations of difference within repeated and familiar narrative forms (46). In turn, the narrative is a construction that provides the audience a context to make sense of the signs presented within a given text and "a framework for audiences to use to make sense of events" (52). Relating specifically to this project, dominant cultural narratives are scripted through heteronormative assumptions, specifically the uncontested premise that straight time is the natural and irrefutable foundation and path to future. As argued in Chapter 3, the cultural production ritualistically represents those who deviate from heteronormative models of future as tragic victims, reifying heteronormativity's uncontested correctness. Tragic framing reiterates and retells a "narrative of reassurance" (52), or more specifically, a narrative of heteronormative reassurance that solidifies the authority of straight temporality.

At the heart of this analysis is the theorizing of a queer temporality within the cultural production that motions to alternative and potentially queer notions of futurity. The book questions how one might locate queer temporalities within the Hollywood master narrative, a rigid and tragic ritual that honors the totalizing illusion of straight time's correctness and is defined through a linear conception of future. If the culturally produced narrative of future parallels the common student narrative of, "In fifteen years, I will be married with children," then the cultural production is premised upon a limiting and tragic foundation of straight time. Future, for queers, is locked into narrative punishment for those who fail to successfully access homonormative inclusion into dominant frameworks of identification.

Enlisting a Burkean comic ethic of both/and, this chapter rejects the tragic either/or formation that queers must either accept the tragic punishment of age and rejection set forth in Chapter 3 or fight for the homonormative inclusion critiqued in Chapter 4. Extending beyond victims of time or faithful servants to the perpetuation of heteronormativity's reign, Burkean theorizing of the comic corrective is placed into dialogue with contemporary conceptions of queer time to locate productive articulations of queer futurity. In the first section of the chapter, Burkean perspective by incongruity and de Lauretis's notion of the elsewhere (25) are enlisted as theoretical tools to challenge dominant and linear conceptions of straight time through nonlinear movement. Rejecting the primacy of a linear framework, where sequential events follow one another in a swift and progressive logic, comic criticism draws attention to the potentials for extending the temporal margins of a suspended moment—seeking to move a narrative across rather than ushering it forward. The subsequent sections locate queer and comic gestures of futurity within popular gay male representation, addressing alternative romantic, familial and community formations, as well as queered articulations of gay male aging and futurity.

Otis's postscript points to "another story," a brief mention to a world that exists at the margins of Hollywood's represented space. Paralleling the crumbs, hints, and signals that once privately spoke to gay audiences in a time when the explicit representation of a happy gay male or female was unthinkable, the dinner party—a wink to queer time, queer futures, and queer orientations towards aging—is not fully absent from the cultural screen. While unintelligible to those confined to straight temporal engagement, the dinner party offers potentialities. "Potentialities are different [than possibilities] insofar as while they are present they do not exist in present things. Thus potentialities have a temporality that is not in the present but, more nearly, in the horizon, which we can understand as futurity" (Muñoz, "Stages" 11). Adopting Muñoz's call for scouting out queer potentialities "for a 'not here' and a 'not now'" (11), this chapter looks to the margins of popular discourse to locate and theorize the potentiality of queered futures. Although the dominant heteronormative narrative defines queers as "people without a future" (10) or anti-future (Edelman), a Burkean comic corrective offers "another story"—a potentially queer one.

PERSPECTIVE BY INCONGRUITY: LOOKING ELSEWHERE

> Is *this* what the Lone Ranger and Tonto did during the Quaker Oats commercials? (Reid 134)

The 2004 film *De-Lovely* presents a narrative about the life of legendary songwriter Cole Porter and his thirty-four year marriage to Linda Lee Thomas. Without placing labels upon Porter's sexuality, the film openly acknowledges Porter's consistent engagement with same-sex sexual encounters throughout his life, as well as Linda's knowledge of Cole's same-sex desire. The narrative of the film, however, forefronts the relationship between Cole and Linda, privileging their story at the expense of several potential others. Cole's affairs with men exist outside of the represented space of the narrative screen, as the audience watches Cole leave Linda and then return to Linda, venturing off into unrepresented spaces with giddy excitement. Married to the logic of straight temporality, the film is structured through Linda and Cole's first meeting, their courtship, their marriage, the miscarriage of their baby, and their eventual deaths. Cole's sexual encounters with men are marginalized in the narrative constructed—tangential and fleeting—whereas his marriage is centralized within the arc of the story. *De-Lovely* demonstrates the narratizing choices of Hollywood productions and the infinite number of possibilities for how a person's life might be narrated. Given a multitude of moments that shaped and defined the life of Cole Porter, the film molded Porter's life into a familiar Hollywood model that reifies heteronormative systems of relation and temporality.

The possibility exists to read *De-Lovely* as a queer narrative, one where a heterosexual female and a queer male construct a nonnormative romance and marriage with full awareness of the Cole's fluid sexual desires. Such a reading, however, only addresses the base narrative without attending to systematic heteronormative tragedy that is played out within the film.

Extensive filmic attention is granted to Linda's growing loneliness, as Cole's wandering sexual appetites leave her feeling isolated and abandoned. Rather than permitting the viewer access to Cole's "other life," the camera lingers repeatedly upon the narrative world of Linda, begging for empathy and identification. Cole's homosexuality is crafted as selfish and cruel, a compulsive appetite that tests Linda's saintly patience time and time again. When Cole suggests, "They were all about you," claiming every song he ever wrote was for his wife, it is Linda who replies, "Not all, but some." In that statement, Linda briefly rejects the full heteronormative recuperation of Cole's life, winking to the dinner party of Cole's "other" inspirational loves and times the Hollywood viewer is not shown. Linda is painted as the martyr of the film, and on her deathbed, she solicits the help of a younger man to take care of Cole when she is gone. Cole, devastated by the loss of his wife and faced with deteriorating health, tells the young man, "Sweet boy, there is nothing for you here." The film opens and closes with a dream sequence of Cole viewing his entire life from the audience of a theater. The characters of his life perform on stage, yet the men in his life are granted no presence or significance. In the film's final scene, Cole and Linda—young as the day they first met—sit at the piano together.

Confined to a "Will and Grace" construction, where the homosexual male is coded within a heterosexual relationship with a female (Battles and Hilton-Morrow; Shugart), *De-Lovely* actively forecloses what de Lauretis refers to as a potential "view from elsewhere" (25). Theorizing the queer potentials of the "blind spots" or the "space-off" (26), she shifts attention "from the space represented by/in a representation, by/in a discourse, by/in a sex-gender system, to the space not represented yet implied (unseen) in them" (26). *De-Lovely*'s privileging of straight time—reifying the centrality of heteronormative systems as the sole architects of meaningful temporal orientation—crafted Cole's life within a rigidly heteronormative tale. Lingering at the margins of *De-Lovely*, however, are the whisperings and reminders of concurrent narratives referred to, yet not represented. The places Cole runs off to, the men he meets, the experiences they share, and the potential meaningfulness of these space-offs offer additional perspectives to the story of Cole Porter and the heteronormative tragedy presented in the film.

The space-off marks a site of queer potentiality, as it works to problematize and queer the heteronormative narrative of *De-Lovely* through defining the story from another perspective, an elsewhere. In Burkean terms, this device can be articulated as a comic corrective enlisting the strategy of perspective by incongruity. As discussed in Chapter 2, perspective by incongruity works to dismantle rigid binary systems—the foundations of tragic framing—through exposing the false integrity of dichotomous systems. Using intentional incongruity or oppositional pairing, likened to the oxymoron, perspective by incongruity exposes the underlying substance (Burke, *Grammar* 29) shared across seemingly opposing concepts. The key binary formations queer time faces work to place queers in opposition to the very notion of a future, as the primary signifiers of future are constructed through marriage and child.[3]

Given the non-representation of Cole's male lovers, *De-Lovely* permitted a tragic narrative where Linda is crafted as heroine and the seemingly shallow and meaninglessness of Cole's flings—thus his homosexual desire—is cast as an evil threat to their marriage. In turn, Cole's isolation following Linda's death and his renouncing of the "sweet boy" sets a cycle of redemption in motion, where Cole self-inflicts misery and loneliness upon himself in honor of his deceased wife. Had the film complicated this tragic tale, permitting Cole's male lovers a face and a humanity, similar to the extensive narrative time devoted to the development of Linda, this tragic tale would have grown more complicated, as well as more comic. The demonization of homosexuality and the valorization of heteronormativity would become problematized, as *De-Lovely*'s simplistic designations of good and evil would lose coherence. In addition, the straight temporality of the film, which chose to depict Cole's life through a series of heteronormative milestones, would also be complicated. Rather than awkwardly disciplining Cole's life into a blasé formula, relying upon heterosexual romantic relations to mark the beginning and end of adult life in a linear trajectory, the narrative timeline could have moved in multiple directions. Cole's male lovers ran concurrent with the relationship with Linda, yet Linda marks the narrative through line by which Cole's life is articulated. Bringing in additional relationships, loves, experiences, and moments of pleasure offers a perspective by incongruity to the tragedy, but also a temporal extension that problematizes the authority of straight time.

A comic corrective to *De-Lovely* would resist the simplistic casting of Linda and heterosexuality as correct, while also claiming an alternative mode of temporality in Cole's life, one that works outside of the linear heteronormative romance script with Linda. Jack and Ennis's time on *Brokeback Mountain* offers a counter text to *De-Lovely*, where their limited time together, a few days a year, defines the temporality of the narrative progression. Placing these two texts in dialogue, *Brokeback Mountain* defines a queer space-off from heterosexual narrated space and time, a summoning towards queer futurity. The overall film, however, is tied to straight temporality, as time is marked and defined through linear progression of the heterosexual lives *away* from Brokeback. Their romance exists alongside straight time, yet is framed by their marriages, their children, and an imposed temporal progression accessible to heteronormative audience expectations. The final marking of time in *Brokeback*, following the tragic sacrifice of Jack Twist, takes place in a dialogue between Ennis and his daughter, when he agrees to attend her upcoming wedding. The only indication of what is ahead of Ennis is his attendance to this wedding, his continued interpellation into a heteronormative temporality, no matter how much he works to divorce himself from these systems. As the end of the film has Ennis living in the trailer, seemingly in complete isolation from anyone else, there is an implied gesture that Ennis seeks to break away from the world completely. In this respect, *Brokeback* articulates a strong tension between straight and queer time, as the film ends with the sense that Ennis is continually subject to straight time, yet holds onto a temporal orientation defined through Jack's shirt and an image of Brokeback Mountain, forever to hang on his closet door.

Perspective by incongruity offers a theoretical framework to analyze the foreclosures of heteronormative tragedy, but also to potentialize queer extensions and rearticulations of queer comedy. Differing from the notion of symbolic merger, which seeks normative inclusion while perpetuating the violence of tragic framing, comedy works to remoralize corrupted and confining systems (Burke, *Attitudes* 39–44). In the words of Anna Madrigal, the queer den mother in Armistead Maupin's Tales of the City series, "You don't have to keep up dear, you just have to keep open" (*Michael*, 197). Rather than keeping up with time, as an ongoing accumulation of sequential events in a designated narrative progression, to keep open alludes to a comic ethic of fallibility and mistakenness. The Burkean comic frame, as discussed in greater detail in Chapter 2, is guided by a the notion of mistakenness (*Attitudes*, 41), as opposed to tragic formations that promote a rigid designation of right and wrong—mandating punishment (39). Rather than merely symbolically bridging allegiance with an oppressive system, perspective by incongruity offers "seeing from two angles at once" (41)—as with the space-off—and complicates the coherence of a singular telling of good and bad to welcome multiple perspectives for the purposes of education and extension of understandings.

A comic ethic of mistakenness mirrors Anna's call to keep *open* to time, rather than keeping *up* with time, thus permitting a queered temporal orientation towards lateral movement and attention to the space-off. Time and future become normalizing and disciplinary constructs defined through the illusionary absolutism of heteronormative systems. The comic corrective draws attention to the margins of discourse, the margins of represented space, embracing an ethic of ongoing education and exploration for potentialities foreclosed by the dominant heteronormative tragedy. Herein, queer theory and Burke work to articulate a collective project, as the comic corrective to the heteronormative tragedy is the exploration of the space-off. As the heteronormative tragedy is a product of straight time, hijacking and disciplining discursive projections for approaching the future, perspective by incongruity provides a tool for remoralizing the violence of straight time by exposing the corrupt tragedy it seeks to perpetuate.

Revisiting the construction of Nelson in the film *Poseidon*, constructing a lonely and suicidal older gay man was accomplished in a rapid succession of signifiers within three brief scenarios. Reflective of numerous gay male representations in popular media, Nelson is cast as a victim to straight temporality, marking his life as without value. In the same style, *An Empty*

Bed—the story of the aging gay male wandering the streets of New York and reflecting on his life—demonstrates how straight time works to punish queers. The youthist economy of gay male culture fuels this tragic cycle, casting older gay men as the sacrificial lambs to straight time's redemption. Future, in straight time, literally plots a narrative timeline where child and spouse are the sole designations of meaning. For this reason, Nelson's suicidal ideation requires minimal justification. He, like Richard in *The Hours*, has "fallen out of time."

This analysis turns to interrogate the regime of straight temporality at work within the cultural production, specifically gay male representation. Enlisting a queer Burkean analysis, this final chapter seeks to explore gestures to queer temporalities within popular film and television to advance resistant, queer, and creative engagements with future, which seek to remoralize, problematize, and reconstitute the heteronormative tragedy.

QUEER COMMUNITY BUILDING AND COALITIONAL GESTURES

Straight time establishes its dominance through its illusionary perfection, the repeatedly privileged idealization of the heteronormative fairy tale where man and woman meet, fall in love, procreate, and further support the assumed correctness of the straight timeline. The iconic image of this heteronormative perfection is the 1950s white suburban heterosexual couple, a culturally produced image of the heyday of heteronormativity, where life was simple, gender roles were rigidly enforced, and diverse expressions of sexuality were masked in the illusions of "Leave it to Beaver" perfection. Todd Haynes's *Far from Heaven* presents a queered view of 1950s suburbia, complicating heteronormative perfection through a complex negotiation of racial, economic, and sexual discourses. Luciano offers a queer temporal discussion of the film, suggesting "Haynes's film to be attempting—a move, that is from an investigative take on the past to the speculative time of the not-yet" (253), through displacement (253), interrogations of progress (251), the "denaturalization of time" (255), and a critique of the "time-patterns of the straight world" (259). While my own discussion of *Far from Heaven*, for the purposes of this study, departs from Luciano's project, there is a shared interest in how this film gestures "to move toward a future that history has not envisioned" (269).

The filmic narrative opens with the overly pleasant and clichéd perfection of Cathy and Frank, an upwardly mobile white couple, who appear to define the perspective seen in Norman Rockwell's 1950s America. Frank is a successful advertising executive, and Cathy is the exaggerated image of suburban royalty. She keeps a tidy home, always has a freshly made-up face and a stylish gown, and is a featured figure on the society pages of the local newspaper. Cathy and Frank are the representation of heteronormative perfection, the symbolically crafted image of flawlessness, from which all deviance and shortcomings will be measured. Although the film alludes to Frank's homosexuality early in the film, the American dream is fully ruptured when Cathy stops by Frank's office to bring him dinner and discovers—in horror—Frank kissing another man. Melodramatic music accompanies Cathy's traumatic realization, as the introduction of the unspeakable brings campy and overstylized horror into a pristine world of strict heterosexual allegiance. Frank is desperate and enrolls in conversion therapy, declaring, "I can't let this *thing* destroy my life."

At this juncture of the film, *Far from Heaven* presents a perspective by incongruity by placing sanitized and stereotypical images of Rockwell-esque 1950s suburbia in dialogue with homosexuality, extending and problematizing the illusionary images of the iconic heterosexual American past. Quite literally, perspective by incongruity can be understood as a shift of the camera from the represented space—the all-too-familiar cultural narrative of domestic bliss—to the marginal space-off that runs along the narrative, yet is never seen. Moving the camera to the dark margins of Cathy and Frank's secret dispels the perfection myth, dismantling the coherence of the socially elite who are often used to determine and discipline those who are "bad" in relation to their illusionary "goodness." The heightened parody of both Cathy's domestic perfection and the melodramatic horror of Frank's same-sex desire highlight the queering at work. Luciano argues that the film poses a challenge to the progressive logics that so much has changed by turning "classic cinema subtext into contemporary text" (251).

Far from Heaven's queer scope extends far beyond the interrogation of America's homosexual past, offering a multifaceted and intersectional critique of heteronormativity. The narrative shifts the camera angle from Cathy and Frank's homosexual crisis to broader discussions of racism, classism, and gender inequality in 1950s America, as a disillusioned Cathy seeks comfort in her growing friendship with Raymond, her African American gardener. The scandal of Raymond and Cathy's relationship is positioned alongside the scandal of Frank's homosexuality, each complicating the 1950s suburban perfection myth at the core of the film. *Far from Heaven* presents a comic corrective to sedimented cultural narratives by refusing the coherent simplicity of a tragic framing of events. Cathy's position as a female inhibits her ability to live her life by her own desires, as patriarchal and racist discourses simultaneously condemn her for her husband's sexuality and her "kindness to negroes." The positioning of Frank as a victim to social homophobia is complicated by his attempt to control Cathy, his own allegiances to white dominance, and his ability to exploit white, middle-class, patriarchal privilege. At the close of the film, Frank—having fallen in love with another man—is presented as comfortable in his future with continued access to personal and economic security. The film does not seek to privilege one axis of oppression over another, yet offers a complex narrative where discourses of sexuality, race, gender, and class cannot be easily parsed apart. The film works to link "interracial heterosexuality and homosexuality and, by extension, racism and homophobia" (Luciano 262), marking and opening a space to critique how heteronormativity is, at the core, a raced endeavor (Cohen). By refusing to highlight one narrative of oppression, and not relegating additional discourses of power to the blind spot of the represented space, *Far from Heaven* offers a uniquely comic corrective to the heteronormative tragedy. Lacking the assertion of heroes or victims in the story, the film offers a comic narrative of mistakenness that initiates a broader social critique on multiple fronts.

Far from Heaven opens with allegiance to the forward momentum of straight time, as Cathy finds herself blindly moving through life according to socially sanctioned temporal orientation. Cathy's life was a linear sequence of events that prepared her for marriage, children, and the reaping of all the joys that were afforded from faithful commitment to the straight-and-narrow temporal script. Luciano marks how Cathy, "despite her picture-perfect homemaker image . . . appears predisposed to missing beats in the repetitive rhythms of domesticity" (259). Having established this slightly out of step temporal commitment, her divorce from Frank and her relationship with Raymond throw Cathy out of time—disillusioned and distanced from the assumed correctness of straight time. Mirroring Richard's claim about of falling "out of time" in *The Hours*, Thomas uses the phrase "out of time" when discussing queer temporality to mean "[b]eyond memory, beyond origin" (327) as it draws our attention to the "queer sense of being out of sync" (330). At this point, as Cathy falls out of time, the narrative shifts its temporal focus, as the promises of future and bliss deteriorate, just as the stories of her past unravel. Although Frank experiences "a failure or disinclination to live up to the time-patterns of the straight world" (Luciano 259), the film lingers and contemplates Cathy's temporal rupture. In this queer moment of being "out of sync," Cathy's attention moves laterally to the world around her. She literally stops and looks around at the blind spots of her world, no longer able to fix her focus on the path ahead of her. Her tragic linear trajectory is complicated by the comic awareness of her tragic complicity, the lives and struggles that exist at the margins of her white picket fence. The suburban perfection at the top of the film unravels and exposes its space-offs, offering an incongruous perspective where Cathy's life is surrounded by a complex and intersectional field of carnage, perpetuated by the universal violence of heteronormativity (Yep).

The linkage between a queer coalitional approach and an interrogation of straight temporality is vital to the rearticulation of queer images of aging, yet will inevitably implicate and interrogate the privileged foundation of many gay male representations in popular media. Note that it is Cathy, as opposed to Frank, who adopts an intersectional consciousness in *Far from Heaven*, as Frank's homosexuality is coupled with a commitment to patriarchal and racist ideologies. In this respect, Cathy offers a more productive queer mode of resistance than the normative politics of Frank. The film leaves Frank with a male partner, closeted and active in his previous professional life, and seemingly satisfied to continue perpetuating the multiple systems of oppression that serve to benefit his personal progress. Frank is not constructed as unsympathetic, yet he works to symbolically merge himself into a corrupt tragic system, hiding his difference in hopes of seeking normative inclusion.

Homonormative gay male postures are strongly critiqued in *Quinceañera*, an independent film where Gary and James—two upwardly mobile white gay men in their thirties—purchase a home in the increasingly gentrified Los Angeles neighborhood of Echo Park. On their newly purchased property, in the backyard, is a small house and garden where Carlos and his uncle currently live. Carlos is a young queer Latino male whose family has kicked him out of the house for being gay. Gary and James "love their Latin boys" and quickly befriend and seduce Carlos, all the while winking and joking about their conquest to their equally wealthy and white male friends. When Gary—five years younger than James—and Carlos begin sleeping together without including James, thus violating the terms of their relationship, James confronts Gary, and Carlos is cut out of their lives. Furthermore, Gary and James make the decision to evict Carlos's uncle from their property, a home that the uncle has lived in for decades, to build the garden of their dreams. Impervious to the history or experience of Carlos and his uncle, Gary and James exploit racial and economic privilege to literally tear down the lives of their Latino neighbors to make space for the expanding future. Marked as superficially queer in their negotiated sexual relationship, Gary and James embody the critique that many queers of color launch against white male queer positions.[4] *Quinceañera* works to openly mark and implicate the privilege Gary and James exploit, their objectification of Carlos as a younger queer of color, and their firm allegiance to a consumer-driven domestic regime of futurity, rearticulated as a white, normative, gay system of manifest destiny.

Quinceañera offers a perspective by incongruity to the blind spots elided in texts such as *Queer as Folk*, where community is championed in limited and problematic ways. In the final episode of *Queer as Folk*, Michael is asked to speak on behalf of a political organization that seeks to promote a "respectable face" for the gay community. As Michael and Ben have, at this time in the series, adopted Hunter and live their lives in a manner closely aligned with the heteronormative script, Michael presents such a "face." Tensions arise just as Michael begins his speech, when his mother and friends are ushered to the back of the press conference, as the front and visible seats are reserved for couples with children. Speaking on behalf of an organization that claims to stand for the rights of all populations, Michael is a first-hand witness to the literal placement of queered bodies to the margins of represented space. He begins his speech,

> Truth is I'm just like you. [conflicted pause] Actually, that's not the truth. Sure, in a lot of ways, I am just like you. I want to be happy. I

want some security, a little extra money in my pocket, but in many ways my life is nothing like yours. Why should it be? Do we all have to have the same lives to have the same rights? I thought diversity is what this country is all about . . . Being different is what makes us all the same. It is what makes us family.[5]

Michael's plea for acceptance of difference offers a motioning towards one form of queer community building, yet it refuses to interrogate power or privilege in any complex manner. In navigating the ways Michael bridges identification with the (assumed to be white and straight) audience, similarity and difference is marked only in relation to sexuality, evoking a narrow and simplistic articulation of community. The viewer's attention is drawn to how Michael's "queer" friends are cast out of visibility in the press conference, yet the absence of nonwhite, non-middle-class bodies is further marginalized to the space-off. *Quinceañera* and *Far from Heaven* offer productive comic correctives to the limited notions of community promoted in texts such as *Queer as Folk* or *Broken Hearts Club*, always obsessing upon their difference and consistently blinded to their racial, class, and gendered identifications. A queer coalitional community must resist such privileged blind spots in their simplistic narratives, acknowledging that a comic narrative *is* intersectional in nature.

This critique is not designed to demonize or diminish the alternative forms of community promoted in *Queer as Folk* or *Broken Hearts Club*. Rethinking notions of family and kinship, Patrick in *Broken Hearts Club* refers to his cohort of gay friends as "the only ones who make it bearable." In the same film, Dennis, asserts, "The only thing that keep us from complete despair is the friends we develop." Similar expressions are found throughout *Queer as Folk*, where friends within the gay community mark an important site of satisfaction, support, and meaning. Rather than belittle these forms of community, this critique seeks to extend the notion of queer community in broader and more comic ways, incorporating discourses of age, race, class, and gender. This calls for a greater interrogation of Michael's discussion of the gay community, as queer concerns extend beyond simplistic calls for the equality and security of alternative sexualities. Only the white, male, middle-class gay man can afford such a convenient coherence of sexual equality and inequality. In turn, a queer coalitional community seeks to problematize the linkage of future to spouse and child systems, and to rearticulate futurity and potentiality through an alternative—if not complimentary—future defined by social justice. Rejecting a linear path of straight time in favor of a comic corrective to the lateral and undefined potential of queer time, such a rethinking of queer community asks that how and where we invest in future undergo radical rethinking.

The articulated project places a hefty burden upon Hollywood productions, which refuse the possibility of radical rearticulations of community in favor of minor deviations from already familiar and normative models.

In short, very few—if any—mainstream texts are capable of embodying and representing queer coalitional gesture, without limitations, constraints, and perpetual blind spots. The productivity of this analysis is in locating the gestures as points of departure, each flawed in multiple ways, yet hinting at articulating moments of comic transcendence and rearticulation—subtle motions to the queer potentiality at the margins.

QUEERED FAMILY IN QUEER TIME

> *JONATHAN:* Doesn't this all feel strange?
> *BOBBY:* No. It's perfect just the way it is. (*A Home at the End of the World*)

The heterosexual family is the cornerstone of straight time, a reproducing system of culturally constructed meanings that discipline queer lives as antithetical to the concept of future. The term "family" marks a contested site in contemporary discourses, as the violent assertion of "family values" works to honor the correctness of heterosexual, state-sanctioned, procreative unions, whereas gay political efforts assert "family" as a generic term for gay and gay-supporting collectives. The usage of the term does not fall neatly into this either/or formation, however, as the term "family" is simultaneously a tool of conservative oppression and a site of potential rearticulation. Marking the distinction between the "biological" families—in relation to "logical" families (*Michael* 81)—Maupin's Anna Madrigal overtly privileges a notion of family you build and create as your own, as opposed to the relations you happen to be born into.

Foundational to the heterosexual family narrative is the notion of generativity, marking the satisfaction older generations experience in interacting and mentoring younger members of the family. Erikson's concept is used to describe a tension in later life between generativity and despair, marking a unique obstacle for aging sexual minorities (Kimmel 271). As the access to relations of generativity for gay men are less likely to be related to one's offspring (271), this poses obstacles to the way heterosexual research in gerontology seeks to account for meaningfulness for aging populations. This process of committing to future generations of a society, according to Erikson's conception, is not restricted to parenting (De Vries and Blando 15) and has been discussed in terms of artistic contribution, political involvement, and career choices (16–7). Still, given the youthist/ageist systems within gay male culture, a community-based model of generativity is impaired by the social meanings and mythologies attached to the aging process. Within the increased visibility of gay male characters in popular media, however, there has also been a growing visibility for nontraditional constructions of kinship that articulate queered notions of family.

The film *A Home at the End of the World* adapts Michael Cunningham's queer contemplation of home and family for a mainstream audience. Bobby and Jonathan are childhood friends with a history of sexual experimentation and intimacy. Whereas Jonathan marks himself as gay in his adult life, Bobby occupies a less rigid queer position where his sexuality remains individualized and fluid. Bobby and Claire—Jonathan's female roommate and best friend—develop a romantic relationship and conceive a child, complicating Jonathan and Claire's initial plans to raise a child of their own. Together, the three of them leave New York City and plan to raise the baby together, creating a home for themselves in upstate New York. Conflicts of temporal orientations lead to the breakdown of their queer creation of home, as the tension between straight time and queer time become enmeshed with gendered disparities and heteronormative commitments.

Their country home and the Home Café, a restaurant Bobby and Jonathan open in their small upstate town, become the locations for the characters to create a queer space to reimagine family. Likened to *Brokeback Mountain*, the film shifts the camera to the space-off, exploring queer potential in a rural space seemingly removed from the rigidity of straight time. The film examines the possibility of creating an isolated queer space, yet falters, for "the term *queer* itself marks this stance of being always already within, in bed with, complicit and contaminated by, the normative with which it engages" (Boellstorff 241). Claire grows disenchanted by their threesome arrangement, surprising herself by the longing she feels for a life more complicit with her lingering heteronormative attachments. She asks Bobby to leave with her and the baby, arguing, "I think maybe I'm not this unusual. I think maybe it's just my hair." Claire is not naïve about the restrictive limitations of marriage and child, as Alice, Jonathan's mother, informs her that the "normal thing" is not all it is set up to be. Alice confesses, "The world just starts to shrink around you." Still, gendered roles and the overall anxiety of their "unusual arrangement" lead Claire to leave with the baby and not return. Jonathan faces a different temporal map, as he discovers he has contracted HIV. As Halberstam writes, "[Q]ueer time perhaps emerges most spectacularly, at the end of the twentieth century, from within those gay communities whose horizons of possibility have been severely diminished by the AIDS epidemic" (*Queer* 2).[6] As Claire adopts a straight logic of time by choosing a life where she can raise her child in a more traditional environment, and Jonathan is forced to rethink "the conventional emphasis on longevity and futurity" (2), it is Bobby who articulates a uniquely queer approach to engaging time, family, and future.

Claire comments that Bobby could live anywhere and be okay, not relying on the conventions and structures that seem to burden and discipline Claire and Jonathan throughout the film. In the final scene, Jonathan and Bobby spread their father's ashes (biologically Jonathan's father), and during that act, Bobby thinks back in time to when he and Jonathan where teenagers, dropping acid in a cemetery. Bobby instructs Jonathan not to fear the dead, as they only want what everyone else wants. Jonathan asks, "What do we want?" Bobby replies, "I don't know, man. I mean, our lives, right? Like this whole big beautiful world and everything that can happen." As the acid kicks in and Jonathan grows uneasy, Bobby calms him, saying, "All's well little brother. There is nothing to fear." Bobby's dialogue in this scene, as well as his overall engagement with time and space paraphrase the words and worldview of his older brother who died as a teenager. In the flashback to the cemetery, we are reminded that Bobby is now exactly who Bobby has always been, unchanged and resistant to space, time, or age. Bobby embodies the "stretched-out adolescences of queer culture makers that disrupt conventional accounts of subculture, youth culture, adulthood, and maturity" (Halberstam, *Queer* 153). Adopting playfulness and a commitment to potentializing alternative modes of existing in the world, Bobby is incongruously childlike and adult, carefree and creative with his temporal engagement and ruled by relational loyalty rather than social narratives of appropriateness. He occupies a unique location between categories of sexuality, temporal scripts, and intelligible subjectivities, longing to create a home and a family that to many seems neither logical nor biological.

Related articulations of queer family emerge in the films *Boy Culture*, *Latter Days*, and *Broken Hearts Club*, where families, similar to Maupin's Tales of the City cohort, build communities centered on shared marginalized sexualities. In *Boy Culture*, X plays a beefy callboy who takes in the younger Joey, referring to him as "Junior" and "The Beaver." X's performance of parent to the young Joey, who is always trying to seduce X, offers an image of generativity and mentorship within generations in gay male culture. *Latter Days* closes with Aaron and Christian breaking bread at a Thanksgiving table of queer friends, where Lila, the restaurant owner and mother figure to several of the younger men, declares, "You always have a place at my table." Although the narrative of *Latter Days* follows the romance of two young white males—one a West Hollywood bar boy and the other a Mormon missionary—the final table image offers a coalitional gesture of men and women of multiple ages, races, and sexualities. The image provides a strong counter argument to the "family values" and homophobic Mormon doctrine, which forced Aaron to leave his biological family and his church family.

Rejecting the need for a biological/logical divide of family, which erases the cultural and individual importance many queers place upon biological family, *Quinceañera* offers a queer articulation of family formation within biological family. Kicked out of his parent's house, Carlos moves in with his unmarried and potentially queer uncle[7] who offers him a home and continued family connection. In addition, Carlos's teenage cousin becomes pregnant, and her family rejects her as well. As a family tied by blood, as well as by a shared experience of being disciplined by conservative cultural norms, the three family members forge and construct a unique bond with one another, taking care of each other and supporting one another where their immediate families would not. This construction of family shifts the emphasis of family on heteronormative time to what Boellstorff refers to as falling time, or a coincidental time, that "does not 'accumulate' or 'build,' it is always in a kind of meantime" (240).[8]

Chapter 4 problematized the ways the gay male/ straight female relationship works to perpetuate patriarchal control over the female character in unproductive and oppressive ways, yet this relationship requires a brief reconsideration within this discussion. Jen on *Dawson's Creek* follows a similar pattern to Grace on *Will & Grace* and multiple other representations of the devoted female friend to the identifiable gay male (Shugart). Although Jack on *Dawson's Creek* belittles and often dismisses Jen to satisfy his fight for normative inclusion, the character of Jen, in her efforts to forge a queer family with Jack, presents a useful discussion. Similar to Bobby in *A Home at the End of the World*, Jen Lindley works to dismantle the notion of queerness from the gay body. As Jack pined away at the misery and isolation of not having a boyfriend, Jen constantly argues, "Best friends are nothing to sneeze at,"[9] arguing the significance of relations outside of cultural romantic scripts. United as "outsiders," Jen is marginalized in her school for being a girl with a sordid sexual past, labeled and demonized for her violation of the feminine gendered roles. Jen struggles to show Jack both the limitations of the heteronormative scripts he longs for and the beauty and potentiality of creating their own way of existing in the world and in time. Although the majority of the representation of their relationship is edited within the heteronormative confines of the *Dawson's Creek* narrative, there is consistent reference to their relational elsewhere alongside the narrated space. For example, in one episode it is revealed that Jen and Jack have a designated a spot where they would routinely meet at night to lay on a blanket and star gaze. However, this space is only made visible within the represented narrative to introduce the heterosexual relationship that interrupts it. In an effort to win favor with his new football buddies, Jack sends Henry to their secret place to meet Jen, as Henry has a crush on Jen. Expecting Jack to arrive for their usual private meeting, Henry appears, disrupting the metaphorical dinner party and violating Jack and Jen's space. Furious and deeply disappointed, Jen explains that there is something sacred about "our place," which he betrayed on a whim.[10] Although Jen continues to forgive Jack for his dismissal and disrespect to their family-through-outsider relationship, marking the importance of gender roles in this relational representation, Jen's unwavering conviction to alternative modes of relation signal a queered sensibility. It is in reference to her past that she asserts, "People grow up and realize 'die young and make a good corpse' is not all it's cracked up to be"[11] Arguably the queerest character on the show, Jen Lindley died in the final episode of cancer.[12] As Jen is a single mother, Jack lobbies for the right to raise her daughter, to which Jen agrees. By sacrificing the queered character of Jen,

Jack gained normative identification and access to straight time through the role of fatherhood.[13]

These texts, while always limited by the Hollywood conventions, motion to alternative ways to conceive of family that extend and expand reductive and tragic articulations of "family," "family values," and "future." Teasing out and branching off from linear models of straight time, such articulations of family present, however subtly, queered temporal engagements that shift the camera to the underrepresented margins of the cultural screen. Future is crafted through an extended repertoire of elements,[14] begging the extension of the limitations of formulaic genre to broaden and expand their range of vision. Through this lateral move to the space-off, branched narratives of family assist the potentializing of queer presents to reinvision queer futures.

QUEER ROMANCE AND GAY MARRIAGE

> *Married* married or just . . . regular? (*Michael*, Maupin 3)

> It won't be long before it [gay marriage] happens here. It's beginning, and we're a part of it. (Ben, *Queer as Folk*)[15]

The queering of marriage, as well as family, marks a comic project that destabilizes the illusionary perfection of heteronormativity, while simultaneously problematizing the demonization of queer critique. Within the contemporary landscape of gay and queer representation, the institution of marriage is interrogated and extended from both within and outside the system, challenging the stability and correctness of marriage by gay characters as well as queer allies. The most directed critiques of marriage on *Sex and the City* are not from Stanford or Anthony, the two gay men on the show, yet are posed through the storylines of the heterosexual women who are also faced with the disciplinary violence of heteronormativity (Yep). In one episode, Carrie is forced to remove her potentially dirt and germ carrying Manolo Blahnik shoes at a baby shower, symbolizing the ongoing mandate for all subjects to accommodate the sacred Child. When her shoes are stolen from the party, the pregnant host, who herself once strutted down the streets of Manhattan in designer shoes, refuses to pay for Carrie's "extravagant lifestyle," commenting that Carrie is devoid of a "real life." This "real life" is something the host links to her marriage and child, "shoe shaming" Carrie for her choice to remain single.[16] The show extends the violence of heteronormative systems outside of gays and lesbians to demonstrate Yep's discussion of heteronormativity's impact on all sexual subjects. Carrie, at first shamed, reflects upon the money, time, and energy she spends celebrating the marriages and children of all of her friends, yet her choice to not marry is shunned, belittled, and infantilized. Pointing out how Hallmark does not make cards for *not* marrying the wrong guy, the episode interrogates cultural celebration of child/spouse systems and the cultural disciplining of heteronormativity's nonconformists.[17]

Within gay male representation, there are multiple representations that reject the monogamous foundations of marriage, coupling, and straight linear trajectories of happily ever after and seek to redefine romantic[18] commitment through alternative scripts. On *Noah's Arc*, Jenito and Ricky begin dating, and Ricky, the "slut" of the program, is conflicted by his feelings for Jenito and his sexually adventurous personality. Jenito argues, "Look, no bullshit. No bogus shows of fearlessness. No fake vows of monogamy that we both know you can't keep. Let's just promise to be as honest with each other as we dare and as kind to each other as we deserve and see how it goes."[19] Rejecting a "till death do us part" temporality, this alternative relational temporality affords a space for potentiality, queer extension, and lateral movement that directly violates the rigidity of marriage scripts. Extending his claim, Jenito asserts, "Fidelity is not love. It's laziness and fear."[20] Rewriting scripts and experimenting with relational formations that cannot be determined in advance represents an interesting and exploratory discussion of queer love. Similar to Brian and Justin on *Queer as Folk*, who refuse "to live with someone who sacrificed their life and called it love to be with me,"[21] these texts seek to interrogate the heteronormative violences imposed through marriage and straight temporal scripts.

The debates around family and queerness center on the ongoing discussion of "gay marriage," marking a rift between gay assimilationists and homophobic religious conservatives, as well as gay assimilationists and many queer activists. Whereas there is a well-established critique of marriage at the foundations of queer theorizing (Warner, *Trouble*), there has been an emergence of queer thinkers who suggest that outright queer resistance to marriage be problematized (Boellstorff; Seidman). Seidman argues, "Marriage is here to stay for the immediate and near future; this reality must be the starting point of any serious political discussion" (191). Boellstorff extends beyond Seidman's claim to accept marriage as a beginning point to question the queer theoretical resistance to same-sex marriage (232). Posing the question, "Why would queer theorists want to be in agreement with George W. Bush about anything?" (236), Boellstorff questions their shared positions (although differing reasons) on the legalization of same-sex marriage. While conscientious of the limitations and problematics of entering into a system of recognition through state legitimation, Boellstorff departs from Butler's and Warner's "apocalyptic framework of straight time" by questioning the potential for "reverse discourse" and the "queering of the dominant" (233).

In Burkean terms, Boellstorff challenges the tragic framing of same-sex marriage recognition by questioning the potential for comic transcendence. Using the example of capitalism as a corrupt and exclusionary system— likened to systems of marriage—Boellstorff argues that our engagement within commodified systems is more complicated than a rigid binary of engaging or not engaging within the system. He draws attention to Warner's criticism of the linkage of homosexuality and capitalism, yet Warner "does not offer as a solution to capitalism's ills the recommendation that we stop buying commodities" (233). Citing Warner's own argument for seeking out strategies of resistance from within a system of power, where there is an array of possibilities between simply sustaining and not sustaining a system (234), Boellstorff posits a similar consideration of engaging within systems of marriage. Such a strategy seeks to queer marriage through comic extension and transcendence, actively engaging in the fears conservatives have launched against gay marriage for decades: allowing gays to marry *will* fundamentally change the institution. The perfected illusion of marriage and the tragic demonizing of the anti-marriage queer offers a potential for a comic corrective to expose the shared substance that is symbolically crafted into a rigid oppositional binary.

The normalization of gay men into systems of homonormative marriage systems is most commonly portrayed through absence, such as in *Will & Grace*, where the final episode leads the viewer to believe Will achieved his long-term goal of marriage and child. The wedding, however, is absent, begging audiences to simply "fill in" the unrepresented, yet present, event with familiar texts of what a marriage has looked like in previous representations. In *Queer as Folk*, however, Michael and Ben's wedding[22] poses a challenge to the restrictive logic that gay marriage offers no potential for resistant—as well as comic—disruption. Brian, true to his "queer" politics, refers to the proposed wedding as "pathetic." Michael, excited by the prospect, confesses, "It wasn't a story I told myself like straight kids did." Their wedding is an impromptu celebration while the couple visits Montreal for a charity bicycling event. The familiar shot of rings being exchanged, the crying mother, and the supportive community of onlookers seems to parallel and adopt the expected depiction of marriage, gay or otherwise. Viewing this ceremony, however, there is something unmistakably queer in its effect, embedded in the performance of the marriage itself. Offering a perspective through incongruity, the mere sliding of rings onto male hands—in that singular moment—both mirrors and extends how marriage is constituted within discourse. While juxtaposing two gay males who, by the logic of the heteronormative tragedy, are without future engaging in a commitment to the future, there appear to be traces of queer resistance within the performance. Mirroring and exposing the limitations of the conventions simultaneously, the event is both remarkable and unremarkable, for it both emulates and rejects the scripts at the same time. At the moment in the ceremony when the witnesses are asked to speak their objections, "or forever hold their peace," Brian leans in the direction of the justice of the peace, marking his disapproval. Deb, Michael's mother, playfully threatens, "You say one word and you'll be holding more than your peace." The queer critique of marriage was present within the ceremony, represented through

Brian, who stood as Michael's best man. In addition, the union rejected illusions of "happily ever after," as Ben and Michael's return through American customs quickly marked the refusal of the U.S. to honor them as a couple, marking their marriage as contested and politicized.

This representation of gay marriage walks a delicate balance, where normalizing institutions are inevitably reified, but not without the space for a comic corrective. On the television screen, gays are marrying, and this act does pose a threat to the sacred demarcation of marriage as tragically restricted to bodies of the "opposite" sex. This argument is not to suggest gay marriage is always a site of resistance, nor does it seek to belittle the importance of queer critiques of marriage, as the very presence of this critique within the *Queer as Folk* ceremony was pivotal to its queering potential. Dismantling the rigidity of anti-marriage queer positions and pro-marriage assimilationist ambitions, a queer critique is embedded within this representation, a dialogue within the ceremony, rejecting the simplified and tragic either/or stance of marriage in favor of a comic corrective of both/and. The marriage is enacted through a queered sensibility, politicized through its border crossing, as well as extending the culturally sedimented images of what marriage looks like. In turn, it potentially extends the linear fixity of what marriage might be and could mean, opening avenues of alternative articulations and meanings.

EXTENDING THE SCRIPTS OF GAY MALE AGING

> This was all I needed for my heart to swell: a plan for the future, the promise of new memories, one more shot at the pipe dream of forever. (Maupin, *Michael* 239)

In 2007, eighteen years after the last installment of the Tales of the City series, Armistead Maupin released the novel *Michael Tolliver Lives*, following up on his beloved characters from the apartment complex at 28 Barbary Lane. At the conclusion of the sixth novel, Michael Tolliver, a gay male who has lost friends and lovers to the AIDS pandemic, is HIV-positive and left to an uncertain future. The very title, *Michael Tolliver Lives*, marks a declaration of the survival of a man whose story once seemed limited to his twenties and early thirties. The book opens with Michael recounting the ongoing hailing by old friends, commenting, "You're supposed to be dead" (1). While brushing with death repeatedly in his life, Michael Tolliver is alive and well at fifty-five years old, now eligible for the senior discount at Denny's (168). The very expectation that Michael is supposed to be dead informs and shapes his engagement with time and future, mirroring how Halberstam theorizes queer time as a problematizing of the naturalization of reproductive time (*Queer* 4), prolonged subcultural involvement (161), and mapping of alternative notions of adulthood and maturation (174). She locates the emergence of queer time as a response to the AIDS crisis, where the temporal conventions of child-raising, biological family, and inheritance were reconsidered in the face of questioned longevity and futurity (2). Working outside the "paradigmatic markers of life experience" (2), Michael Tolliver continues to live a life of joy, friendship, romance, sex, and potentiality.

Enlisting a discussion of alternative modes of thinking about gay aging—or potentially queer configurations of aging—the youthist economy of gay male culture presents a primary consideration. Halberstam's discussion of queer temporality as stretched out adolescence and extended subcultural involvement marks an important distinction between gay temporality and her queer time. Gay cultural time, as discussed at length in Chapter 3, operates in a tragic frame where youth is highly privileged and aging is demonized through predatory myths and subcultural exclusion. As Dave, the aging gay male stripper in Rechy's *Bodies and Souls*, is described, he felt "cheated by a world he helped to create and which he was not sure he understood anymore, knew only that it was now preparing, indefinitely, to shut him out, discard him" (160). This brings about a complex tension between gay and queer modes of temporality, as gay time is rigidly punished through linear heteronormative scripts and queer temporality seeks to embody an oppositional engagement to reproductive heterosexual temporalities.

In an effort to bridge these discussions, this section shifts its attention to the notion of generativity to examine the ways generational dialogue within popular gay media representation can help articulate queer temporal modes. As generational exclusion and youth worship are central to the perpetuation of the heteronormative tragedy, alternative representations of generativity offer queered potentials for thinking about gay and queer subcultural formations, unexplored relationship models for intergenerational community, and a dismantling of the ageist/youthist system within gay male representation.

Noah's Arc chronicles the lives of four gay friends, three African American and one Latino male, in West Hollywood, California. Although this text has been criticized for its reification of a homonormative, apolitical, and consumer-driven gay male identity (Yep and Elia, "Performing"), the text challenges dominant gay male representation in two significant ways. First, the show centers on the lives of gay men of color, and while the show has been critiqued for eliding racial issues and forefronting discourses of sexuality (Yep and Elia, "Performing"), the continual representation and focus upon gay men of color on a television series should not be dismissed. Although representation does not equal progress (Dow; Shugart), the repeated marginalization of gay men of color and the perpetuation of linking gayness to the white male body is challenged by the very existence of this series. Second, in the two seasons of *Noah's Arc* reviewed for this study, negative discussions of age, ageism, and youthism are completely absent from the text. Noah's birthday celebration is simply a celebration, lacking any mention of the dread, fear, or resentment for growing older.[23] Radically different from the negative ageist discourses that carry through the entire series of *Queer as Folk*, aging just happens—birthdays just "fall" on certain days (Boellstorff)—without attention to their placement on heteronormative temporal timelines. For example, whereas *Queer as Folk* engages the birthday celebration as a simultaneous looking backward to what is now lost and gone and a dreaded look forward for the misery ahead, adopting a straight timeline as the temporal map, Noah's birthday simply happens. It does not rely on the linear contextualization of what came before and what is to follow in order to mark the meaning of the event. In addition, while age is rarely discussed, the four main characters on *Noah's Arc* seem to occupy a broad range of ages, as Chance was once Noah's college professor before they became friends. Countering *Queer as Folk*, where Ted's four-year seniority was an ongoing source of mockery and belittlement, the importance of age on *Noah's Arc* is minimal to the characters' ongoing narratives. No characters, regardless of age, are marked as being more or less included in their gay subcultural involvement, yet they choose to move in and out of these settings with a greater sense of agency. What is offered in *Noah's Arc*, besides a representation of gayness outside of white male bodies, is a community of men who transcend the tragic constructions of aging commonly represented in the cultural production of gay males.

Although the existence of gay men beyond their forties remains unrepresented in *Noah's Arc*,[24] *History Boys* offers alternative models of generativity through the interaction of three generations of gay men. Rather than dismissing age as a primary point of discussion, *History Boys* forefronts youthist and ageist discourses, yet offers a complex investigation of these themes in new and productive ways. Set in a British grammar school in the 1980s, the film tells the story of a group of young men struggling to prepare for university entrance exams. Hector, who has homosexual desires for the boys and is also married, is the general studies professor. Hector emphasizes their education of cultural literacy by having them memorize scenes from Bette Davis films and additional pieces of popular—and queer—culture. The headmaster of the school, an uptight and conservative man determined to get the boys into prestigious universities to increase the institution's credibility, hires Mr. Irwin, an early-thirties gay male who is supposed to sharpen the boys' writing skills before exams. In the group of young boys is Posner, a small Jewish boy who is coming to terms and negotiating his own homosexuality, as well as a longtime crush on Dakin, his classmate.

Forefronted in the film's narratives are the differing ways these men navigate and define their sexuality, as well as how each negotiates their youthist desires for "the boys." Hector embodies a temporal queerness, as an overweight gray-haired male who dwarfs the small motorcycle he drives around town. The juxtaposition of his body on the motorbike demonstrates an extended adolescence that is also enacted in his character. Dismissed by the headmaster as trivial, as well as perverse, Hector's notion of a general studies education is queer to the standards of the institution, believing the boys are best served by memorizing poetry and enacting scenes from *Now, Voyager*. Hector occupies the position of a joke and beloved mentor to the boys all at once, as each of the boys understand what it means to accept a ride home on Hector's motorbike. With a student on the back of his bike, Hector, grinning ear to ear without shame or apology, routinely reaches his arms back and gropes the boys' genitals. By this description, Hector can easily be assumed to be a villain, a predator, and an exemplar of the monstrous aging gay male discussed in Chapter 3. The narrative of the film rejects this simplistic casting of Hector, however, as it complicates the tragic frame through a comic corrective. Hector is flawed, and his actions arguably problematic, but he is not cast as evil. The film represents a kind, loving, impassioned educator with strong integrity who loves ideas, his students, and the process of education.

The closest character to a villain in the film is the narrow-minded headmaster who criminalizes Hector and projects the very judgments expected from dominant cultural production. Hector attempts to interrupt the headmaster during his disciplinary session, offering a historical lesson about how renaissance men and boys commonly engaged in sexual mentorship, but the headmaster yells at him to be quiet. The headmaster's frustration with Hector is played as humorous, a joke, to which the audience is asked to identity with Hector in this scenario. The headmaster fires him for his perverted behavior that "isn't normal." Hector shows little remorse. In turn, the headmaster threatens to tell his wife about his perversions. Hector, in jolly indifference, replies that she most likely will not be all that interested. The charges of sexual pervert and predator, while not irrelevant, are rendered comic by the narrative structure, as the boys rally behind their beloved yet perverse, foolish, and flawed mentor who is always true to who he is. Had the narrative offered this story through the eyes of the headmaster, situating the audience in the tragic frame of judgment, *History Boys* might have resembled multiple previous texts. This film, however, shifted the camera and the narrative to the space-off, allowing Hector to be human, complicated, lovable and problematic, and thus a more comic representation.

Through perspective by incongruity, the text allows the representation of elsewheres rarely offered within the dominant cultural production. Posner is both concerned yet unapologetic for his love of Dakin, and he sings soft ballads in class directly to Dakin without fear. Upon graduation, Dakin gives Posner his "reward," offering Posner a quick hug that fails to satisfy Posner's fantasy. Furious, Posner protests, "That's it?" The boys, rather than mocking Posner, tease Dakin for offering up such a pathetic embrace, until he caves and holds Posner close until he is satisfied. Dakin, himself, while engaging in sexual relations with women, is queer in his attraction to Mr. Irwin, whom he flirts with and develops a crush on upon his arrival.

Dakin tells Irwin that he is "not too old" and is willing to let Irwin suck him off as a thank you for all of his help. This offering can be viewed as Dakin's way of fulfilling homosexual desire under the guise of an appreciative gesture, but it is more productively understand as an articulation of the youthist discourse at work in the film. The film centers on the power of "the boys," the privileging of youthful bodies in gay male culture. Both beloved and a "sad fuck," Hector becomes Irwin's cautionary tale. Irwin is instructed by a colleague, "You don't want to be like Hector. He's a joke." Although enticed by Dakin, Irwin is warned that to succumb to his invitation will make him the fool.

At the close of the film, the boys have arranged for Hector to keep his job, and Irwin has agreed to meet Dakin to graciously accept his "thank you" gift. Seated on his motorbike, Hector, clearly not scared by the disciplinary action of the school for his previous sexual exploits, asks the boys who would like a ride home. To the cheering celebration of the boys in a queer championing of their sexually nonnormative mentor, Irwin agrees to accept a ride home with Hector. The celebration of Hector and Irwin, who is soon to be groped, is the last scene for Hector, as a motorcycle accident leads to the death of the beloved general studies teacher with a desire for male-genital fondling. The final scene takes place at Hector's funeral, yet the boys, still in their youthful bodies, speak from their futures and reflect on the lives they have lived in the decades since passed. Posner, following in the footsteps of his mentor Hector, becomes a teacher, expressing a desire to "pass it on." The majority of the boys respond that they are happy, whereas Posner states that he is not happy, "but not unhappy about it." Posner says that he does not touch the boys, as Hector once did, yet implies it is a struggle and an ongoing choice that he makes.

Perhaps alarming and perverse when recounted on the page in black-and-white text, Posner's—as well as Irwin's and Hector's—struggle with worshipping the beauty of "the boys" refuses to dismiss the ever-presence of youth worship at the center of gay cultural formations. Still, while placing this discussion at the forefront of the film, it refuses it to adhere to tragic and simplified frameworks of understanding. The underlying tension is that heteronormative understandings of aging and sexuality fail to account for or address a broad range of potential experiences relating to sexuality and aging. In the classrooms of *History Boys*, intimacy and generational interactions extend beyond mere groping and physical contact to encapsulate a broad range of potential intimacies and pleasure. While not divorced from physical sexuality, there is a space of pleasure marked through the sharing of knowledge, the exploration of culture, the collective pedagogical experience, and intergenerational mentorship that is sensual, intimate, and erotic, marking comic departures from the heteronormative script. Rather than adopting or promoting a simplified narrative of heteronormative generativity, as with the grandfather-to-grandson scripts, *History Boys* offers a more complex and comic brushstroke to what a queered generativity might

140   *Queer Temporalities in Gay Male Representation*

look like—as well as marking the obstacles that it may face by normative systems of judgment.

In *Shortbus*,[25] there is a moment when the young and attractive Ceth engages in a brief discussion with a man well over sixty. The man comments that "New York is one of the few places they let in the new and the old," indicating a sense of alienation based on his age. The older man, who was once a politician, confesses a deep guilt for not doing enough to help the community through the AIDS crisis. Ceth listens to the man speak about experiences before he was born, leans into the man, and then kisses him softly on the lips, and they hold each other for a moment. Their interaction is not particularly sexual, although it is sweet, tender, and sensual. This narrative break nods to a queered formation of generativity, one where the youthist logics, predatory myths, and heteronormative scripts of generational roles can be reconsidered through queer temporal articulation. The heteronormative tragedy is propelled through youthist exclusion of age and aging, whereas normative pleas seek to pattern gay lives within straight time. A queer generativity asks for a model for queered generational engagement that seeks to extend outside of straight temporality and generativity to promote and explore alternative conceptions of futurity, community, and dialogue. Working alongside Halberstam's call to interrogate the youth/age binary (*Queer* 2), and understanding—yet cautious—of her dismissal of longevity and safety as guiding values, this project seeks to point to queer engagements with time that respect and celebrate queer age, rather than punish it.

A queer model of generativity seeks to transcend the tragic ritual of gay male aging by exploring alternative meanings of gay bodies in relation to time, age, and future. Furthermore, by problematizing how youth is privileged in gay discourse, as well as the predatory demonization of age, a queer generativity seeks to consider intergenerational relations that operate outside of the rigidity of heteronormative modes of temporality. The film *Another Gay Movie* presents four gay male high school graduates who make a pact to have anal sex before they leave for college. As a playful hijacking of the traditional heterosexual teen male sex comedy, such as the *Porky's* or *American Pie* franchises, *Another Gay Movie* is a sex comedy about teenage gay boys. Within the narrative, however, is a series of "older" gay male representations, including the closeted bisexual father of one of the boys, the high school teacher who secretly lives the life as an S&M Web cruiser with the screen name Rodzilla, two NAMBLA men who dismiss high school boys as too old for them, and Richard Hatch from *Survivor* fame, who plays himself. In addition, directly parodying the *American Pie* films is "Muffler's grandfather,"[26] who is represented as an older gay male with a George Hamilton tan and a white boatman's cap. Nico, the most effeminate of the boys, seeks out Muffler's grandfather at the conclusion of the film, flirting with him, and calling him "silver foxy." The grandfather replies, "Aged eighteen years, just the way grandpa likes it." Muffler's grandfather announces, "Fasten your seatbelt sonny, it's gonna be a bumpy ride," and the two, along with the rest of the cast at various locations at the party, succeed in their sexual quest at the conclusion of the film.

What makes *Another Gay Movie* relevant to exploring a queered generativity is the constraints placed upon the interactions between the older and younger gay men in the film, most specifically the disciplinary power afforded to youth within gay intergenerational interactions. Older gay male sexual expressions, as demonstrated with the closeted bisexual father who shamefully cruises the rest-stop toilets, are constructed as predatory and pathetic. Only through Nico continually marking himself as attracted to older men are his sexual encounters with Richard Hatch and Muffler's grandfather permissible, and Nico is clearly marked as the aggressor. These older men are readily available and willing to accept the affections of Nico, awaiting his attentions, yet are forbidden to initiate dialogue with the younger boy. Adopting the "sexualizing daddy" double bind of the early issues of *Instinct* magazine (Goltz, "Laughing), older gay men are only permitted a sexuality that is sanctioned and controlled by gay youth. For the older man to assert sexual desire without youth instigation and ongoing permission quickly relegates the older gay man to sedimented stereotypes of the sexual predator.

The title *Another Gay Movie* plays upon Hollywood's dismissal of gay representation but is also titled with an element of sarcasm. The film, like many of the texts previously discussed, does provide a queering of the dominant narrative, so much that the 1980s teenage sex comedy is told with a gay twist. Where it falls short in terms of queering the dominant systems of power—outside of the obvious reification of gayness as white, male, and middle-class identity—is the overarching temporal formula of *American Pie*, which remains uninterrogated. Specifically, straight time drives *Another Gay Movie*, as the temporal structure follows the story of young boys who graduate high school, prepare for college, and narrate their future through the sole hope to "find husbands someday." Although the title is playful and sarcastic, the film fails to provide "another story," as motioned to at the close of *Happy Endings*. While playfully subversive and unapologetic on multiple levels, in terms of temporal modes, the film is simply "another gay movie."

The lingering question throughout this chapter is whether there is an inherent heteronormativity embedded within narrative structures, suggesting that notions of modernity, progress, and chronology are inescapably tied to straight time. The theoretical question of how one might queer time, or adopt a queer engagement with time, is carried through this discussion, merely hinted at through texts such as *Noah's Arc*, *Shortbus*, and *History Boys*. Halberstam suggests that the project of queering time begins with a dismantling of the youth/adult binary and the epistemology of youth (*Queer* 175), crafting a resistant position where subcultural involvement be explored as a potential lifelong commitment, rather than a fleeting and temporal stage of life (174). Boellstorff offers the problematic that Halberstam's attempt to theorize a queer temporality is still implicated within straight formations of time, merely slowing down or extending a queered adolescence while still remaining situated "within straight time's linear framework" (230). Edelman calls for queers to reject future, embracing a negative relation to future. In response to this call, Muñoz argues that any political resistance of queerness requires a future focus ("Cruising"), refusing to sacrifice the future and a politics of hope. He further suggests that Edelman's theorizing of reproductive futurism—the notion that the future is hijacked in the name of the Sacred Child, marking queers as anti-future—simplifies the concept of the child in terms of primarily white privileged babies (363). This lively and generative discussion within contemporary queer theory, to which this study is deeply indebted, seeks to work through the temporal limitations within straight time and explore the temporal potentialities of queer time. Aligning with Muñoz's refusal to hand over the concept of futurity to normative, white, reproductive futurity, which directly extends and problematizes Edelman's theorizing, this project aims to locate productive gestures toward queer temporal futurity as a way of offering a comic corrective to tragic formations of gay male aging. The next section of the chapter examines the queer potential of the space-off for articulating alternative temporal frameworks of futurity that exist within, and transcend through, tragic configurations of straight time.

QUEER TEMPORALITY AS COMIC CORRECTIVE

> I sometimes wonder what this country would be like if the puritans stayed at home. (Alfred, *Kinsey*)

> It's my only life, and I need it to be mine. (Olim, *Touch of Pink*)

> What about everything in my tired pathetic life that I happen to love? (Christian, *Latter Days*)

This study opened with a seemingly simple question that asked what it means to be an aging gay male in America. Looking to popular media as a site of gay male identity construction, gay male aging is presented as a distinct cultural process, a tragic ritual where gay youthist worship leads to gay ageist sacrifice due to the fixed logic of straight temporality. In a project designed to locate queer temporal articulations that offer a comic corrective to the tragedy of straight time, there is a multitude of tragic binary formations embedded within the cultural production, erecting tensions between young/old, queer/normative, future/queer, and the older gay male as asexual assimilationist or deviant predator. The very notion of future is reductively signified through Child, heteronormativity, maturation, marriage, assimilation, and the linear logic of straight progressive time, enacting the governing tragic configuration where queers are anti-future. In discussing her engagement with queer temporality, Halberstam states, "I hear a loud voice in my head saying fuck family, fuck marriage, fuck the male teachers, this is not my life, that will not be my time line" (Dinshaw et al. 182). Part of her critique of these issues emerges from her argument that "[f]or queers, the separation between youth and adulthood quite simply does not hold" (*Queer* 174). She argues the dangers of this configuration, which always equate adulthood with reproduction and traditional models of family (176). Halberstam's engagement with this topic offers a productive theorizing of queer temporality that resists the heteronormative imperative of straight time. Straight time, as this book has worked to argue, works to craft a cultural script that systematically punishes the gay male through a heteronormative temporality. In this respect, the current study works with and alongside Halberstam's[27] (and Edelman's) critique, as working within the markers of straight time perpetuates a tragic system. Halberstam's call for an extended conception of subcultural involvement to challenge and disrupt the progressive momentum of heteronormative time, however, is complicated by the youthist dimensions of gay male culture and gay cultural representation. Herein marks an important tension, as seen in the "final dance" of Brian Kinney in Chapter 3. "Older" gay men are constructed as less valuable in mainstream gay cultural constructions, marking their continued participation in youth-centered bar and club culture as a tragic failure. Discourses of youth/maturation underscoring Halberstam's critique define maturation through limited heteronormative systems that perpetuate and uphold the authority of straight time, while further demonizing potentialities of queer world-making. As argued in Chapter 3, youthism and ageism in gay male representation work to support and uphold one another, while simultaneously reifying youth/maturation systems and heteronormative violence. Halberstam's and Edelman's call to deconstruct child/youth discourses pose an important project, one that extends beyond straight couples and their baby strollers to the central values and systems embraced and enacted *within* gay male culture and gay male cultural production.

However, as argued in Chapter 4, this project must be further complicated, for the systems that define the child, youth, age, progress, and maturation are raced, classed, and gendered systems. As Muñoz's response to Edelman ("Cruising") asserts, straight time is a privileged and oppressive temporal trajectory that is, by no means, isolated to discourses of sexuality. As my project turns attention to mainstream representations of gay men, where I can and cannot directly align myself with Halberstam and Muñoz requires some attention. Halberstam's discussion stems from, and is grounded in, transgendered experiences, and Muñoz's research openly pledges a specified commitment to queers of color. These bodies, lives, and experiences are problematically absent from the vast majority of gay male representations in mainstream culture, cast elsewhere to the space-offs of gay and queer cultural production. Theorizing queer temporality from the locations of subcultural spaces, marginalized communities, and Hollywood representations mark differing projects, aligned in several core commitments, but operating from differing points of reference. What can be productively forged in these discussions is a queer engagement with gay aging construction, an interrogation of how youth/maturation in gay male representation enacts heightened narratives of violence and how homonormative pleas for identification by privileged gay male constructions are complicit in heteronormative tragedy and queer temporal foreclosures.

This study places it pedagogical objectives in the forefront, attempting to offer a critical framework to understand how the Hollywood master narrative is driven by a temporal mode that reproduces queer tragedy. While this project seeks to offer queer alternatives to the tragedy of gay male aging and the violences of youth/adult formations, such deeply indoctrinated logics as youth, youthfulness, and age are not likely to quickly disappear. As gay youth[28] are always already interpellated into a straight temporality, it is important to note that pop cultural representations of gay and queer lives offer, for many, the only access to alternative considerations of time, aging, and future (the closest thing to the subcultural club spaces from which Halberstam theorizes). The gay cultural constructions of youthism and ageism are by no means queer, yet they present temporal constructions that can be complicated and extended through queer intervention via a comic corrective. The current project has set the objective of theorizing and exploring the potential for queer temporalities through and alongside heteronormative narratives. Accepting the limitations and foreclosures of mainstream representation, this shift reframes the inquiry to explore what *might* queered aging and future look like, and where could we ground these theoretical abstractions within the dominant cultural production.

Anti-child and anti-future postures are readily present within gay popular culture, as seen in the animated parody show *Rick & Steve: The Happiest Gay Couple in the World*. Dana comments, "We only call babies miracles 'cause it sounds better than an accident."[29] In the same episode, a television advertisement within the animated world claims, "Abortions won't solve all your problems, only the really big ones. Dial 1–800-BYE BYE BABY." Mirroring the Brian Kinney anti-child approach to queer resistance, anti-child positions fall into the tragic pitfalls previously discussed. One text that offers a more comic interrogation to heteronormative systems is *Kinsey*, the biographical story of the infamous sex researcher Alfred Kinsey. The film refuses to glamorize heterosexual sex, presenting it as awkward, painful, and no more natural or correct than any variety of sexual expression. Alfred's father instructs him at the open of the film, "Don't rush it. Once you have children you are tied down forever. Your life is over." This statement offers a useful counter-narrative to the heteronormative assumption that absence of children is the end of life. Later in the film, Alfred is seduced by one of his research assistants, a much younger male who has developed a crush on Alfred. Reflecting the historical impact of Kinsey's research, the film sought to deeply problematize the coherence of fixed or stable sexual orientations, embracing and exploring the fluidity and constructed nature of sexuality categorizations. Although the narrative normalizes and recuperates the centrality of the heterosexual married couple at the conclusion, Kinsey offers greater attention to what *De-Lovely* worked to foreclose—a narrative that broke from a heteronormative temporality within to explore sites of queer sexuality and heterosexual investigation.

One trend that has existed throughout this chapter is the presence of queer work being more directly performed by—for lack of a better terminology—non-gay identified characters. From *Sex in the City* and *Dawson's Creek*, to *Far From Heaven* and *A Home at the End of the World*, there is a trend of heteronormative interrogation taking place from those who exist within dominant sexual subject positions. As set forth in the previous chapter, gay characters are often tamed and normalized for dominant consumption, refusing the blurring of the homo/hetero binary or critique of heteronormative systems. Characters such as Kinsey or Carrie Bradshaw can perform heteronormative critique more easily from their privileged position of heterosexual identification and are afforded greater license to enact queer resistance, for the dominant narrative assumes their normative recuperation through the "natural" maturation process.

Karen Walker, the boozed-up and pill-popping millionaire on *Will & Grace*, occupies this privileged position of queer critique and has been labeled the show's most queer representation (Battles and Hilton-Morrow 96–7; Mitchell 86). Reversing the standard formula that has relegated gay characters to the support of sitcom narratives for decades, Karen Walker plays the "straight" sidekick at the periphery of the storyline. While married for the majority of the show's run, Karen's sexuality is constantly lingering within a queer fluidity (Mitchell 90), as she has moments of sexual tension with every person she surrounds herself with. Karen depicts disgust for children, problematizes traditional ideologies of marriage, femininity, and maternity (Battles and Hilton-Morrow 97), rejects dominant modes of maturation, and floats through days, weeks, and months in an inebriated haze that renders time and progression irrelevant. Although her economic status affords this intoxicated departure from linear time, the grounding of Karen in heterosexuality permits her a position to enact multiple queer criticisms that the normative-pandering Will could never perform.

In the series finale of *Will & Grace*,[30] as the show juggles multiple storylines about the on-again-off-again relationship between the two lead characters, there is a queer interruption to the narrative that halted the show for several minutes. Amidst Will and Grace's scenes of child-rearing, marriage, and progressive linear life following a normative trajectory, Jack and Karen sit quietly in their living room together. Throughout the entire series, Jack and Karen are the comic relief of the show, and any depth or complexity for these characters is marginalized to forefront the narratives of Will and Grace. Marking an incongruous "dinner party" perspective, the audience is granted a glimpse of their lives away from the ongoing drama of supporting the show's primary narrative. Karen asks Jack to sing a song on the piano. Jack agrees, and the two of them sing "Unforgettable" together. The audience is caught off guard for a moment, waiting for the expected punch line, as this is always expected when these two characters are placed in the narrative frame. There is no joke, however, and they simply sing the song, from beginning to end, uninterrupted and without punch line. Watching the episode and seeing these characters sing in sincerity is an incongruous moment where the characters of Karen and Jack seem to slip away, becoming unfamiliar. The importance of this moment is that it becomes Jack and Karen's final representation outside of their involvements in the narratives of Will and Grace, a space that winks to an alternative to the Will and Grace spouse-and-child futurity privileged within the show. Pulled through episode after episode on Will and Grace's temporal watch, Karen hilariously asks Jack in the final episode, "Do you find them exhausting?" Highlighted in the series finale, Jack and Karen mark an alternative engagement with time and future, temporally hijacking the flow of the episode to declare their own space and time.

In the film *Camp*, Michael wakes up to find that the entire camp has dressed in drag in honor of his birthday. Michael is asked to make a wish, and he replies, "Right at this moment I have everything I want, so I'll give my wish to you guys." Michael's relinquishing of his wish can be read as another example of deified gay male performance. After all, Michael's life in the film has been nothing but an accumulation of disappointments and trauma. Still, the relinquishing of the wish is offered because he has everything he wants in this very place and time. Beyond simply being validated, as well as his gender performance accommodated and honored by his camp friends, Michael looks around the setting with amazement and contentment. The wish, a calling to the future and a desire for progress or progression is discarded in an effort to suspend and maintain his temporal present. A breech from the overall narrative structure of young musical theater youth dreaming of stardom and relationships on the horizon, Michael calls attention to the now and the moment at hand, rejecting its alignment with the ongoing narrative. For a brief segment, Camp Ovation becomes another space where time operates in different ways, before the film editing cuts to the next scene and the narrative moves forward. Michael's rejection of his wish testifies to his privileging of the event as it happens, a magical moment somehow removed from the pain of yesterday and what might occur in the next day to come.

Returning to the emergence of queer temporality in the earlier days of the AIDS outbreak, when temporal attention shifted from longevity and future to the now, the "live for today" approach championed in *Rent* and Ben and Michael's *Queer as Folk* relationship needs further attention.

Rent's "No day but today" mantra can be read as either a literal claim that there is no future at all, or a queer engagement with time working to call attention from the linear workings of straight time to a lateral orientation of the scope and breadth that exists in the now. The former presents a problematic compliance with the heteronormative tragedy, although the latter seeks to articulate a productive direction for discussion. Similar to Cathy's break from linear time in *Far from Heaven*, the "no day but today" orientation to time adopts a comic rupture to temporal engagement. The danger, however, is the risk of slipping into an outright rejection of futurity through a privileging of the now. As *Rent* offers, "There is no future. There is no past. Thank God this moment's not the last." The distinction of living in the moment and around the moment while maintaining an emphasis on the future is an important one and vital to this project, less this temporal philosophy risks falling back into "live fast and die young" without attention to or concern for health, longevity, or risk. As clearly demonstrated in the earlier chapters of this text, self-destructive and high-risk behaviors enacted by gay youth could be theorized as a queer orientation towards time,[31] yet this study marks them as tragic and thus unproductive. Where queer time orientation becomes productive and occupies a space of potentiality is when this temporal engagement is enacted through queer resistance, rather than passive heteronormative compliance with tragic framing.

An interesting articulation of this approach in popular culture is demonstrated through the character of Omar Little on HBO's *The Wire*. The Robin Hood of the drug world in *The Wire*'s Baltimore, Omar makes his living through the "rip and run," where he pulls his gun on the local drug organizations and steals their money.[32] In turn, Omar returns a portion of his gains to his "people, for a rainy day."[33] Although repeatedly belittled by his foes as "the cocksucker" and "the faggot," Omar makes no apologies for his sexual desire for men. As an African American male, Omar can be easily criticized for reifying a violent notion of gun-toting black masculinity, which is all too common in the contemporary cultural production (*Tough Guise*, Katz). What places Omar Little in a unique category and makes him an important representation worthy of attention is the queer space he occupies within the show's ongoing narrative. Performing a trickster function, Omar mocks the social order from all sides, through the use of perspective by incongruity. Both comic—in the Burkean sense—as well as humorous, Omar is in nobody's camp, defies classifications of good or bad, and exists as a thorn in the side of the competing power structures on the streets of Baltimore. Quite simply, he does not fit neatly into any story, yet when he appears, his emergence is exciting and unpredictable. Existing within a world of drugs, violence, corruption, and betrayal, Omar is pious to his own resistant and individualized constitution of relationships, time, and understandings of social oppression. He humbly testifies, "I've never put no gun on no citizen."[34] He never swears or uses "cuss words," instructing his boyfriend, "Nobody wants to hear those dirty words, especially

148 *Queer Temporalities in Gay Male Representation*

coming from such a beautiful mouth."[35] He is tender in his friendships and relationships, playful in his choice to wear his "I am the American Dream"[36] T-shirt, but is as calm and unemotional as Dirty Harry when he picks up his gun and walks into a job.

As a Burkean demonstration, it might seem that this analysis has simply come full circle, returning to the representation of gay men as violent creatures of the night—now articulated through Omar Little walking the streets at midnight, shotgun in hand, whistling "The Farmer in the Dell."[37] Omar's theme, which he whistles proudly as he prepares an ambush, is most relevant when considering the final verse of the popular nursery rhyme. After "the farmer takes a wife," "the wife takes a child," and a series of relationships are articulated, the song ends when "the cheese stands alone." There are no systems in place to make sense or frame the character of Omar; both feared and mocked, gay and African American, thug and hero, Omar is the alienated "cheese who stands alone." He lives by his own codes and credos, similar to Brian Kinney, yet differing in relevant ways. Where Brian is a victim to heteronormative temporalities and the punishment of gay time, Omar lives outside of straight time, taking up residence in the space-off of a queer temporality.

In Season 2, Omar is summoned to testify as a witness for the state in the prosecution of a prominent drug dealer.[38] Instructed by the police to buy a suit and tie to look respectable in court, Omar struts onto the witness stand wearing flashy garb and a tie wrapped around his neck defiantly, like a disheveled scarf. In outright rejection to performing normative identification in the heteronormative court, he actively mocks the convention through his outfit. The defense attorney asks Omar his age, and Omar confidently replies, "About twenty-nine." The defense attorney, seeking to discredit Omar, sarcastically asks, "About?" Omar simply nods with dismissive confidence, indicating a disinterest in the question, rather than any shame or discomfort with the answer. As the cross-examination continues, Omar unapologetically lays out his career of robbing drug dealers, and the defense attorney calls him "amoral" and "a parasite." Rather than shaming Omar, Omar replies, "Just like you. I got a shot gun, you got a briefcase," which receives chuckles from the jury, shaming the lawyer. In his cool and clever performance, Omar walks into the courtroom, and rather than allowing it to discipline or shame him, he enacts a trickster performance that shifts the interrogation to the legal system itself.

The lawyer asks Omar how he has lived to tell about his work, because he makes a living from stealing from very dangerous people. With a big smile, Omar replies, "A day at a time, I suppose."[39] What is most interesting about this inquiry, along with the questioning of Omar's age, is that the very foundations upon which these questions are premised are, themselves, called into question. Linear time, chronological age, and devotion to future are queered in Omar's answers. His delivery implies a dismissive tone of, "If you ask me stupid questions, based on your reductive worldview, then you will get equally stupid answers." In these moments, Omar is baited by tragic questions, but rather than allowing himself to be positioned on either side of the tragedy, he enacts a comic corrective, exposing the limitations of the inquiries themselves. On the witness stand, a defendant's integrity is called into question by a series of questions that are simply "for the record." However, the "innocent" record is at the heart of this entire theoretical discussion, as the litany of questions that sexual citizens face, and the manner in which those answers are responded to, are anything but innocent. Age, job, plans for future, race, class, gender, and marital status are nothing short of factors of heteronormative identification, constructing the definition and the parameters for proper sexual citizenship within limited temporal frames. These are tragic questions, flawed in the ongoing oppressive and socially constructed belief that they have any meaning at all.

Omar exists in the space-off of dominant systems of intelligibility, and so when he is faced with these questions, he turns the questions back on themselves, exposing their inherent limitations and flaws. Throughout the first three seasons of *The Wire*, Omar appears and disappears in differing places at differing times with no sense of where he is coming from or where he is going, almost like a ghost for whom the walls of conventional narratives fail to contain him. Embodying his "a day at a time" engagement with time, he maintains a loose grip on the notion of the future that is shaped moment by moment, based on the right thing to do at that given time. He places himself at risk and does not flee from danger, but not recklessly or purely for the purposes of engaging in risk for risk's sake. He acts based on what he understands as right or just in the temporal present, allowing the future to be shaped "a day at a time" as well. Omar's trusted confidant Butch makes the suggestion, "Maybe it's time you might think about backing off some," trying to convince Omar that he has enough money to disappear and start a new life. Omar replies, "Back off to what?"[40] Omar's momentum defines a futurity that is performed through the present, a commitment to persevering in the moment, rather than defining future through abstract speculations of what is to come, what ought to come, or fear of what might come. He makes the future "one day at a time," allowing the space for unanticipated potentialities to come into being rather than defining articulated end objectives.[41] In this respect, to "back off" might articulate the form of safety that Halberstam criticizes—the tamed and constrained performances that foreclose queered temporality and support assimilationist faithfulness to heteronormative time. Halberstam cautions us to interrogate how discourses of health and longevity are equated with "the most desirable future" (152). To "back off" for fear of risk marks a position of safety, a passive commitment to a prescribed projection of future that fails to do the work that must be done—the ongoing work of queer coalitional politics. In this sense, "backing off" privileges longevity at the expense of queer commitment. This type of risk prevention, at the expense of a commitment to social justice, presents a space where discourses of rationality and health conflict with and diminish queer work. She calls for us to question how we "pathologize modes of living that show little or no concern for longevity" (152) and how issues of health and safety are used to protect and uphold heteronormative systems. Queering is antithetical to backing off, as queerness defines a perseverance and commitment to the present, a "day at a time" philosophy that seeks to potentialize unforeseen, unforeseeable, and unintelligible futures.

ELSEWHERE IN THE PRESENT

> We make mistakes when we compare with the past instead of the possible. (Gilbert 155)

> It could be worse. I could be going to the prom. (Augusten, *Running with Scissors*)

Perhaps queers, for the time being, are rightfully lingering in the dark alleys of the heteronormative script, threatening the sanctity of their institutions, and seeking to challenge the coherence of their protected meanings. Representations such as Omar Little expose the underlying substance that problematizes the heteronormative tragedy—an exposure that refuses the perfection of straight lives, straight relations, and straight futures. To point to a singular text or narrative that demonstrates what a queer future looks like defeats the very project in itself, as the project exists in the looking, the challenging, and the moment-by-moment articulation that usurps the temporal logic that we must plan our lives according to some progressive scheme of events that somehow achieves a marker of socially successful aging and achievement. As Gilbert reminds us, our knowledge of the future is secondhand knowledge (234), "foresight is just as fallible as eyesight and hindsight" (210–1), and uncertainty breeds happiness where certainty diminishes happiness (209). Straight time is designed around reducing uncertainty and reproducing systems of relation that justify its illusionary perfection. Queer time rejects the linearity of straight time that has been defined, mapped, and constrained by the totalizing dominion of heteronormativity, defining future through the limited systems of child, marriage, and consumption. Dominant Hollywood narratives perpetuate this tragic framing of straight temporality, casting the queer as alien to the discursive construction of future. Assimilationist strategies seek to beg identification with heteronormative systems, enacting a homonormative plea, in an effort to render their futures intelligible within the governing heteronormative paradigm of time and future.

Queer engagements with the future understand the violent and oppressive limitations of straight temporal engagement, shifting the camera angle to the space-off and enacting a perspective by incongruity that seeks to remoralize dominant understandings of time, future, and aging—each presenting a sedimented body of cultural meanings that need to stay open to contestation. This means working in the present, without "backing off"—as Omar argues, "Back off to what?" As heteronormativity marks the ongoing project of hijacking the future, queerness adopts the temporal orientation of working within the present—rejecting the tragic forecasting of heteronormativity's threats, with a "day at a time" orientation towards unforeseen futures. After all, our limited capacity to envision the future—from this moment—has much more to do with where we are today than where we might be tomorrow (Gilbert 123).

In 2007, in Trenton, New Jersey, a conservative group opposed to same-sex marriage ran the following radio ad. It opens with an announcer saying, "If we change the definition of marriage," but the ad is interrupted by the voice of a child. "Grandma, my teacher said if grandpa was a girl that's okay, you can still be married." The announcer continues, stating, "Our kids will be taught a new way of thinking: "God creating Adam and Eve is so old-fashioned." "Thinking the unthinkable: 'If my dad married a man, who would be my mom?'"[42] While clearly set up as an ad to scare conservative voters to avoid having to ponder the "unthinkable," the ad poses a queer question, which enacts a perspective by incongruity that exposes the fallacy in the constituted premise of the question itself. The question marks a trained incapacity to think of relations, family, community, and potentiality in oversimplified and tragic frames.

Had Omar Little been permitted to answer the question, "If dad married a man, who would be my mom?" one could expect a response that reveals the violent limitations embedded within the inquiry. One could expect a similar smile and sarcastic reply to the question of where Omar will be in fifteen years, or what an older gay man in the U.S. looks like. The problem exists in the limitations of answers available, but also the limitations and allegiances posed by these questions, themselves. As Michael Tolliver claims, "My life, whatever its duration, is still a lurching, lopsided contraption held together by chewing gum and baling wire" (Maupin 23). "That life hasn't been perfect, but it has been my life, tailored to my dreams and safely beyond the reach of God's terrible swift sword. My [straight conservative] brother can't say that. Never could" (Maupin 94).

The future, as well as the future of gay male representation, remains uncertain, and there are hints and gestures to suggest multiple potential directions and possibilities. The release of the Academy Award–winning *Milk*, depicting a narrative of Harvey Milk's political career, points us in several complicated and potentially queer directions. Whereas the tragic murder of Harvey Milk is not, in itself, a new or challenging image, the film offers much more than a tale of heteronormative tragedy. The film opens with the announcement of Milk's and Moscone's deaths, informing the audience what is to come before we ever are introduced to Sean Penn's embodiment of Milk. We are given the end, the tragic finale, refusing to allow the death of Milk (for the uninformed audience member) to punctuate and foreclose all the potential impacts the film might produce. Upon Harvey's entrance, as he cruises Scott on the subway stairs, Scott states, "I don't date guys over forty." With playful and unrepentant charm, Harvey informs Scott that he will be thirty-nine for a few more minutes; today is his birthday. They go home together and, following sex, they share a slice of birthday cake in bed. Scott says to Harvey, "Happy birthday, old man." The significance of beginning his story at the age of forty marks a radical shift from the ways we have seen gay male lives narrated in Hollywood. Here/then, at forty, Harvey and Scott decide to begin their lives together and "drop out" by moving to San Francisco.

The discourses surrounding the audiencing of *Milk* have repeated a familiar script of how "things haven't changed," often drawing parallels between the Brigg's Initiative, Anita Bryant, and the 1970s gay rights movement with the contemporary debates over gay marriage, the passage of Proposition 8 in California, hate crime legislation, Employment Non-Discrimination Act, "Don't Ask, Don't Tell," and Defense of Marriage Act. While these parallels attest to the queering of progressive narratives, drawing attention to how "things have not changed" (Luciano), *Milk* provides an even more compelling challenge to gay temporal progress. *Milk* shows the mobilization and activation of a politicized queer public that is not interested or invested in normative assimilation. Harvey Milk's message is about demanding respect and human rights for queers, but without the normalizing or assimilationist rhetoric that exists in homonormative politics of today (Duggan). Addressing his crowd as "my fellow degenerates," Milk is interested in gaining legal protections, but not claiming or enforcing a straight temporality or morality upon queer lives. A far cry from the box office success *Mamma Mia!*, which offers an additional gay male representation over forty, whose body was tossed into the heterosexual celebration of love and romance to briefly complicate and resolve the story. Milk set forth a political agenda that sought to unite all the "us's" through a narrative of hope. Rejecting the negativity of Edelman's polemic, he works alongside Muñoz's refusal to abandon hope or the future. "Without hope life is not worth living. You gotta give them hope." Further challenging narratives of progress, not only was Milk's political platform queer, by way of celebrating and respecting all forms of gender and sexual expression, but he also developed coalitional rhetoric that sought to embrace a broad platform of racial and economic difference. The film offers an alternative past that allows us "to move toward a future that history has not envisioned" (Luciano 269).

In addition, *Milk* provides an alternative model for generativity, most notably in Harvey's relationships with Cleve and Danny, as younger boys who flocked to Harvey's camera shop. Cleve firsts dismisses Harvey as an "old man," in whom he is "not interested." However, Cleve turns to Harvey, following a breakup, where he confesses, "I actually thought we were going to spend the rest of our life together." Rejecting this temporal map of love and happily ever after, Cleve, simultaneously, moves past his limited characterization of Harvey as a perverted old man who only wants his body. A relationship is formed, which is neither particularly paternal nor sanitized, where Cleve begins to articulate his sexuality in politicized terms. They form a mentoring relationship as allies, workers, and family.

Perhaps most significant of all is both how and when *Milk* constitutes a meaningful life (Goltz, "Investigating"). The film clearly takes the position that Harvey Milk mattered, but the film does not end with images of Scott or Cleve, but of real footage of thousands of mourners walking the streets of San Francisco with candles. Although romantic love and queered notions of familial kinship were central to the story *Milk* presented, Harvey's meaning was constructed though his political commitments—not that those could be or ever should be divorced from the love and connection he felt with the queered family he created. Forefronting politics and a politicized sexual identity, *Milk* offers an alternative articulation of future meaning through the story of a man killed in 1978.

Although Harvey Milk, like so many gay bodies on the Hollywood screen, was dead before the final frame, this historical film opens up numerous spaces of potential for thinking outside heteronormative futures and the violences they enact. At forty-eight, at his final birthday party, Harvey explains his new partner to Scott, asking, "Where is an ugly old man like me going to find a handsome young man like that?" Scott lovingly replies, "You're not that old," marking a progression and rejection of the ways he framed Harvey years earlier. Although Scott's projection, "It looks like you are going to make it to fifty, after all, Mr. Milk" fails to come true, the film returns us to Scott and Harvey's first night together, on his fortieth birthday, towards the end of the film. After watching the political career of Harvey Milk take off, we return to the sight of a forty-year-old man who does not feel he has done anything with his life. Harvey's story begins *after* our cultural script suggests it will end. We are shown how little forty years can mean, and the amazing potential that eight years can afford. Time, scripts, straight narratives, and stories of progress break down, as we witness history and potential articulations of futurity simultaneously. A corrective to what Halberstam calls "this new emphasis on youth" (176) that highlights time in the present and the future, while ignoring the past, *Milk* gestures to a different temporality. In the past, rather than the present or the future, we see new potentialities.

Whereas the historical tale of Harvey Milk queerly offers the potential for alternative articulations of future, the tragic circularity of the "progressive" present continues to construct itself. The television show *Brothers & Sisters* has brought Uncle Saul out of the closet, which introduces a gay male character played by a seventy-year-old actor to primetime television. While the mere existence of this character is a relevant and important point to mention, his story has yet to violate predictable patterns. His "coming out" occurred following what was alluded to as a suicide attempt, and his sexuality and new boyfriend are almost completely relegated to the space-off. Saul is only written into storylines to offer help and assistance to the preservation and maintenance of the Walker family. His other life still remains a ghostly mystery, haunting the margins of the televised frame. Kevin and Scotty, also on *Brothers & Sisters*, are now coupled, married, urban, and "normal." In one episode, the mere solicitation for a three-way by another man (whom they both desired) shamed them into an argument, guilt, self-identified near-breakdown, and apology. Basked in soft white daylight, with gentle music in the background, they reconcile their brief temptation with a three-way. Scotty says, "So we move on, monogamous, domesticated, married." Kevin nods in agreement with each word, followed by a warm vocal confirmation of "Yeah." Scotty smiles reassuringly, asserting, "I wouldn't have it any other way."[43]

The mediated future of the aging gay male is uncertain, as the cultural production of gayness is always in assimilation with, in resistance against, and transcending through the logics of heteronormativity. There remains, however, a potential and a pleasure in the space-off of the Hollywood master narrative, which gestures to a dinner party taking place in the unrepresented space of the elsewhere. Much like all the barely invisible and unrepresented lives that exist at this very moment, those lives where gays, queers, and queer gays are doing future elsewhere in this moment (rather than moment by moment), there exist comic correctives and incongruous perspectives to every tragedy projected on screens and televised within our homes. They remain at the horizon of cultural discourse, where unlimited archives of "another story" linger at the margins of intelligibility, foreclosed through the litany of tragic questions that circulate around age, marital status, gender, sexuality, race, class, and plans for the future.

Queers are subjected to the heteronormative court, interpellated into an ongoing cross-examination that is premised upon correctness of the heteronormative plea. These questions will continue to face queers, wielded from left and right as straight time works to discipline queers into a rigid conception of temporality and future. Enacting a heteronormative plea of assimilation through identification perpetuates a tragic system, reproducing heteronormative violence, while reinscribing the illusionary perfection of a corrupt and limited conception of future. Rejecting the plea, however, relegates the defendant to a culturally produced cautionary tale of horror, subject to narratives of perpetual loss, misery, and the "harder road." The heteronormative court will always cast queers as aliens to the future, but it is not *the* future to which queers are alienated, but *one* conception of future, marked and charted through linear heteronormative systems. Heteronormativity's dominion relies upon its false promises of perfection and predictability, its charted and linear articulation of future, which provides answers to all of its questions. Where do you expect to be in fifteen years? Thirty years? The questions themselves are in service to the heteronormative court, self-sealing and circular inquiries that promote the ongoing tragedy and one conception of temporality and future. The questions beg for lazy and directed answers, coerced through fear, while lacking creativity and refusing an eye on potentialities. The questions place queers on the stand—accountable to judge, jury, court, and self—demanding a response to a flawed and biased inquiry for the purposes of upholding the regime of heteronormative temporal correctness. The inquiries will continue to be launched, yet each time these questions are posed, the tragedy they adhere to and the foreclosures they enact are exposed, leaving open the opportunity for a redirected question and further interrogation. As seen through the character of Omar Little, there is potential resistance and comic correction in a smirk, a smile, and a refusal to answer stupid and violent questions. Where will you be in fifteen years? To answer this question, perhaps one ought defer to Debbie, Michael's mother on *Queer as Folk*, who advises, "If you've got one foot in yesterday, and another foot in tomorrow, you'll piss on today."[44] The future is a discursive production, and the ability to conceive of a future or predict a future is always subject to the foreclosures at the margins of intelligibility. Constrained by heteronormative discourse, any direct answer is subject to the very trappings of the question itself. When faced with the question of the future, perhaps it is best to simply respond with a "Yes," accompanied by a smile that leaves them guessing. Such a response aims to liberate the question from the answers (and the answers from the questions).

Notes

NOTES TO CHAPTER 1

1. "Larry King Live" and "Weekend Update" were telecast on *Saturday Night Live* on NBC, November 3, 2008. The episode was directed by Don Roy King with guest star Brian Williams.
2. The use of the term "future" in this study refers to a projected image of forthcoming events and lives that, however impossible to predict, are aspired to and expected based upon cultural forecasting through representation and mythology. In this sense, the future is articulated as a discursive production, as well as a prediction, that works to articulate and discipline the margins of intelligibility for what is to come.
3. "Must See TV" is a slogan used by the National Broadcast Company (NBC) to promote their weekly primetime line-up.
4. The claim that older persons, particularly older heterosexual men, are coded with asexuality is open for some debate. Whereas there is a tendency in our culture to desexualize or assume older populations are devoid of sexual drive and are asexual, there remain gendered mythologies in the culture of the "dirty old man," regardless of their sexual object choice. In their discussion, however, de Vries and Blando are addressing how a predatory and hypersexualized stigma is placed upon the older gay male body that is disproportionate to the ways the culture frames older heterosexual males.
5. There has been a debate around whether or not gay men experience the phenomena of "accelerated aging" (Bennett and Thompson 66; De Vries and Blando 20; Friend 244; Hostetler 147). The accelerated aging hypothesis remains highly contested (Berger and Kelly 61), but the research strongly indicates, strictly in their usage of the term, that the self-labeling of the word "old" is deployed at earlier ages than in heterosexual communities.
6. It is important to note that this project is interrogating mainstream representations of gay male culture and thus refuses any claim that mainstream representations of gay male culture accurately or fully depict the reality of gay lives. Whereas youthism has been found to be prevalent in gay cultural representation and within lived experience, alternative "scenes" in the community absolutely exist. Bear culture, as one example, challenges and problematizes the worship of young hairless men, yet this dimension of the gay male community is rarely represented on the Hollywood screen. The absences from the cultural production draw attention to the ways gay culture is constructed and produced in limiting and exclusionary ways that fail to account for articulations of aging and future outside of a violent grammar of gay male sexuality. This attention to the tensions between the images of

representation and the "realities" of lived experience (Walters 10) addresses a different, yet very important, discussion.
7. The use of the term "gay" within a queer-informed project could be misunderstood as a contradiction in logic, or a conflation of two differing concepts. The use of the term "gay" in this text is specific and carefully considered, based on the goals and intentions of the work. As a general definition, this research approaches the term "gay" as a label used to identify a social identity discursively constructed around same-sex desire, an identity marker that interpolates an individual into a system of sexual categorization. The use of the term claims no essential gay identity (Fuss) and does not refuse the socially constructed nature of sexual categorization (Foucault; Katz, *Invention*) but is used to identify an identity or identification that groups or individuals take on, or are assigned, for personal, social, or political purposes.
8. In recent discourse, the greatest tensions and discussions of the term "gay" are in relation to the more recently reappropriated non-identity of "queer." Queer emerges as a direct response to many of the criticisms launched at the deployment of "gay," questioning its essentialist claims, its marginalization of multiple axes of social oppression (intersections of race, gender, class), the ways it has been depoliticized, and the problematic privileges the term assumes and erases. Outside the academy, the terms are often distinguished by viewing "gay" as a social identity and "queer" as a politicized identity. However, this is a very problematic and reductive distinction. Queerness is a non-identity by its very nature, as the term stands in the place of any fixed notion of sexual categorization (Gamson, "Sexualities"). Queer directly interrogates identity politics, challenging the sedimented assumption of essential homosexual identity, which is foundational to gay liberation debates. Queer also rejects gender categorization, as queerness is about the aspiration of a gender-free world (Butler, *Bodies*). Queer theorists launch direct attacks against normalizing efforts of conservative gay agendas, criticizing the racial, economic, and gendered neglect that homonormative politics perform in their efforts to fit in, questioning the very exclusions homonormative politics perpetuate and benefit from (Duggan; Halberstam, "Shame"; Perez). Politically, this research project is strongly aligned with queer objectives, with strong attention to hetero- and homonormalizing strategies, constructions of white privilege, and an investigation of potential configurations or gestures to futures that offer queer possibilities. Chapter 2 presents a more detailed discussion of the queer theoretical work at the foundation of this study.
9. Although Halberstam is critical of utilizing adult/youth distinctions, which reify an antagonistic relationship between two falsely constructed "groups" (*Queer* 176), the marking of "youth" is reflective of the language in the research cited in this discussion. In addition, Halberstam has alluded to a concern for projects, such as mine, that isolate gay youth health issues as a primary rationale for research (Dinshaw et al. 182; *Queer*). Whereas in support of her critical exploration of youth/maturation formations, and seeing my work as tied in strongly to her objectives, this project remains committed to addressing the discursive violence of future that shapes and narrates the experiences of "younger" queers.
10. As a project informed by cultural studies and ideological criticism, the attention of the project moves away from discussion of aesthetics and artistry to place ideological discussions at the fore. This note is not to claim that there is a grand divide between ideological discussions and aesthetic merit, as it can well be argued that nuanced and emotionally complex representations complicate the ideological workings of a text. The statement is merely to mark the primary attention and intention of the research, as it is most invested

in locating recurrent and resistant themes attached to gay aging and future across the breadth of mainstream cultural production.

NOTES TO CHAPTER 2

1. The name "John Reid" was a pen name for the author of the memoir. In later editions of the text, as well as its sequel *The Best Little Boy in the World Grows Up*, the pen name was changed and the texts were published by the author "Andrew Tobias writing as John Reid."
2. The body of work interrogating the normalizing and exclusionary practices of media representation is far too vast to review in this chapter. There is a strong body of literature tied to issues of race (Hall; hooks; Locke; Pieterse; Shome; Zook), economic homogenization and privilege (Butsch; Brookey; Cloud; Jordan), and gender (Fiske; Katz, *Tough*; Kilbourne; Trujillo).
3. Earlier projects, prior to the establishment of queer criticism, such as Russo's *Celluloid Closet*, provided a foundational critique of the limited ways that Hollywood films allowed gay representation. Russo overviews a century of filmmaking, marking the limited presence of overt references, as well as a strong history of coded references, to gays and lesbians since the beginning of film. What emerges is a limited typology of roles available until the late 1970s, limiting queers to the humorous and flamboyant sissy (4), the mentally ill and depressed pervert (193), or the bloodthirsty killer (182) who preys upon the innocent.
4. Fejes and Petrich's 1993 publication provided a detailed overview of gay and lesbian media criticism from the 1970s to the early 1990s, offering an extensive literature review in the areas of film, television, news media, pornography, and the gay consumer market. They assert that gay and lesbian media studies seeks to explore how "media images and meanings create definitions of homosexuality, homosexuals, and the homosexual community, and what are the consequences" (396). They argue the present task of gay and lesbian media scholars is an interrogation of the ways heterosexism functions in all areas of media (412).
5. The term "audiencing" is commonly used in performance studies literature to address the active process of interpretation and meaning-making from the position of audience. Rather than being an audience member, the term draws attention to the active and individualized experience each audience members engages through the process of constructing meaning moment by moment, thus granting space for audience agency, resistant modes of engaging texts, and active participation in textual dialogue.
6. Foundational to the queering of media is Doty's *Making Things Perfectly Queer*, where he carefully navigates his distinctions between queer audiencing and gay or lesbian audiencing. He asserts that "sexually parallel areas of textual production or reception" (xviii), whether gay or straight, are not what he refers to as queer audiencing. "'Queer' is used to describe the nonstraight work, positions, pleasures, and readings of people who either don't share the same 'sexual orientation' as that articulated in the texts they are producing or responding to (the gay man who takes queer pleasure in a lesbian sitcom, for example) or who don't define themselves as lesbian, gay, bisexual (or straight for that matter)" (xviii). However, he defines queer texts or queer textual elements as those "with reference to a range or a network of nonstraight ideas" (xviii). Doty's work is framed as a cultural and political project, aimed at understanding the multitude of ways "in-between" texts of mass culture are audienced. Written in the early 1990s, he anticipated the

eventual establishment of "academic and nonacademic discourses to challenge and redefine those ways of seeing and using mass culture that now [early 1990s] invoke mass culture queerness only to deny/dismiss/contain it in order to maintain straight culture's pleasures and profits" (104).

7. The position that sexuality is a product of social construction is now a common foundation within gay and lesbian and queer studies, often attributed to Foucault's tracing of the invention of the homosexual identity to the late 1800s (43). Whereas the notion of homosexuality as a social construction is widely supported, when and how homosexual and heterosexual identities came into existence is a point of contest and discussion (Jagose 10–6). Foucault's claims have since been both extended and complicated by theorist/historians such as D'Emilio, Halperin, Weeks, and Katz (7–21).

8. Originally known as the Hays Code, the Motion Picture Production Code took different names throughout its life until its termination in the late 1960s (Russo 31).

9. Centering this discussion on heteronormativity should not be seen as a move to privilege sexuality above the multiple intersecting axes of power that shape and define hegemonic forces, such as race, class, gender, and ability, as these systems of domination are not so easily parsed out. Heteronormativity is inescapably tied to multiple discourses of domination, and the intersection of these systems will be addressed throughout the study. The current discussion of heteronormative orientation provides us a point of entry into Burkean frameworks and thus offers a foundation to build and extend these discussions.

10. Acceptance frames are poetic structures that work within the status quo. These frames include tragedy, comedy, and epic systems, each working under the logic that there is a right or better way to do things. In *Attitudes toward History*, Burke also discusses rejection frames and transitional frames; however, acceptance logics are most effective for discussing historical representation in popular media.

11. The iron law of history accounts for three tragic vehicles for purging guilt, where "someone or something must suffer if the world is to be set right" (Carlson and Hocking 206). Factional scapegoating marks the villain, and this is the governing form of victimage in early gay and lesbian representation. The second form of tragic victimage is mortification, self-punishment, and this is explained later in this chapter. Additionally, there is the universal scapegoat who represents humanity as a whole, a symbolic representation of the "everyman" (*Attitudes* 188). Burke uses the example of Ashenbach from Mann's *Death in Venice* as a universal scapegoat, as the text solicits the reader's identification with Ashenbach and his "erotic criminality" (189). Universal scapegoating is discussed further in the next two chapters.

12. In each era of increased visibility for homosexuals in mainstream media, reported hate crimes show a parallel increase, according to police records (Gross, *Up*; Russo; Seidman 8; Walters 9).

13. The work of queer media criticism has expanded to include multiple scholars from various disciplines (see also Bad Object Choices; Battles and Hilton-Morrow; Brookey; Brookey and Westerfelhaus; Dow; Erni; Fejes and Petrich; Gever, Grayson and Parmar; Peele).

14. In his discussion of 1980s gay representations, such as *Making Love*, *Victor/Victoria*, and *Personal Best*, Russo asserts that these films offer more sympathetic portrayals from the sickly or vilified models. Still, "even when gays and lesbians were presented in a non-problematic manner, the issues of gay/lesbian culture, community, identity, history, and oppression and discrimination are minimized or totally obscured" (Fejes and Petrich 398).

15. Erni coined the term "queer media criticism" (162) in the field of communication in his 1998 study of Michael Jackson. He suggests the field is rooted in queer, as well as cultural theory (160). He makes no claim to have discovered queer media criticism as a field of research, because the foundational work for both queer theory and gay and lesbian media criticism had been going on for a couple of decades.
16. It needs to be addressed that many of the studies that have contributed to the body of work on 1990s representations of gayness and the foundations of queer media criticism in Communication have recently been critiqued by Schiappa for implicitly or explicitly advancing "norms of representational correctness" (9). Schiappa calls for rhetorical critics of mediated texts to enhance their claims through audience study (31), suggesting that textual analysis is merely one form of audience analysis, and rhetorical critics run the risk of missing "the cultural and political work a text may perform among the general population" (65). Given the focus of my book project, which analyses the narrative structures and meanings surrounding age and future of over 100 films and 25 full television series, I am not focusing upon what he claims to be a simplified model of "good texts cause good effects, and that sociopolitically bad texts cause bad effects" (11). Rather, my study seeks to mark and analyze larger narrative patterns in pop cultural discourse that extend across multiple texts, marking themes, commonplaces, and foreclosures. My project is not concerned with texts "getting it right," but rather with investigating what meanings are forefronted and what other potential meanings are absent from the cultural discourse. However, I do have some concerns about his characterization of previous research in the field of queer media studies and his generalized critique of "representational correctness." While I agree that audience analysis could provide convincing arguments for how particular audiences engage a particular text in a particular moment, he bypasses and simplifies the work of critical rhetoric, which calls for a telos of perpetual criticism (Ono and Sloop; McKerrow). Instead, he argues much rhetorical work, whether intentional or not, holds to a fixed and simplified evaluative criteria of "accuracy" of representation, "purity" in the liberatory potential of the work, and "innocence" of offense (9). Critical rhetoric, critical research, and queer media studies share a commitment to the work of producing generative and emancipatory knowledges, engaging texts in a far more complex manner than good/bad or right/wrong representation. I find Schiappa's critique to be more invested in the good text/bad text binary to make his charge than seeing this dynamic play out in the rhetorical work he characterizes as such. One of his final suggestions is for critics to "praise the good stuff" (165), suggesting critics need to be marking productive sights of representation, for producers will never be able to get it perfect. I do not agree with the logic that critical rhetoricians and/or queer media critics are interested in perfection, simplified distinctions of good or bad, or blanket reviews. Specifically giving attention to Dow, Battles and Hilton-Morrow, and Shugart, what is obscured in Schiappa's articulation and critique of these works is the queer underpinnings of their discussion. For example, Schiappa cites a study by Ortiz and Harwood that indicates audiences responded more favorably to the gay character of Will Truman and thus were more willing to interact with gay men (or at least less unwilling) based on their viewing (83–4). Schiappa uses this data to counter claims by several textual analysts, arguing that the "Ortiz and Harwood results directly challenge the idea that the relationship [between Will and Grace] promotes heteronormativity" because exposure to the show indicated "lower social distance toward gay people" (84). I am unconvinced by this line of argumentation for several

reasons. Reporting reduced homophobia or "decreased prejudice" (85) is *not at all* the same are challenging heteronormativity, as these are two *very* different ideas. Will Truman, as many critics have previously articulated (as well as myself, in Chapter 4), works to uphold and normalize many tenants of heteronormativity. It is not surprising, nor contrary to the work of Shugart or Battles and Hilton-Morrow, that many heterosexual audiences found Will Truman to be a "positive" representation. The repeated critique is that Will *is constructed for normative audiences to like him*, downplaying his sexuality and forefronting his asexual, masculine, and heteronormative identifications. One of the critical concerns of my project is the problem with Will becoming "what a gay guy looks like," as he is so normatively relatable, and that relatability works to privilege some gay identities at the expense of many others. A queer critique often works to challenge the dominant reading of the text, questioning the very assumptions, identifications, and ideologies that work to make Will Truman likeable, friendly, and relatable, because these audience identifications work to construct the "good gay" who has been subject to great scrutiny by queer media critics. In turn, those gay men who fail to be "like Will" (men of color, lower class, more sexually open, more flamboyant, non-monogamous, etc.) may not receive as high of a likability score or perhaps might receive higher anxiety-inducing scores in audience analysis research. While engaging Schiappa's entire discussion is not in the scope or focus of this study (particularly as this study engages multiple texts, rather than the singular text work he critiques; 13), it is important to mark that queer media criticism's concern for normalizing strategies and assimilationist efforts are not engaged or represented in his conception or critique of queer/critical work. This absence in his argument seems to miss the important contributions of this scholarship and fails to account for why I find it important and productive to engage with and build upon. I do, however, agree with Schiappa that certain types of claims by rhetorical critics can be bolstered and strengthened through the audience analysis work he calls for. Such a claim echoes previous assertions by Kellner, addressing the importance of audience analysis, textual analysis, and the political economy to critical cultural studies.

17. Queer theorist Judith Halberstam takes up several of these issues in her discussion of gay shame, the theorizing that claims abject childhoods provide the energy to construct queer momentum ("Shame" 221). Halberstam argues that shame always ends up being thrown upon someone else (224), perpetuating a tragic system. She insists this approach obscures queer agendas by demonizing sissiness in the allegiance to an oppressive masculinity (226), projecting shame onto raced bodies (229), as well as further idealizing gay youth and interiority (222). In short, gay shame further supports tragic systems by constructing symbolic mergers with systems of whiteness and patriarchy, rejecting an intersectional queer politic in favor of normative alliance.
18. Cornell uses the word ethical "to indicate the aspiration to a nonviolent relationship to the Other and to otherness in the widest possible sense" (78). Ethics, by Cornell's conception, is not a system of rules or behaviors but "an attitude toward what is other to oneself" (78). Specifically, the ethic of fallibilism "implies a challenge to one's basic organization of the world" (78), a concept originally developed by Peirce. For the purposes of this project, the challenge is posed to restrictive orientations, allowing a space for mistakenness and comedy.
19. The ethic of musement is a second Peircean concept, which Cornell adopted in her conception of an ethical feminism (78).

NOTES TO CHAPTER 3

1. Season 3, Episode 10.
2. Throughout the entire Nightmare on Elm Street series, Freddy Krueger's anthem is repeated. Often sung by young children playing jump rope, the song goes, "One, two, Freddy's coming for you. Three, four, better lock your door. Five six grab your crucifix. Seven, eight, better stay up late. Nine, ten, never sleep again."
3. Season 1, Episode 12.
4. Season 1, Episode 3.
5. Season 6, Episode 6.
6. Season 1, Episode 6.
7. Season 1, Episode 12.
8. Season 6, Episode 11.
9. Season 1, Episode 22.
10. Season 4, Episode 18.
11. Season 2, Episode 6.
12. Season 1, Episode 22.
13. For an additional discussion of suicidal gay males in popular media, see the discussion on *Poseidon* later in the chapter.
14. Season 11, Episode 2.
15. Season 1, Episode 3.
16. The use of parody in these texts can be read through the Burkean frame of burlesque, as Paul's dismissal and the tragic performance of the suicidal gay friend are sped up to a pace of absurdity (*Attitudes* 54). The use of caricature and polemic in this representation gestures to the limitations of this extreme, offering the potential for discounting (55) the tragic reification. The film does not present a sense of mistakenness or complication to the tragic gay male narrative, thus failing to provide a comic corrective through perspective by incongruity and the reconstitution of the heteronormative tragic orientation.
17. Season 2, Episode 10. The trivializing and dismissal of gay corpses might be thought as a form of perspective by incongruity, although such a response is perfectly aligned with the orientation of heteronormativity. While unexpected, and seemingly incongruous, the flippant dismissal and mockery of gay corpses reifies and substantiates the heteronormative tragedy, constructing dominant identifications, rather than rupture and rearticulation.
18. Season 1, Episode 18.
19. Season 3, Episode 5.
20. Season 1, Pilot and Episode 2.
21. Drug use marks another theme that links gay male living with self-destruction in several of the texts, yet drugs are also constructed as central to the glamour of gay metropolitan living. The texts assume an unclear distinction between the playful pill-popping of Terry Crabtree in *Wonder Boys* and the strung out dog walker in *A Guide to Recognizing Your Saints*. The former reifies the notion that cocaine, GHB, ecstasy, and crystal meth are as much a part of "gay culture" as drag performances and flavored vodka. In these circumstances, drugs are rarely criticized, but are ever-present, claiming an "honest" representation of gay reality. On *Queer as Folk*, Brian snorting a bump of cocaine on the dance floor of Babylon is as common as 1980s dance remixes, shirtless men, and bulging Speedo shorts. The scale is tipped, however, when Ted uses drugs in Season 3, quickly falling into addiction, stealing money, losing control, and hitting rock bottom. Suddenly everyone is quick to judge drugs. Even Brian hypocritically dismisses Ted, telling his friends, "Forget about him. He's dead." This sets up an unclear standard where

164   *Notes*

drugs are normalized within the culture, shared communally with friends, but quickly turn to simplistic storylines of the weak addict who went astray. The gay male performs a dangerous dance between glamour and destruction, romanticizing life on the edge, yet demonizing those who lose their delicate balance and are no longer fabulous.

22. Season 5, Episode 13.
23. Season 5, Episode 19.
24. Season 1, Episode 1.
25. Season 1, Episode 10.
26. Season 4, Episode 10.
27. Season 3, Episode 7.
28. Season 3, Episode 11.
29. Season 1, Episode 4.
30. Season 4, Episode 13.
31. Season 1, Episode 14.
32. Season 2, Episode 4; Season 3, Episodes 4–5.
33. Season 3, Episode 4–5.
34. Season 4, Episode 3.
35. Season 4, Episode 19.
36. Season 3, Episode 19.
37. While an ongoing theme, one example is in Season 3, Episode 9, when Marco has to endure Spinner's homophobia and explain that he is not a sexual predator, nor is he interested in Spinner.
38. Season 3, Episode 4.
39. Season 4, Episode 5.
40. Season 3, Episode 22.
41. Season 5, Episode 5.
42. Season 3, Episode 22.
43. Season 1, Episode 2.
44. Season 1, Episode 9. This analysis makes no argument about the aesthetic merit of these texts, as *Six Feet Under* provides one of the most complicated and rich representations of gayness yet to be seen on TV. However, what is perpetuated in this show, and many others of varying quality and sophistication, is the notion of gay misery. David cries to Keith, "I don't know why it's so hard for me?" Calmly, Keith responds, "It's hard for all of us."
45. Season 1, Episodes 12–4.
46. See Chapter 4 for a detailed discussion of the rigid hetero/homo binary formation within normalized gay male representation.
47. Season 4, Episode 19.
48. Season 3, Episode 2.
49. Season 1, Episode 16.
50. Season 1, Episode 6.
51. Season 1, Episode 11.
52. Season 1, Episode 21.
53. Season 1, Episode 3.
54. Season 1, Episode 1.
55. Season 1, Episode 6.
56. Season 2, Episode 16.
57. Season 1, Episode 22.
58. Season 3, Episode 3.
59. The notion that gay men experience "accelerated aging" remains a contested concept in studies of older gay men and gay culture (Bennett and Thompson; Brown et al.). However, within the cultural production of gay men in this research, there is reoccurring theme of deploying the term "old" at significantly

Notes 165

lower ages than heterosexual characters in the same texts. This study does not claim that accelerated aging is either correct, nor a misconception, but does locate multiple texts within gay popular culture, which reify the accelerated aging script.

60. Season 1, Episode 14.
61. Season 5, Episode 18.
62. Season 1, Episode 1.
63. Season 3, Episode 10.
64. Season 1, Episode 5.
65. Season 1, Episode 6.
66. Season 1, Episode 4.
67. Season 2, Episode 10.
68. Season 2, Episode 8.
69. Season 2, Episode 14.
70. Season 1, Episode 20.
71. Season 1, Episode 11.
72. Season 2, Episode 7.
73. Season 2, Episode 4.
74. Season 2, Episode 11.
75. Season 1, Episode 21.
76. Season 4, Episode 3.
77. Season 2, Episode 14.
78. Season 4, Episode 7.
79. Season 1, Episode 9.
80. Season 3, Episode 12.
81. Season 1, Episode 20.
82. Season 1, Episode 20.
83. In the examples of *Dante's Cove*, *Queer as Folk*, and *Broken Hearts Club*, the stories are initiated based on the arrival of these characters. Each of these texts begins with the younger boy entering an existing scene, location, or friend group, but it is their arrival that drives the stories. In the final episode of *Queer as Folk*, the series ends with Justin leaving Pittsburgh, and Michael and Brian returning to their routine of dancing at Babylon. In the deleted scenes for the final episode on the DVD, however, there is a brief scene of a new young boy stepping onto Liberty Avenue for the first time, mirroring the opening of the series five years before. Although deleted, this scene simply emphasizes the centralized positioning of Justin in the show, marking his absence as the end of the story. In turn, the arrival of a new golden boy, walking into Babylon, alludes to the potential of Brian picking up a new kid and perpetuating the same cycle, and forefronting the fact that the lead characters are in the same place as the opening of the series.
84. Season 1, Episode 2.
85. Season 2, Episode 4.
86. Season 1, Episode 3.
87. Season 1, Episode 19.
88. Season 1, Episode 11.
89. Season 2, Episode 13.
90. Season 1. Episode 16.
91. Season 1, Episode 12.
92. Season 1, Episode 20.
93. Season 1, Episode 8.
94. Season 1, Episode 9.
95. Chapter 4 spends a significant amount of time theorizing representations, such as David Fisher, who seek access to heteronormative systems through

firm allegiance to straight time. The representations, their rhetorical strategies, and the critical concerns they create are given a more detailed treatment in the next chapter.
96. Season 2, Episode 8.
97. Season 2, Episode 11.
98. Season 1, Episode 4.
99. Season 1, Episode 3.
100. Season 1, Episode 5.
101. Season 4, Episode 4.

NOTES TO CHAPTER 4

1. Season 3, Episode 22.
2. Queer theorists and queer media critics have built a solid foundation of research interrogating the dangers, pitfalls, concessions, and perpetuated oppressions of assimilationist tactics and representations. The emergence of increased gay visibility in the 1990s ushered in a strong wave of developing queer criticism which sought to challenge the compliance of gay normalization with neo-liberal politics (Duggan), heteronormative systems of oppressions (Warner, "Introduction"; Yep), patriarchy (Shugart), racism (Yep and Elia, "Quaring"), whiteness, essentialized gender and sexuality (Butler, *Bodies*; Sedgwick), and the foreclosure of queered potentiality (Muñoz, "Impossible"; Muñoz, "Stages"). See Chapter 2 for a detailed overview.
3. Season 1, Episode 3.
4. Season 6, Episode 6.
5. Queer theorists have sought to rethink and re-explore the potentials for alternative kinship formations that extend beyond nation, biological family, and borders for the potential of a queer form of kinship. For example, Chela Sandoval discusses how third world feminism calls citizen-subjects who have traditionally been separated through systems of gender, sexuality, race, nation, and culture to join in a "trans-difference" coalition that interrogates and transcends traditionally limited notions of kin and kinship (23).
6. Season 3, Episode 9.
7. Season 2, Episode 4.
8. Season 1, Episode 3.
9. Season 3, Episode 10.
10. Gay men running to the altar—while depicted in shows such as *Queer as Folk*, *Noah's Arc*, and *Will & Grace*—is not without criticism. The romantic picnics in the country, the sentimental pet names, and the proud declarations of fidelity are always subject to the critique of Brian Kinney, the show's self-proclaimed voice of queer sexual politics. In Episode 5 of Season 1, as Michael prepares to go to out to dinner with David, Brian comments, "A real date . . . It's so hetero." When asked if Brian has ever gone on a date, himself, he replies, "Once. I ended up fucking the waiter." Later in the same episode, Justin—Brian's boyfriend—tells Brian, "I need you." Brian dismissively replies, "Where did you learn to talk that like that? Watching some teen drama?" The character of Brian Kinney and the "queer" politics of *Queer as Folk* are given specific attention in the final section of this chapter.
11. Season 1, Episode 1.
12. Season 2, Episode 4.

13. Preceding Edelman's critique of reproductive futurism, Erni also discusses a "queer-phobic culture that brands queer people as an automatic threat to children and adolescents" (173).
14. Season 1, Episode 12.
15. This tension between youth-defined clubs and adult-defined suburbia parallels Halberstam's critique of the disciplinary function of the youth/adult binary, where she conceives of queer time as a sustained and extended subcultural commitment.
16. Season 3, Episode 3.
17. Season 1, Episode 3.
18. For some additional texts that center around gay males and children, see Michael and Brian's children with Melanie and Lindsay on *Queer as Folk*, Jonathon and Bobby in *A Home at the End of the World*, Gil and Charlie in *Happy Endings*, Jack with Elliot on *Will & Grace*, and Jack in the final episode of *Dawson's Creek*.
19. Season 6, Episode 11.
20. This episode of *Queer Eye for the Straight Guy*, titled *Queer Eye for the Red Sox*, aired in 2005 and is available on DVD.
21. Embedded in this statement is the adherence to the cultural logic that the young boys are assumed to be heterosexual. "Hanging out with the gays" marks the Fab Five's sexual deviation, while simultaneously reifying the assumed heterosexuality of the entire baseball team. The underlying assumption that maintains this tragic narrative is the refusal to problematize the cultural logic that all children are inherently heterosexual (Fejes and Petrich 409).
22. Season 1, Episode 4.
23. Season 4, Episode 23.
24. Season 3, Episode 2.
25. Season 6, Episode 23.
26. Season 2, Episode 3 of *Queer as Folk*.
27. *Queer as Folk's* representation of "Gay as Blazes" is a sarcastic parody, which eventually works to expose all of the upstanding and "normal" gay men as sexual hypocrites, a repeated plotline that runs throughout the entire series. Later in the chapter the queer politics of *Queer as Folk* will be given specific focus.
28. Season 2, Episode 1.
29. Season 2, Episode 11.
30. It is important to note that the rigid discipline of sexual categories operates differently for male and female representation. For example, Karen Walker on *Will & Grace* is often flirting with multiple sexual partners regardless of age, gender, or sexuality. Although married, multiple situations allude to same-sex desire with Rosario, Grace, and even Martina Navratilova. Given that masculine gendering is more carefully guarded than feminine gendering in our culture, the potential for a male character to occupy the queer space of Karen Walker is far more difficult, as men who express, flirt with, or even allude to same-sex desire are quickly labeled as gay. This will be addressed further in Chapter 5.
31. Season 1, Episode 1.
32. At the time of this research project, *Sweet Home Alabama* had the highest domestic gross of all the films studied with explicit gay representation. Since that time, the film adaptation of *Mamma Mia!*, which has Colin Firth playing a gay male named Henry, earned over $160 million at the U.S. domestic box office, beating out *Sweet Home Alabama* by approximately $40 million. *Mamma Mia!* is briefly addressed in the conclusion of this study.

33. The use of gay characters to demonstrate the righteousness of their heterosexual allies is a common theme extending across multiple texts. For example, the self-hating Jack of *Dawson's Creek* just wants to play football, but when the opposing team finds out there is a gay player, they intentionally attack him on each play. Dawson, the hero of the show, arrives in the locker room at halftime with a plan. The players wipe mud all over the back of their jerseys, so that the other team cannot spot Jack on the field. Dawson's brilliant plan is taken a needless step further, as the entire football team puts on lipstick to further hide Jack, taunting their homophobic opponents to "find the homo now." The lipstick, while not necessary for disguising Jack (equating his gayness to femininity and assuming it somehow was literally written across his face) served as a gesture to show the loyalty and open-mindedness of Dawson and the football team.

34. In latter seasons of *Brothers & Sisters*, Kevin and Scotty get married, following a period of time where Kevin confronts and deals with his own shame. However, as Scotty returns to the show, there noticeable shift in his performance, as much of his flamboyance and playfulness is no longer present. While this shift is never marked, Scotty is narrated as having matured and gotten his life together since his first introduction into the series in Season 1.

35. The "not *too* gay" plea is constructed through the spoken allegiance and nonverbal conformity to traditional masculine performance. The masculine gay male bridges identification and helps promote the image of a "normal" guy who "happens to be gay" (Conway 77). Jack on *Dawson's Creek* struggled for multiple seasons to blend in with the guys, and would grow angry and frustrated when his gayness was marked or discussed. After his fraternity opts to bunk him in a single room, as the fraternity brothers were hesitant to room with him, Jack complains, "I haven't done anything but try and fit in around here and you make me feel like some kind of quarantined freak" (Season 5, Episode 11). Although Jack's father was first afraid of Jack's gayness, believing there would be too many differences for them to get along, Jack's playing football changed his fathers mind. "When I saw you in that Jersey, I saw myself in you" (Season 3, Episode 2). Jack's first crush on the show was Ethan, the "straightest gay guy" he had ever met (Season 3, Episode 10), offering a gay man who was not too gay for Jack to identify with. Jack's later boyfriend, Toby, is disciplined for not performing traditional masculinity, when Jack criticizes, "Don't get all 'girl-friendy' on me now" (Season 5, Episode 5). In short, traditional masculinity is used to construct audience identification, while also reifying the devaluation of alternative and more feminine gay male performances.

36. Season 3, Episode 8.

37. The most common device to create this audience connection is the "coming out" sequence where the gay character faces the judgment and fear of rejection for loved ones for announcing their same-sex attraction. The "shame scene" performs an acknowledgment of violation, a mandatory performance of guilt for that shame, and offers the dominant foundation from where understanding can be constructed. In texts such as *All Over the Guy* and *Another Gay Movie*, this model is tweaked by offering parents who are not shocked, ashamed, or judgmental of their gay children. Still, the gay children, themselves, continue to perform the obligatory script of self-loathing. When the parents are quick to accept their sexuality, the child acts frustrated, angry, and confused, as their narrative of shame-leading-to-eventual-acceptance is denied.

38. Season 1, Episode 12.

Notes   169

39. Season 7, Episode 8.
40. Season1, Episode 1. David delivers this line to Keith when Keith shows up to support David during his father's funeral. At this point in the series, David is still closeted to his family, thus marking Keith's mere presence at a family event as politicized.
41. Season 1, Episode 16.
42. Season 4, Episode 10.
43. Season 4, Episodes 2–5.
44. Season 3, Episode 13.
45. Season 4, Episode 8.
46. Season 1, Episode 8.
47. Season 5, Episode 16.
48. Season 6, Episode 7.
49. The "flaming" and "sissy" model of gay representation rarely is designed to solicit audience identification, yet works to designate and situate "the normal gay" as the reasonable and respectable character. This trend has been discussed at great length through the pairing of Will and Jack on *Will & Grace*. In films such as *Mean Girls*, you see the stereotypical gay character at the periphery of the narrative, enduring the repeated one-liners or "you've really out-gayed yourself" and "you are too gay to function." In these instances, such as *Reno 911!*, *Be Cool*, *Best in Show*, *The Producers*, and *Deuce Bigalow: European Gigolo*, the gay male remains a sight gag or a predictable one-liner, marked as ridiculous, shallow, and divorced from any political agenda or effort at audience identification. The gay male remains the ridiculous Other.
50. The discussion of gay male sexuality is complicated by limited and heterosexist conceptions of what "gay sexuality" or "gay intimacy" may entail. While inclusive of anal penetration, oral sex, and various configurations of petting, rubbing, and pulsating, it is important to leave a broad net of possibilities and potentials for what might fall into the realm of gay sexuality and intimacy outside a limited laundry list of configurations. This critique of privatized and desexualized gay representation is broadly addressing the depiction of same-sex intimacy, eroticism, bodily contact, and the sharing of bodies. It does not in any way wish to place a stamp on erotic potentialities and possibilities, demarcating some prescribed notion of queer sexual expression.
51. Season 1, Episode 4.
52. Season 3, Episode 12.
53. Season 3, Episode 13.
54. Season 2, Episode 1.
55. Yep lays out a detailed discussion of the violence heteronormativity inflicts on all sexual subjects, regardless of their espoused sexual identity. Rather than approaching heteronormative violence from a minoritarian perspective, heteronormative systems impose confines, limits, and violently enforced restrictions on "heterosexual women" (19), "real men" (20–1), and LGBTQ populations (21–5).
56. Carlson's ("you know") Burkean study of *Rhinelander v. Rhinelander* demonstrates the rhetorical strategies of bridging devices in a literal court case. The defendant was a woman of mixed racial blood, who was prosecuted by her husband for "pretending" to be white. In her analysis of this trial, Carlson demonstrates how social structures of racism were maintained by the defense—as the social context of the time would not allow the racial hierarchy to be questioned—through situating gender at the center of the discourse. Gender was used as a bridging device (122), establishing identification with

the court, while posing no threat to the racial hierarchy. By shifting perspectives of the defendant from racial to gender frames, the defendant was evaluated by the "ideals of white womanhood" (125). Once the discourse shifted to gender, the violations against womanhood worked against the plaintiff, "who was obviously less than 'white' in his heart" (125). The Andrew Tobias, "best little (gay) boy" model speaks for "respected, contributing gay men and lesbians" (*Grows* 264). These "decent, productive tax-paying professionals" (119) enlist class, whiteness, and traditional gender performances as bridging devices to plead affinity with existing—and oppressive—social hierarchies. As the Rhinelander defense claimed, "Many a white heart beats under a dark skin" (Carlson, ["you know"] 123), the "best little (gay) boy" argues that the civilized, respectable, hard-working, successful, monogamous, romance-invested homosexual shares the heterosexual heart.
57. The show *Queer as Folk* is offered much attention in this analysis for several reasons. As a show centering exclusively on the lives of gay men, with over one hundred hours of episodes, the sheer volume of the series is equal to fifty major motion pictures. The only other show with this level of attention dedicated to gay male characters is *Noah's Arc*, which at the time of the study has only produced eight hours of episodes. In addition, the show presents and extremely relevant cultural text, as gay bars across the U.S. and abroad hosted weekly "*Queer as Folk* nights," the show is Showtime's most successful series to date, and the entire series continues to be produced on DVD. In this section, the show presents a unique discussion as Brian Kinney embodies the politics of a queer theory primarily focused on discourses of sexuality. Seemingly resistant, and defining a vernacular understanding of what a "queer politics" might look like to mainstream audiences, *Queer as Folk* claims to forefront what might be argued as "queer" and "progressive" representation. For this reason, the show is being analyzed directly, but is also a text to discuss the limitations of the queer politics it asserts, thus presenting a concrete example to engage a theoretical discussion.
58. Season 3, Episode 4.
59. Season 2, Episode 1.
60. Season 2, Episode 16.
61. Season 4, Episode 7.
62. Season 2, Episode 11.
63. Season 2, Episode 10.
64. Season 2, Episode 7.
65. Season 1, Episode 3.
66. Season 3, Episode 2.
67. Season 3, Episode 2.
68. Season 3, Episode 5.
69. Season 1, Episode 11.
70. Season 1, Episode 12.
71. Season 3, Episode 1.
72. Season 1, Episode 14.
73. Season 3, Episode 4.
74. Season 2, Episode 2.
75. Season 5, Episode 6.
76. Season 3, Episode 5.
77. Mirroring this construction of the female body as abnormal in dominant media, gay males in popular culture often ridicule, demonize, and mock the female body as repulsive or flawed. In Episode 16 of the second season of *Sex and the City*, Samantha is asked to have a three way with two of her gay male friends. The sexually confident and aggressive Samantha agrees to the

experience, and everything is going well until the two guy men slowly move their heads down to her vagina. The passion disappears, and the two men, with sour expressions on their faces, comment hesitantly, "It's very pretty." When Grace finds out that Will slept with another woman to confirm his gayness, she complains, "I thought it was my naked body that makes you feel nothing" (Season 3, Episode 8). While waiting for Grace to be inseminated with his sperm, Will flips through a book with images of birthing. He jokes, " It looks like a bad guy from a science fiction movie" (Season 4, Episode 25). Here gay identity is constructed through repulsion to the female body, constructed as alien, foul, and subject to ridicule.

78. Season 8, Episode 23.
79. Season 6, Episodes 23–4.
80. Season 5, Episode 12.
81. Season 5, Episode 13.
82. These exact lines are repeated from the final episode in Season 1, where Michael finds Brian hanging himself on his thirtieth birthday.

NOTES TO CHAPTER 5

1. For a few examples of the interrupted dinner party, see *My Best Friend's Wedding*, *Three to Tango*, and Vic and Rodney's dinner party in Episode 5 of the fourth season of *Queer as Folk*.
2. Judy Chicago's "The Dinner Party" is a famous feminist art installation that was created between 1974 and 1979. Creating a space that celebrates the lives of women who have been obscured, marginalized, or completely erased from historical narratives, "The Dinner Party" was constructed by a large collaborative team who embroidered, sewed, hand painted, and wove intricate and individualized place settings to mark the contributions of notable women in history.
3. This is not making the claim that coupling, marriage, or procreation are inherently heteronormative in and of themselves, as the chapter seeks to problematize this simplicity. The future, however, through heteronormative scripts is defined primarily through these systems—at the foreclosure of others—and seeks to define regimented and restrictive potentials for what marriage and child relations might look like.
4. As wealthy and white gay men, Gary and James embody the dangers of gay political stance that ignores the privileges attached to race and class positions. Carlos is objectified as a "hot little Latin boy" in the film, denied the respect or integrity of a full person, and treated as an eroticized sexual object for white gay male consumption (Perez). For further information, see Perez; Carbado; Johnson; and Ferguson, "Race-ing."
5. Season 5, Episode 13.
6. Locating the emergence of queer time in the outbreak of the AIDS pandemic, there are several mainstream texts that demonstrate and enact this temporal engagement. Such films include, but are not limited to, *Longtime Companion*, *Parting Glances*, *An Early Frost*, *Philadelphia*, *Jeffrey*, *Love! Valor! Compassion!*, and *It's My Party*.
7. The uncle in the film is never marked as "gay" or mentioned to have any same-sex sexual desire. The character can be read as a queer character, insomuch as he lives his life outside of the heteronormative family and marriage script, has created an ornate and somewhat fantasy-like backyard in his home, and moves through space and time on a different register than the rest of his family in the film.

8. *Six Feet Under* and *Queer as Folk* each offer additional articulations of queer family in multiple formations, particularly dealing with adoption and the child. David and Keith's decision to adopt two older sons—both old enough to attend school—presents a text where an interracial gay couple performs an ongoing tension between how a family "should" act and how they make do, based on their own experiences and understandings of family. *Queer as Folk* has Michael and Ben adopt Hunter, a teenage street hustler who used to work the corner outside of their apartment. Working to extend and redefine notions of parenthood, child, and family, the text presents another representation of nonnormative family that mirrors and resists heteronormativity simultaneously—an additional perspective by incongruity.
9. Season 3, Episode 5.
10. Season 3, Episode 5.
11. Season 4, Episode 4.
12. Season 6, Episode 23/24.
13. There is the possibility of a second reading of Jack's newfound fatherhood, as an extension of Jack and Jen's queer relation. As Jack has consistently struggled to locate and define himself through heteronormative identification, however, Jack's wanting to raise Jen's daughter seems to follow the identification trajectory, offering a "happy ending" for Jack's ongoing aspiration to be "normal." Jen's willingness to have Jack raise her daughter—a gay male who is her best friend—provides an additional example of Jen's willingness to resist and question oppressive scripts, such as the "harder path" of having gay parents.
14. Film genres are comprised of their repertoire of elements, such as the narratives, iconography, characters, and locations that define the genre (Lacey 48). Films will pull from this repertoire to construct a film that fits within its established genre, yet attempt to organize or shift them in such a way as to appear novel or fresh (48).
15. Season 4, Episode 14.
16. Season 6 (Part 1), Episode 9.
17. It is important to note that at the conclusion of *Sex and the City*, Carrie does couple with Mr. Big and it is implied that she and Big will "settle down." Whereas the series offered several productive questions about heteronormative discipline, Carrie's narrative is recuperated into a familiar arc by the end of the series.
18. The notion of romantic love, regardless of gender, cannot be divorced from the heteronormative temporal scripts, as the illusionary promises of romance are embedded in straight time. The use of the term "romance" in this analysis does not seek to dismiss the limitations of the concept, nor to exclude the potential rejection of romance narratives altogether. For example, in Maupins's *Michael Tolliver Lives*, Michael discusses two of his friends, Leo and Bill who happily cohabitated as friends, never lovers. "As far as I can tell, they both relinquished romance without a fuss . . . They will grow old together, those two, tucked in their separate beds (with their separate collections of porn)" (255). While this section of the chapter focuses on negotiations within the romantic relationship, the abandoning of romance, altogether, offers an additional departure worthy of queer investigation.
19. Season 2, Episode 2.
20. Season 2, Episode 7.
21. Season 5, Episode 13.
22. Season 4, Episode 13.
23. Season 1, Episode 5.

24. In Episode 1 of Season 1, as Chance is moving out of his home, there is a brief interaction with a much older landlord who could be read as gay. Although not explicitly marked, based on his interaction, I read the man as gay and there was a brief scene that reflected a caring and supportive friendship between him and Chance.
25. *Shortbus* offers an image of an underground sex club in New York, and the lives of those who are part of its community. In the world of the film, sexualities, sexual expressions, and sexual experimentations are a site of play and exploration for the main characters, depicting a queer subculture very in line with Halberstam's notion of queer temporality. *Shortbus* can be argued to exist primarily in the space-off, turning the camera to lives and sexualities that are almost always marginalized in mainstream cinema. The characters exist in a temporal space unmarked or unregulated by heteronormative time, enacting a collective resistance through their participation in their subcultural commitment. Whereas the film could be discussed in several of the sections of this chapter, the scene with Ceth and the older gentleman offers the most productive signal to the queer generativity explored in this section.
26. In the original *American Pie* film, from where *Another Gay Movie* parodies "Stiffler's Mom" with "Muffler's Grandfather," Stiffler's mother plays a character likened to Mrs. Robinson—a sexualized older female who seduces the younger man. In this instance, the sexual interaction between the older female and the younger man is constructed as a form of straight male conquest, introducing the acronym MILF ("Mother I'd Like to Fuck") into the vocabulary of popular culture. In *Another Gay Movie*, however, Muffler's Grandfather exists as a "gay twist" on *American Pie*, used to solicit humor. The older gay male sexual encounter is a joke, a punch line, rather than a conquest. The film relies upon the sedimented stereotypes that are signified by the older gay male body discussed previously in *Boat Trip* and *Boy Culture*. In *American Pie*, the younger heterosexual boy gained respect and praise for "bedding" an attractive, aggressive, and experienced older women, whereas Nico's sexual encounter paints an older gay male waiting for permission and awarded the attention of a young male. The discourses surrounding gay youth and "older" gay men present an obstacle to a queer model of generativity, as the sexual expression of older gay males is carefully policed by demonizing mythologies.
27. Where this study potentially breaks from Halberstam, however, is one of the foundational issues within the study's rationale—the devaluation of health and longevity present in gay youth culture. Halberstam poses the question to why we "pathologize modes of living that show little or no concern for longevity" (*Queer* 152), and this study is, perhaps, complicit of this emphasis on health and longevity for gay male and lesbian populations. However, I do not read Halberstam as condemning concerns of health or longevity, so much as asking us to interrogate the assumptions and values that often guide these concerns and how they are enmeshed and rooted in straight temporal commitments and foreclosures.
28. One of the guiding rationales for this study is situated in the investment in gay youth, the majority of whom are raised in heterosexual homes and come to understand themselves *as* youth within dominant systems of temporality. Their identity and their temporal engagement is shaped within these institutions and systems from a young age, and so—while it is potentially dangerous to rally around the concept of youth for the ways it works to solidify its fixity and interpellation into straight temporal frameworks—their identity is shaped and defined by these systems.
29. Season 1, Episode 3.

30. Season 8, Episodes 23/24.
31. Whereas Halberstam calls for an interrogation of the emphasis on youth, self-destruction, longevity, and the "pathologizing of modes of living that show little or no concern for longevity" (*Queer* 4), a full departure from these concerns marks a highly questionable and self-defeating trajectory. See also note 28 from Chapter 5.
32. The representation of a gay male thug or mobster is not without precedent, as seen in the films *The Mexican*, *The Sopranos*, and *Kiss Kiss Bang Bang*.
33. Season 2, Episode 10.
34. Season 2, Episode 6.
35. Season 1, Episode 5.
36. Season 2, Episode 10.
37. Omar repeatedly whistles this popular children's song when he is on the prowl, particularly when he has a wrong to right. The final chorus when "the cheese stands alone" is also referenced in through in the title *I Am the Cheese*, a famous novel by Robert Cormier about isolation and alienation.
38. Season 2, Episode 6.
39. Season 2, Episode 6.
40. Season 2, Episode 10.
41. In the final season of *The Wire*, Omar Little is killed off, just two episodes before the series finale. His death seemed to violate all the ways this character was introduced, as well as the ways he navigated space and time throughout the series. Walking into a corner shop to purchase a pack of cigarettes, a child no older than twelve shoots him in the head from behind. For a man who was a target and outlaw, who always seemed three steps ahead of everyone else, he allowed himself to be vulnerable in broad daylight. Furthermore, he seemed inexplicably unaware of the threat, which fails to make sense with how the character had been established. In his final episodes, he hobbled around the city, on a crutch, injured and lacking the mobility and smoothness that had come to be expected from the character. In this respect, prior to his death, Omar stopped resembling Omar and, perhaps, provided an indication of his fate. The choice of having a younger child shoot Omar from behind seems a loaded choice, providing potential counter-arguments to the innocence of the Child, or a retaliation and destruction of Omar through the revenge of the Child as queer punishment. It is in the last moment we see Omar, when he is being zipped up into a body bag at the morgue, that his age is revealed. His name card reads his birth year was 1960.
42. Reported by the news center staff as the *365.com* Web site. See <http://www.365gay.com/Newscon07/11/112907jersey.htm> for a detailed report.
43. Season 3, Episode 21, titled "S3X." The episode originally aired on ABC on April 19, 2009.
44. Season 2, Episode 6.

Bibliography

All Over the Guy. Dir. Julie Davis. Videocassette. Lions Gate Home Entertainment, 2001.
Another Gay Movie. Dir. Todd Stephens. Videodisc. TLA Releasing, 2006.
Bad Education (La Mala Educaci—n). Dir. Pedro Almod—var. Videocassette. Sony Pictures Home Entertainment, 2004.
Bad Object-Choices (Organization). *How Do I Look?: Queer Film and Video.* Seattle: Bay Press, 1991.
Baldwin, James. *Giovanni's Room: A Novel.* 1956. NY: Delta Trade Paperbacks, 2000.
Barker, Judith. "Lesbian Aging: An Agenda for Social Research." *Gay and Lesbian Aging: Research and Future Directions.* Eds. Gilbert Herdt and Brian de Vries. NY: Springer Publishing, 2004. 29–72.
Bateman, Robert Benjamin. "What Do Gay Men Desire? Peering Behind the Queer Eye." *The New Queer Aesthetic on Television: Essays on Recent Programming.* Eds. James R. Keller and Leslie Stratyner. Jefferson, NC: McFarland & Company, 2006. 9–19.
Battles, Kathleen, and Wendy Hilton-Morrow. "Gay Characters in Conventional Spaces: *Will & Grace* and the Conventional Comedy Genre." *Critical Studies in Media Communication* 19 (2002): 87–105.
Be Cool. Dir. Gary Gray. Videodisc. Metro-Goldwyn-Mayer, 2005.
Becker, Ron. *Gay TV and Straight America.* New Brunswick: Rutgers UP, 2006.
Before Night Falls. Dir. Julian Schnabel. 2000. Videodisc. New Line, 2001.
Beirne, Rebecca Clare. "Embattled Sex: Rise of the Right and Victory of the Queer in *Queer as Folk.*" *The New Queer Aesthetic on Television: Essays on Recent Programming.* Eds. James R. Keller and Leslie Stratyner. Jefferson, NC: McFarland & Company, 2006. 43–58.
Bennett, Keith C., and Norman L. Thompson. "Accelerated Aging and Male Homosexuality: Australian Evidence in a Continuing Debate." *Gay Midlife and Maturity.* Ed. John Alan Lee. NY: Hayworth, 1991. 65–76.
Benshoff, Harry M. *Monsters in the Closet: Homosexuality and the Horror Film.* Manchester: Manchester UP, 1997.
Berger, Raymond M. *Gay and Gray: The Older Homosexual Man.* Urbana: U of Illinois P, 1982.
———. "Realities of Gay and Lesbian Aging." *Social Work* 29 (1984): 57–82.
Berger, Raymond M., and James J. Kelly. "What Are Older Gay Men Like: An Impossible Question." *Midlife and Aging in Gay America.* Eds. Douglas C. Kimmel and Dawn Lundy Martin. NY: Harrington Park Press, 2001. 55–64.
Bergling, Tim. *Reeling in the Years: Gay Men's Perspectives on Age and Aging.* NY: Harrington Park Press, 2004.
Best in Show. Dir. Christopher Guest. Videodisc. Warner Bros., 2001.

Boat Trip. Dir. Mort Nathan. Videodisc. Lions Gate, 2003.
Boellstorff, Tom. "When Marriage Falls: Queer Coincidences in Straight Time." *GLQ: A Journal of Lesbian and Gay Studies* 13.2–3 (2007): 227–48.
Boy Culture. Dir. Q. Allan Brocka. 2006. Videodisc. TLA, 2007.
Boy Meets Boy (Season 1). 2003. Videodisc. New Video Group, 2004.
Boys in the Band. Dir. William Friedkin. 1970. Videodisc. Paramount, 2008.
The Breakfast Club. Dir. John Hughes. 1985. Videodisc. MCA Universal, 1998.
Brokeback Mountain. Dir. Ang Lee. Videodisc. 2005. Focus Universal, 2006.
Broken Hearts Club: A Romantic Comedy. Dir. Greg Berlanti. 2000. Videodisc. Sony, 2001.
Brookey, Robert Alan. "A Community Like *Philadelphia*." *Western Journal of Communication* 60.1 (1996): 40–56.
Brookey, Robert Alan, and Robert Westerfelhaus. "Pistols and Petticoats, Piety and Purity, *Too Wong Foo*, the Queering of the American Monomyth, and the Marginalizing Discourse of Deification." *Critical Studies in Media Communication* 18 (2001): 141–56.
Brothers & Sisters (Season 1–2). Videodisc. Buena Vista/ Touchstone, 2007–2008.
Brown, Lester B., et al. "Gay Men: Aging Well!" *Midlife and Aging in Gay America*. Eds. Douglas C. Kimmel and Dawn Lundy Martin. NY: Harrington Park Press, 2001. 41–54.
Brummett, Barry. "Rhetorical Theory as Heuristic and Moral: A Pedagogical Justification." *Communication Education* 33 (1984): 97–108.
Burke, Kenneth. *A Grammar of Motives*. 1945. Berkeley: U of California P, 1969.
———. *A Rhetoric of Motives*. 1950. Berkeley: U of California P, 1969.
———. *Attitudes toward History*. 1959. 2nd rev. ed. Boston: Beacon, 1961.
———. *Counter-Statement*. 1931. Berkeley: U of California P, 1968.
———. *Language as Symbolic Action; Essays on Life, Literature, and Method*. Berkeley: U of California P, 1966.
———. *Permanence and Change*. 1954. 2nd rev. ed. Los Altos, CA: Bobbs-Merrill, 1965.
———. *Philosophy of Literary Form*. 1941. 3rd Ed. Berkeley, CA: U of California P, 1973.
———. *The Rhetoric of Religion*. 1961. Berkeley, CA: U of California P, 1970.
Butler, Judith. "Against Proper Objects." *Feminism Meets Queer Theory*. Eds. Elizabeth Weed and Naomi Schor. Bloomington: Indiana UP, 1997. 1–30.
———. "Bodies That Matter." *Bodies That Matter: On the Discursive Limits Of "Sex"*. NY: Routledge, 1993. 27–55.
———. *Undoing Gender*. NY: Routledge, 2004.
Butsch, Richard. "Ralph, Fred, Archie, and Homer: Why Television Keeps Re-Creating the White Male Working-Class Buffoon." *Gender, Race, and Class in the Media*. Eds. Gail Dines and Jean M. Humez. 2nd ed. Thousand Oaks, CA: Sage, 2003. 575–85.
Camp. Dir. Todd Graff. 2003. Videodisc. MGM, 2004.
Carbado, Devon W. "Privilege." *Black Queer Studies: A Critical Anthology*. Eds. E. Patrick Johnson and Mae G. Henderson. Durham: Duke UP, 2005. 190–212.
Carlson, Cheree A. "Limitations of the Comic Frame: Some Witty American Women in the Nineteenth Century." *Quarterly Journal of Speech*.74 (1988): 310–22.
———. "You Know It When You See It: The Rhetorical Hierarchy of Race and Gender in 'Rhinelander v. Rhinelander.'" *Quarterly Journal of Speech*. 85 (1999): 111–28.

Carlson, Cheree A., and John E. Hocking. "Strategies of Redemption at the Vietnam Veteran's Memorial." *Western Journal of Speech Communication* 52 (1988): 203–15.

The Celluloid Closet. Dirs. Rob Epstein and Jeffrey Freidman. 1996. Videodisc. Sony Pictures, 2001.

Chuck & Buck. Dir. Miguel Arteta. Videodisc. Lions Gate, 2000.

Cloud, Dana L. "Rhetoric and Economics: Or, How Rhetoricians Can Get a Little Class." *Quarterly Journal of Speech* 88 (2002): 342–62.

Cohen, Cathy. "Punks, Bulldaggers, and Welfare Queens: The Radical Potential of Queer Politics?" *Black Queer Studies: A Critical Anthology.* Eds. E. Patrick Johnson and Mae G. Henderson. Durham: Duke UP, 2005. 21–51.

Cohler, Bertram J. "Saturday Night at the Tubs: Age Cohort and Social Life at the Urban Gay Bath." *Gay and Lesbian Aging.* Eds. Gilbert Herdt and Brian de Vries. NY: Springer Publishing, 2004. 211–34.

Commando. Dir. Mark L. Lester. 1985, Videodisc. 20th Century Fox, 1999.

Connie and Carla. Dir. Michael Lembeck. Videodisc. Universal Pictures, 2004.

Consequence (Die Konsequenz). Dir. Wolfgang Peterson 1977. Videodisc.Water Bearer, 2006.

Conway, Richard J. "A Trip to the Queer Circus: Reimagined Masculinities in *Will & Grace.*" *The New Queer Aesthetic on Television: Essays on Recent Programming.* Eds. James R. Keller and Leslie Stratyner. Jefferson, NC: McFarland & Company, 2006. 75–84.

Cooper, Dennis. *Closer.* NY: Grove Press, 1989.

———. "Time is a Construct." *PoemHunter.com.* 5 Mar. 5 2008 <http://www.poemhunter.com/poem/time-is-a-construct/>

Cornell, Drucilla. "What Is Ethical Feminism?" *Feminist Contentions: A Philosophical Exchange.* Eds. Seyla Benhabib et al. NY: Routledge, 1995.

Crenshaw, Kimberlé. "The Intersection of Race and Gender." *Critical Race Theory: Key Writings That Formed the Movement.* Eds. Kimberlé Crenshaw et al. NY: New York Press, 1995. 357–83.

Cruising. Dir. William Friedkin. 1980. Videodisc. Warner Home Video, 2007.

Cruz, Michael J. *Sociological Analysis of Aging: The Gay Male Perspective.* NY: Harrington Park Press, 2003.

Dante's Cove (Seasons 1–2 and Original Pilot). 2005. Videodisc. Liberation Ent., 2007.

Dawson's Creek (Seasons 1–6 Plus Series Finale). 1998–2003. Videodisc. Sony, 2007.

The Deep End. Dirs. Scott McGehee and David Siegel. 2001. Videodisc. 20th Century Fox, 2002.

Degrassi: The Next Generation (Seasons 1–5). 2001–2005. Videodisc. Funimation, 2004–2007.

De Lauretis, Teresa. "The Technology of Gender." *Technologies of Gender: Essays on Theory, Film and Fiction.* Bloomington: Indiana UP, 1987. 1–30.

De-Lovely. Dir. Irwin Winkler. MGM Home Entertainment, 2004.

Desperate Housewives (Seasons 1–2). Videodisc. Buena Vista Home Entertainment, 2005–2006.

De Vries, Brian, and John A. Blando. "The Study of Gay and Lesbian Aging: Lessons for Social Gerontology." *Gay and Lesbian Aging.* Eds. Gilbert Herdt and Brian de Vries. NY: Springer Publishing, 2004. 3–28.

Dinshaw, Carolyn, et al. "Theorizing Queer Temporalities: A Roundtable Discussion." *GLQ* 13.2–3 (2007): 177–95.

Dorfman, Rachel, et al. "Old, Sad, and Alone: The Myth of the Aging Homosexual." *Journal of Gerontological Social Work* 24 (1995): 29–45.

Doty, Alexander. *Making Things Perfectly Queer: Interpreting Mass Culture*. Minneapolis: U of Minnesota P, 1993.

Dow, Bonnie J. "Ellen, Television, and the Politics of Gay and Lesbian Visibility." *Critical Studies in Media Communication* 18 (2001): 123–40.

Drawn Together (Season 1). 2004. Videodisc. Comedy Central, 2005.

Deuce Bigelow: European Gigolo. Dir. Mike Bigelow. Videodisc. Sony Pictures, 2005.

Duggan, Lisa. "The New Homonormativity: The Sexual Politics of Neoliberalism." *Materializing Democracy: Towards a Revitalized Cultural Politics*. Eds. Russ Castronovo and Dana D. Nelson. Durham: Duke UP, 2002. 175–94.

Dyer, Richard. *The Matter of Images: Essays on Representation*. London: Routledge, 2002.

Dynasty (Season 1). 1981. Videodisc. 20th Century Fox Home Entertainment, 2005.

Edelman, Lee. *No Future: Queer Theory and the Death Drive*. Durham: Duke UP, 2004.

Ellis, Alan L. *Gay Men at Midlife*. NY: Harrington Park Press, 2001.

An Empty Bed. Dir. Mark Gasper. Videodisc. First Run Features, 2006.

Entourage. (Seasons 2–4). 2004–2006. Videodisc. HBO, 2006–2008.

Erni, John Nguyet. "Queer Figurations in the Media: Critical Reflections on the Michael Jackson Sex Scandal." *Critical Studies in Media Communication* 15 (1998): 158–80.

The Family Stone. Dir. Thomas Bezucha. 2005. Videodisc. 20th Century Fox, 2006.

Far from Heaven. Dir. Todd Haynes. 2002. Videodisc. Universal, 2003.

Fejes, Fred. "Advertising and the Political Economy of Lesbian/Gay Identity." *Gender, Race, and Class in the Media: A Text Reader*. Eds. Gail Dines and Jean M. Humez. Thousand Oaks, CA: Sage, 2003. 212–22.

Fejes, Fred, and Kevin Petrich. "Invisibility, Homophobia, and Heterosexism: Lesbians, Gays and the Media." *Critical Studies in Media Communication*.10 (1993): 395–422.

Ferguson, Roderick A. "Of Our Normative Strivings: African American Studies and the Histories of Sexualities." *Social Text* 84/85 (2005): 85–100.

———. "Race-ing Homonormativity: Citizenship, Sociology, and Gay Identity." *Black Queer Studies: A Critical Anthology*. Eds. E. Patrick Johnson and Mae G. Henderson. Durham: Duke UP, 2005. 52–67.

Ficera, Kim. "Don't Quote Me: Anti-Gay Violence Isn't Funny, Capiche?" 2007. *Afterelton.com*. 21 Aug. 2007 <http://www.afterelton.com /TV/2007/8/joegannascoli?page=0%2C2>.

Fiske, John. "Gendered Television: Femininity." *Gender, Race, and Class in the Media*. Eds. Gail Dines and Jean M. Humez. 2nd ed. Thousand Oaks, CA: Sage, 2003. 469–75.

Foster, Guy Mark. "Desire and the 'Big Black Sex Cop': Race and the Politics of Sexual Intimacy in HBO's *Six Feet Under*." *The New Queer Aesthetic on Television: Essays on Recent Programming*. Eds. James R. Keller and Leslie Stratyner. Jefferson, NC: McFarland & Company, 2006. 99–112.

Foucault, Michel. *The History of Sexuality*. Vol. 1. 1978. Trans. Robert Hurley. NY: Vintage Books, 1990.

Fox, Ragan Cooper. "Gay Grows Up: An Interpretive Study on Aging Metaphors and Queer Identity." *Journal of Homosexuality* 52.3/4 (2007): 33–61.

Freebie and the Bean. Dir. Richard Rush. 1974. Videodisc. Warner, 2009.

Freud, Sigmund. *Three Essays on the Theory of Sexuality*. 1962. NY: Basic Books, 2000.

Friend, R. A. "Gayging: Adjustment and the Older Gay Male." *Alternative Lifestyles* 3 (1980): 231–48.

Friends: The Complete Series. 1994–2004. Videodisc. NBC, 2006.
Fuss, Diana. "Lesbian and Gay Theory: The Question of Identity Politics." *Essentially Speaking: Feminism, Nature and Difference.* NY: Routledge, 1989. 97–112.
Gabbay, Sarah G., and James W. Wahler. "Lesbian Aging: Review of a Growing Literature." *Journal of Gay and Lesbian Social Services* 14.3 (2002): 1–21.
Gamson, Joshua. "Sexualities, Queer Theory, and Qualitative Research." *Handbook of Qualitative Research.* Eds. Norman K. Denzin and Yvonna S. Lincoln. 2nd ed. Thousand Oaks, CA: Sage, 2000. 347–65.
———. "Sitting Ducks and Forbidden Fruits." *Gender, Race, and Class in the Media.* Eds. Gail Dines and Jean M. Humez. 2nd ed. Thousand Oaks, CA: Sage 2000. 553–74.
Gever, Martha, John Greyson, and Pratibha Parmar. *Queer Looks: Perspectives on Lesbian and Gay Film and Video.* NY: Routledge, 1993.
Gilbert, Daniel. *Stumbling on Happiness.* NY: Vintage, 2005.
Giles, Howard, et al. "Future Selves and Others: A Lifespan and Cross-Cultural Perspective." *Communication Reports* 16.1 (2003): 1–22.
Goltz, Dustin B. "Investigating Queer Future Meanings: Destructive Perceptions of 'the Harder Path.'" *Qualitative Inquiry* 15.3 (2009): 561–86.
———. "Laughing at Absence: *Instinct* Magazine and the Hyper-Masculine Gay Future?" *Western Journal of Communication* 71.2 (2007): 93–113.
———. "Perspectives by Incongruity: Kenneth Burke and Queer Theory." *Genders Online Journal* 45 (2007). 12 Oct. 2007 <http://www.genders.org/g45/g45_goltz.html>.
Gorman, Michael E, and Keith Nelson. "From a Far Place: Considerations About HIV Among Midlife and Older Gay Men." *Gay and Lesbian Aging.* Eds. Gilbert Herdt and Brian de Vries. NY: Springer Publishing, 2004. 73–96.
Groomsmen. Dir. Edward Burns. Videodisc. Bauer Martinez Studios, 2006.
Gross, Larry. "Gideon Who Will Be 25 in the Year 2012: Growing up Gay Today." *International Journal of Communication* 1 (2007): 121–38.
———. "Minorities, Majorities and the Media." *Media, Ritual and Identity.* Eds. Tama Liebes and James Curran. NY: Routledge, 1998. 87–102.
———. "Out of the Mainstream: Sexual Minorities and the Mass Media." *Media and Cultural Studies: Keyworks.* Eds. Meenakshi Gigi Durham and Douglas M. Kellner. Malden: Blackwell, 2001. 405–23.
———. "The Paradoxical Politics of Media Representation." *Critical Studies in Media Communication* 18.1 (2001): 114–19.
———. *Up from Invisibility: Lesbians, Gay Men, and the Media in America.* NY: Columbia UP, 2001.
———. "What Is Wrong with This Picture? Lesbian Women and Gay Men on Television." *Queer Words, Queer Images: Communication and the Construction of Homosexuality.* Ed. Jeffrey Ringer. NY: New York UP, 1994. 143–58.
A Guide to Recognizing Your Saints. Dir. Dito Montiel. 2006. Videodisc. First Look International, 2007.
Hajek, Christopher, and Howard Giles. "The Old Man Out: An Intergroup Analysis of Intergenerational Communication among Gay Men." *Intergenerational Communication* (2002): 698–714.
Halberstam, Judith. *In a Queer Time and Place: Transgender Bodies, Subcultural Lives.* NY: New York UP, 2005.
———. "Shame and White Gay Masculinity." *Social Text* 84/85 (2005): 219–34.
Hall, Stuart. "The Whites of Their Eyes: Racist Ideologies in the Media." *Gender, Race, and Class in the Media.* Eds. Gail Dines and Jean M. Humez. 2nd ed. Thousand Oaks, CA: Sage, 2003. 89–93.
Happy Endings. Dir. Don Roos. Videodisc. Lions Gate Home Entertainment, 2005.

Bibliography

Harris, Mark. "Entertainer of the Year: J. K. Rowling " *Entertainment Weekly* 30 Nov. 2007: 35–8.
Harry Potter and the Prisoner of Azkaban. Dir. Alfonso Cuar—n. Videodisc. Warner Bros. Entertainment, 2004.
Hart, Kylo Patrick R. "Representing Gay Men on American Television." *Gender, Race, and Class in the Media*. Eds. Gail Dines and Jean M. Humez. 2nd ed. Thousand Oaks, CA: Sage 2000. 597–607.
Hellbent. Dir. Paul Etheridge-Ouzts. 2004. Videodisc. Liberation Ent., 2006.
Herdt, Gilbert H., and Brian de Vries. *Gay and Lesbian Aging: Research and Future Directions*. NY: Springer Pub. Co., 2004.
The History Boys. Dir. Nicholas Hytner. 2006. Videodisc. 20th Century Fox Home Entertainment, 2007.
A Home at the End of the World. Dir. Michael Mayer. Videodisc. Warner Independent, 2004.
hooks, bell. "Eating the Other: Desire and Resistance." *Media and Cultural Studies: Keyworks*. Eds. Meenakshi Gigi Durham and Douglas M. Kellner. Malden: Blackwell, 2001. 424–38.
Hornby, Nick. *A Long Way Down*. NY: Riverhead Books, 2006.
Hostetler, Andrew J. "Old, Gay, and Alone? The Ecology of Well-Being Among Middle-Aged and Older Single Gay Men." *Gay and Lesbian Aging*. Eds. Gilbert Herdt and Brian de Vries. NY: Springer Publishing, 2004. 143–76.
The Hours. Dir. Stephen Daldry. 2002. Videodisc. Paramount, 2003.
I Now Pronounce You Chuck and Larry. Dir. Dennis Dugan. Videodisc. Universal, 2007.
Isherwood, Christopher. *A Single Man*. 1964. NY: Quality Paperback Book Club, 1992.
Jackson, Ronald L. "White Space, White Privilege: Mapping Discursive Inquiry into Self." *Quarterly Journal of Speech* 85 (1999): 38–54.
Jagose, Annamarie. *Queer Theory: An Introduction*. NY: New York UP, 1996.
Johnson, E. Patrick. "'Quare' Studies, or (Almost) Everything I Know About Queer Studies I Learned from My Grandmother." *Text & Performance Quarterly* 21.1 (2001): 1–25.
Jordan, A. B. "Social Class, Temporal Orientation, and Mass Media Use Within the Family System." *Critical Studies in Mass Communication* 9 (1992): 374–87.
Katz, Jonathon Ned. *The Invention of Heterosexuality*. NY: Plume, 1996.
Kellner, Douglas. "Cultural Studies, Multiculturalism, and Media Culture." *Gender, Race, and Class in the Media: A Text Reader*. Eds. Gail Dines and Jean M. Humez. Thousand Oaks, CA: Sage, 2003. 9–20.
Kelly, J. "The Aging Male Homosexual." *The Gerontologist* 17 (1977): 328–32.
Kertzner, Robert, Ilan Meyer, and Curtis Dolezal. "Psychological Well-Being in Midlife and Older Gay Men." *Gay and Lesbian Aging*. Eds. Gilbert Herdt and Brian de Vries. NY: Springer Publishing, 2004. 97–116.
Kilbourne, Jean. "'The More You Subtract, the More You Add': Cutting Girls Down to Size." *Gender, Race, and Class in the Media*. Eds. Gail Dines and Jean M. Humez. 2nd ed. Thousand Oaks, CA: Sage, 2003. 258–67.
Kimmel, Douglas C. "Issues to Consider in Studies of Midlife and Older Sexual Minorities." *Gay and Lesbian Aging*. Eds. Gilbert Herdt and Brian de Vries. NY: Springer, 2004. 265–84.
Kinsey. Dir. Bill Condon. 2004. Videodisc. 20th Century Fox, 2005.
Kiss Kiss Bang Bang. Dir. Shane Black. 2005. Videodisc. Warner Home Video, 2006.
Kissing Jessica Stein. Dir. Charles Herman-Wurmfeld. 2001. Videodisc. 20th Century Fox, 2002.

Kooden, Harold, and Charles Flowers. *Golden Men: The Power of Gay Midlife.* NY: Avon Books, 2000.
L.I.E. Dir. Michael Cuesta. 2001. Videodisc. New Yorker Video, 2002.
Lacey, Nick. *Introduction to Film.* NY: Palgrave Macmillan 2005.
Lacroix, Celeste, and Robert Westerfelhaus. "From the Closet to the Loft: Liminal License and Socio-Sexual Separation in *Queer Eye for the Straight Guy.*" *Qualitative Research Reports in Communication* 6.1 (2005): 11–9.
Lantana. Dir. Ray Lawrence. 2001. Videodisc. Lions Gate Films, 2002.
Laramie Project. Dir. Moisés Kaufman. 2001. Videodisc. HBO Home Video, 2002.
Latter Days. Dir. C. Jay Fox. 2003. Videodisc. TLA Releasing, 2004.
Lee, John A. "Foreword." *Gay Midlife and Maturity.* Ed. John Alan Lee. Binghampton, NY: Harrington Park Press, 1991. xiii–xix.
Little Miss Sunshine. Dirs. Jonathon Dayton and Valerie Faris. Videodisc. 20th Century Fox, 2006.
Locke, Brian. "Here Comes the Judge: The Dancing Itos and the Televisual Construction of the Enemy Asian Male." *Gender, Race, and Class in the Media.* Eds. Gail Dines and Jean M. Humez. 2nd ed. Thousand Oaks, CA: Sage, 2003. 651–55.
Love and Death on Long Island. Dir. Richard Kwietiowski. 1998. Videodisc. Lions Gate, 2003.
Luciano, Dana. "Coming Around Again: The Queer Momentum of *Far From Heaven.*" *GLQ* 13.2–3 (2007): 249–72.
Lucky Number Slevin. Dir. Paul McGuigan. Videodisc. The Weinstein Company, 2006.
MacDonald, Ron, and Trudi Cooper. "Young Gay Men and Suicide." *Youth Studies Australia* 17 (1998): 23–8.
Making Love. Dir. Arthur Hiller 1982. Videodisc. 20th Century Fox, 2006.
Mambo Italiano. Dir. Émile Gaudreault. 2003. Videodisc. Samuel Goldwyn Films, 2004.
Mamma Mia! The Movie. Dir. Phyllida Lloyd. Videodisc. Universal, 2008.
Manalansan, Martin F. "Race, Violence, and Neoliberal Spatial Politics in the Global City." *Social Text* 84/85 (2005): 141–56.
Manchurian Candidate. Dir. John Frankenheimer 1962. Videodisc. MGM/UA Home Entertainment, 2004.
Maupin, Armistead. *Michael Tolliver Lives.* NY: Harper-Luxe, 2007.
McIntosh, Peggy. "White Privilege and Male Privilege." *Race, Class, and Gender: An Anthology.* Eds. Margaret L. Anderson and Patricia Hill Collins. NY: Wadsworth. 1993. 76–87.
McKerrow, Raymie. "Critical Rhetoric: Theory and Praxis." *Contemporary Rhetorical Theory: A Reader.* Eds. John Louis Lucaites, Celeste Michelle Condit and Sally Caudill. NY: Guilford Press, 1999. 441–63.
Mean Girls. Dir. Mark Waters. Videodisc. Paramount Home Entertainment, 2004.
The Mexican. Dir. J. H. Wyman. 2000. Videodisc. Dreamworks Video, 2001.
Midnight Cowboy. Dir. John Schlesinger. 1969. Videodisc. MGM/UA Home Entertainment, 2006.
Milk. Dir. Gus Van Sant, 2008. Videodisc. Universal, 2009
Minnegerode, F. A. "Age Status Labeling in Homosexual Men." *Journal of Homosexuality* 1 (1976): 273–76.
Miss Congeniality. Dir. Donald Petrie. 2000. Videodisc. Warner Bros., 2004.
Mitchell, Danielle. "Straight and Crazy? Bisexual and Easy? Or Drunken Floozy? The Queer Politics of Karen Walker." *The New Queer Aesthetic on Television.* Eds. James R. Keller and Leslie Stratyner. Jefferson, NC: McFarland and Company, 2006. 75–84.

Bibliography

Morrison, Linda, and Jeff L'Heureux. "Suicide and Gay/Lesbian/Bisexual Youth: Implications for Clinicians." *Journal of Adolescence* 24 (2001): 39–50.

Muñoz, José Esteban. "Cruising the Toilet: Leroi Jones/Amiri Baraka, Radical Black Traditions, and Queer Futurity." *GLQ: A Journal of Lesbian and Gay Studies* 13.2–3 (2007): 353–67.

———. *Disidentifications: Queers of Color and the Performance of Politics*. Minneapolis: U of Minnesota P, 1999.

———. "Feeling Brown: Ethnicity and Affect in Ricardo Bracho's 'the Sweetest Hangover (and Other STD's).'" *Theatre Journal* 52 (2000): 67–79

———. "Impossible Spaces: Kevin McCarthy's Chameleon Club." *Gay & Lesbian Quarterly* 11.3 (2005): 427–36.

———. "Stages: Punks, Queers, and the Utopian Performance." *The Sage Handbook of Performance Studies*. Eds. D. Soyini Madison and Judith Hamera. Thousand Oaks, CA: Sage, 2006. 9–20.

My Best Friend's Wedding. Dir. P. J. Hogan. Videocassette. Sony Pictures, 1997.

Mysterious Skin. Dir. Gregg Araki. 2005. Videodisc. Strand Releasing, 2005.

Nero, Charles I. "Why Are Gay Ghettos White?" *Black Queer Studies: A Critical Anthology*. Eds. E. Patrick Johnson and Mae G. Henderson. Durham: Duke UP, 2005. 228–48.

The Next Best Thing. Dir. John Schlesinger. Videodisc. Paramount, 2000.

Nicholas, Jonathon, and John Howard. "Better Dead Than Gay." *Youth Studies Australia* 17 (1998): 28–34.

The Night Listener. Dir. Patrick Stettner. 2006. Videodisc. Miramax Films, 2007.

A Nightmare on Elm Street. Dir. Wes Craven. Videocassette. New Line Entertainment, 1984.

Nine Dead Gay Guys. Dir. Lab Ky Mo. 2003. Videodisc. TLA Releasing, 2004.

Noah's Arc (Seasons 1–2). Dir. Patrick Ian Polk. 2005–2006. Videodisc. MTV Networks, 2006–2007.

Ono, Kent A., and John M. Sloop. "Commitment to Telos—a Sustained Critical Rhetoric." *Communication Monographs* 59.1 (1992): 48–60.

Ott, Brian L., and Eric Aoki. "The Politics of Negotiating Public Tragedy: Media Framing of the Matthew Shepard Murder." *Rhetoric & Public Affairs* 5.3 (2002): 483–505.

Peele, Thomas. "Introduction: Popular Culture, Queer Culture." *Queer Popular Culture: Literature, Media, Film, and Television*. Ed. Thomas Peele. NY: Palgrave Macmillan, 2007. 1–8.

Perez, Hiram. "You Can Have My Brown Body and Eat It Too!" *Social Text* 84/85 (2005): 171–92.

Philadelphia. Dir. Jonathan Demme. 1993. Videodisc. Sony Home Entertainment, 1997.

Pieterse, Jan Nederveen. "White Negroes." *Gender, Race, and Class in the Media*. Eds. Gail Dines and Jean M. Humez. 2nd ed. Thousand Oaks, CA: Sage, 2003. 111–15.

Police Academy. Dir. Hugh Wilson. 1984. Videocassette. Warner Home Video, 1997.

Porfido. Giovanni. "*Queer as Folk* and the Spectacularization of Gay Identity." *Queer Popular Culture: Literature, Media, Film, and Television*. Ed. Thomas Peele. NY: Palgrave Macmillan, 2007. 57–70.

Poseidon. Dir. Wolfgang Peterson. Videodisc. Warner Home Video, 2006.

The Producers. Dir. Susan Stroman. 2005. Videodisc. Universal Pictures, 2006.

Queer as Folk: The Complete Series. 2000–2005. Videodisc. Showtime, 2007.

"Queer Eye for the Red Sox." *Queer Eye for the Straight Guy*. Dir Steven Kijak et al. 2003. Videodisc. Genius Entertainment, 2005.

Quinceañera. Dirs. Richard Glatzer and Wash Westmoreland. 2005. Videodisc. Sony Pictures, 2007.
Rand, Ayn. *The Fountainhead*. 1943. 50th Anniversary Ed. NY: Signet: The Penguin Group, 1993.
Rawls, Todd W. "Disclosure and Depression among Older Gay Men and Homosexual Men: Findings from the Urban Men's Study." *Gay and Lesbian Aging*. Eds. Gilbert Herdt and Brian de Vries. NY: Springer, 2004.
Reality Bites. Dir. Ben Stiller. 1994. Videodisc. Universal, 1998.
Rechy, John. *Bodies and Souls*. NY: Grove Press, 1983.
Reid, John (Andrew Tobias). *The Best Little Boy in the World*. 25th Anniversary ed. NY: Ballantine Books, 1998.
Remafedi, Gary. *Death by Denial: Studies of Suicide in Gay and Lesbian Teenagers*. Boston: Alyson Publications, 1994.
———. "Sexual Orientation and Youth Suicide." *Journal of the American Medical Association* 282 (1999): 1291–2.
Reno 911! (Season 1–2). 2003–2004. Videodisc. Comedy Central, 2004–2005.
Rent. Dir. Chris Columbus. 2005. Videodisc. Sony Pictures Entertainment, 2006.
Rick and Steve: The Happiest Gay Couple in the World (Season 1). Videodisc. MTV, 2007.
Rofes, Eric E. *I Thought People Like That Killed Themselves: Lesbians, Gay Men, and Suicide*. San Francisco: Grey Fox Press, 1983.
Román, David. "Negative Identifications: HIV-Negative Gay Men in Representation and Performance." *Queer Representations: Reading Lives, Reading Cultures: A Center for Lesbian and Gay Studies Book*. Ed. Martin Duberman. NY: New York UP, 1997. 162–76.
Romesburg, Don. "Suicidal Tendencies in Gay Youth." *Advocate* 5 April 1994: 5.
Ross, Marlon B. "Beyond the Closet as Raceless Paradigm." *Black Queer Studies: A Critical Anthology*. Eds. E. Patrick Johnson and Mae G. Henderson. Durham: Duke UP, 2005. 161–89.
The Rules of Attraction. Dir. Roger Avary. 2002. Videodisc. Lions Gate Films, 2003.
Running with Scissors. Dir. Ryan Murphy. 2006. Videodisc. Sony, 2007.
Russo, Vito. *The Celluloid Closet: Homosexuality in the Movies*. Rev. ed. NY: Harper & Row, 1987.
Sandoval, Chela. "Dissonent Globalizations, Emancipatory Methods, Social Erotics." *Queer Globalizations: Citizenship and the Afterlife of Colonialism*. Eds. A. Cruz-Malave and M. Manalansan. NY: New York UP, 2002. 20–32.
Sater, Steven. *Spring Awakening*. NY: Theatre Communications Group, 2007.
Saturday Night Live. Dir. Don Roy King. Guest Star Brian Williams. NBC, 3 Nov. 2007.
Saved! Dir. Brian Donnelly. 2003. Videodisc. MGM, 2004.
Schiappa, Edward. *Beyond Representational Correctness: Rethinking Criticism of Popular Culture*. NY: State U of NY P, 2008.
Sedgwick, Eve Kosofsky. *Epistemology of the Closet*. Berkeley: U of California P, 1990.
Seidman, Steven. *Beyond the Closet: The Transformation of Gay and Lesbian Life*. NY: Routledge, 2002.
Sender, Katherine. "Gay Readers, Consumers, and a Dominant Gay Habitus: 25 Years of the *Advocate* Magazine." *Journal of Communication* 51 (2001): 73–99.
Sex and the City: The Complete Series. 1998–2004. Videodisc. HBO, 2005.
The Shield (Season 1). 2002. Videodisc. 20th Century Fox, 2003.
Shock to the System: A Donald Strachey Mystery. Dir. Ron Oliver. 2006. Videodisc. Regent Entertainment, 2007.

Shome, Raka. "Race and Popular Culture: The Rhetorical Strategies of Whiteness in *City of Joy*." *Communication Quarterly* 44.5 (1996): 502–18.
Shortbus. Dir. John Cameron Mitchell. 2006. Velocity/Videodisc. ThinkFilm, 2007.
Shugart, Helene A. "Reinventing Privilege: The New (Gay) Man in Contemporary Popular Media." *Critical Studies in Media Communication* 20 (2003): 67–91
Six Feet Under: The Complete Series. 2001–2005. Videodisc. HBO, 2006.
Sloop, John M. "Disciplining the Transgendered: Brandon Teena, Public Representation, and Normativity." *Western Journal of Speech Communication* 64.2 (2000): 165–89.
———. "In a Queer Time and Place and Race: Intersectionality Comes of Age." *Quarterly Journal of Speech* 91.3 (2005): 312–26.
The Sopranos (Season 6, Part 1). Videodisc. HBO, 2006.
South Park (Season 7). 1997. Videodisc. Comedy Central, 2006.
South Park (Season 11). 2001. Videodisc. Comedy Central, 2008.
Spin City: Michael J. Fox's All-Time Favorites Vol. 2. Videodisc. Dreamworks Home Video, 2003.
Storey, John. *Cultural Theory and Popular Culture*. 3rd ed. Harlow, England: Pearson, 2001.
Suddenly Last Summer. Dir. Joseph L. Mankiewicz 1959. Videodisc. Sony Pictures, 2000.
Sweet Home Alabama. Dir. Andy Tennant. 2002. Videodisc. Buena Vista Pictures, 2003.
Talk to Her (Hable Con Ella). Dir. Pedro Almod—var. 2002. Videodisc. Sony Pictures Classics.
Talladega Nights: The Ballad of Ricky Bobby. Dir. Adam McKay. Videodisc. Columbia Pictures, 2006.
Thomas, Kate. "What Time We Kiss: Michael Field's Queer Temporalities." *GLQ* 13.2–3 (2007): 327–51.
Three to Tango. Dir. Damon Santostefano. 1999. Videodisc. Warner, 2000.
Tobias, Andrew. *The Best Little Boy in the World Grows Up*. NY: Random House, 1998.
Tompkins, Phillip K., and George Cheney. "On the Limits and Sub-Stance of Kenneth Burke and His Critics." *Quarterly Journal of Speech* 79 (1993): 225–31.
Touch of Pink. Dir. Ian Iqbal Rashid. 2004. Videodisc. Sony Pictures, 2005.
Tough Guise: Violence, Media, and the Crisis of Masculinity. Featuring Jackson Katz. Dir. Sut Jhally. Written by Jackson Katz and Jeremy Earp. MEF, 1999.
Trick. Dir. Jim Fall. 1999. Videodisc. New Line Home Video, 2000.
Tropiano, Stephen. *The Primetime Closet: A History of Gays and Lesbians on Television*. NY: Applause Theater and Cinema Books, 2002.
Trujillo, Nick. "Hegemonic Masculinity on the Mound: Media Representations of Nolan Ryan and American Sports Culture." *Critical Studies in Mass Communication* 8.3 (1991): 290–308.
Ugly Betty (Season 1). 2006. Videodisc. Buena Vista/ Touchstone, 2007.
V for Vendetta. Dir. James McTeigue. Videodisc. Warner Bros., 2006.
Vaid, Urvashi. *Virtual Equality: The Mainstreaming of Gay and Lesbian Liberation*. NY: Doubleday, 1995.
Villarejo, Amy. "Tarrying with the Normative: Queer Theory and Black History." *Social Text* 84/85 (2005): 69–84.
Walters, Suzanna Danuta. *All the Rage: The Story of Gay Visibility in America*. Chicago: U of Chicago P, 2001.

Wander, Phillip. "The Third Persona: An Ideological Turn in Rhetorical Theory." *Contemporary Rhetorical Theory: A Reader.* Eds. J. L Lucaites, C. M. Condit, and S. Caudill. NY: Guilford Press, 1999. 357–80.
Warner, Michael. "Introduction." *Fear of a Queer Planet: Queer Politics and Social Theory.* Ed. Michael Warner. Minneapolis: U of Minnesota P, 1993. vii–xxxi.
———. *The Trouble with Normal: Sex, Politics, and the Ethics of Queer Life.* NY: Free Press, 1999.
Wedding Wars. Dir. Jim Fall 2006. Videodisc. Sony, 2007.
Wilde, Oscar. *The Picture of Dorian Gray.* 1890. Barnes & Noble Classics Ed., NY, 2003.
Will & Grace (The Complete Series). 1998–2006. Videodisc. Lionsgate, 2008.
Williams, Raymond. "Culture Is Ordinary." *Resources of Hope: Culture, Democracy, Socialism.* Eds. Raymond Williams and Robin Gable. London: Verso, 1989.
Wilson, Clint C., and Félix Gutiérrez. "Advertising and People of Color." *Gender, Race, and Class in the Media.* Eds. Gail Dines and Jean M. Humez. 2nd ed. Thousand Oaks, CA: Sage, 2003. 283–92.
The Wire (The Complete Series). 2002–2008. Videodisc. HBO, 2008.
Wonder Boys. Dir. Curtis Hanson. Videodisc. Paramount Home Video, 2000.
Yep, Gust A. "The Violence of Heteronormativity in Communication Studies: Notes on Injury, Healing and Queer World-Making." *Queer Theory and Communication: From Disciplining Queers to Queering the Discipline(s).* Eds. Gust A. Yep, Karen E. Lovaas, and John P. Elia. NY: Harrington Park Press, 2003. 11–60.
Yep, Gust A., and John P. Elia. "Performing Black Queer Masculinities in *Noah's Arc.*" *93rd Annual National Communication Association National Convention.* Chicago, IL, 2007.
———. "Queering/Quaring Blackness in *Noah's Arc.*" *Queer Popular Culture: Literature, Media, Film, and Television.* Ed. Thomas Peele. NY: Palgrave Macmillan, 2007. 27–40.
Yoakam, John R. "Gods or Monsters? A Critique of Representations in Film and Literature of Relationships Between Older Gay Men and Younger Men." *Midlife and Aging in Gay America.* Eds. Douglas C. Kimmel and Dawn Lundy Martin. NY: Harrington Park Press, 2001. 65–80.
Zook, Kristal Brent. "The Fox Network and the Revolution in Black Television." *Gender, Race, and Class in the Media.* Eds. Gail Dines and Jean M. Humez. 2nd ed. Thousand Oaks, CA: Sage, 2003. 586–96.

About the Author

Dustin Bradley Goltz is an Assistant Professor in the College of Communication in performance studies and rhetoric at DePaul University. He teaches courses on the performance of literature, queer theory, the performance of gender and sexuality, the rhetoric of popular culture, and performance art. Goltz received his PhD from Arizona State University from the Hugh Downs School of Human Communication and his MFA from the Art Institute of Chicago. He has recently published research in *Text and Performance Quarterly, Genders, Liminalities, Western Journal of Communication,* and *Qualitative Inquiry.* As an artist and a performer, Goltz also produces solo and collaborative multimedia work. Recent projects include *Blasphemies on Forever: Remember Queer Futures, Lines in the Sand: Fear, Loss, and Whiteness in U.S. Media's Representations of Contemporary Mexican Immigration, I Can't (Death) Drive 55;* and *Banging the Bishop: Latter Day Prophecy.*

Index

A
Accelerated aging, 5, 63–64, 157, 164–65
Aging; defined 4–5; conceptions of "old" 7
AIDS, 6, 8, 9, 27, 38, 50, 54–55, 70, 72–73, 79, 129, 135, 146
All Over the Guy, 86, 168n37
Another Gay Movie, 109, 140–141, 168n37, 173n26

B
Bad Education (La Mala Educación), 66
Bad Object-Choices. 160
Baldwin, James. 19, 20, 51, 56, 64
Barker, Judith, 5, 6, 7
Bateman, Robert Benjamin, 39, 86, 101, 102
Battles, Kathleen, and Wendy Hilton-Morrow, 12, 38, 39, 86, 100, 120, 145, 161–162n16
Be Cool, 169n49
Becker, Ron. 27, 38, 100
Before Night Falls, 106
Beirne, Rebecca Clare, 103
Bennett, Keith C., and Norman L. Thompson, 157n5, 164–165n59
Benshoff, Harry M., 48
Berger, Raymond, 5, 6, 7, 8, 10, 79
Berger, Raymond M., and James J. Kelly, 79. 157n5
Bergling, Tim, 7, 61, 64, 73
Best in Show, 67, 107, 169n49
Boat Trip.66, 67, 76, 86, 100, 107
Boellstorff, Tom., 9–10, 16, 17, 47–48, 60, 117, 129, 131, 133–134, 137, 142
Boy Culture, 63–64, 72, 77, 102, 130
Boy Meets Boy, 87, 94–95
Boys in the Band, 3, 20, 21, 23, 24, 28, 34
The Breakfast Club, 25–6
Brokeback Mountain, 4, 20, 24; violence, 51; gay misery. 56, 57; scapegoating; 91; space-off, 121–122, 129
Broken Hearts Club: A Romantic Comedy, 70, 74, 76, 97, 104, 109, 127, 130
Brookey, Robert Alan. 15, 22, 27, 28, 38, 46, 159n2, 160n13; identification, 83, 87, 90, 97
Brookey, Robert Alan, and Robert Westerfelhaus. 12, 26, 27, 38, 96, 160n13
Brothers & Sisters, 90, 95, 97, 153–4, 168n34
Brown, Lester B., et al., 7, 65, 79, 164n59
Brummett, Barry, 43, 44
Burke, Kenneth. 15, 30, 78; alienation, 83, 90; bridging device, 39–40, 42, 83, 84, 87, 93, 104, 105, 169–170n56; casuistic stretching, 39, 84; comic frame, 41, 42–3, 44, 118, 120, 122, 133; guilt, 31–2; hierarchy, 32; identification, 81–4, 88; iron law of history, 28–34, 35, 160n11; mortification., 33, 51, 98; orientation, 30, 47; perfection and the negative, 31, 32; perspective by incongruity, 41–2, 43, 84, 91, 115–23, 151; poetic frames, 47, 160n10; scapegoating, 50, 90, 98, 160n11; substance, 81, 83, 120; symbolic merger, 91; tragic

frame, 30, 32, 35, 47, 49, 63, 69, 70, 83
Butler, Judith, 37, 44, 46, 158n8, 166n2
Butsch, Richard, 159n2

C
Camp, 49, 50, 58, 86, 146
Carbado, Devon W., 110
Carlson, A. Cheree, and John E. Hocking., 160n11
Carlson, Cheree A., 40, 43, 169–170n56
The Celluloid Closet (Film), 34, 35, 46 (see also Vito Russo)
Chicago, Judy., 115–5, 171n2
Chuck & Buck, 59, 85
Cloud, Dana, 159n2
Closet (as metaphor), 19, 24, 40
coalition., 26, 84, 104, 108, 123–8, 130, 166n5
Cohen, Cathy, 25, 37, 104, 125
Cohler, Bertram J., 6, 8, 26
Commando, 22
Connie and Carla, 86
Consequence (Die Konsequenz), 20
Conway, Richard J., 102, 168n35
Cooper, Dennis. 18, 53, 74, 77–8
Cornell, Drucilla, 21, 42, 161
Cruising, 24
Cruz, Michael J., 5, 6, 7
cultural studies, 11–2, 14, 23
critical rhetoric, 43

D
Dante's Cove, 53, 64, 74, 109
Dawson's Creek; violence, 50, 51; self-destruction, 53; harder road, 57, 59; older gay male bodies, 66–7; future, 79; "normal"/identifiable gay male, 81, 86, 92, 98, 168n35; apolitical, 99, 101; patriarchal, 109; finale, 111; Jen Lindley/queer, 131–2, 145, 172n13
Death in Venice, 6
The Deep End, 78
De Lauretis, Teresa, 23; gender construction 12; space-off/elsewhere 28, 41, 44, 46, 115–23
Degrassi: The Next Generation, 50, 57, 100
De-Lovely, 119–21
Desperate Housewives, 95

De Vries, Brian, and John A. Blando, 5, 6, 128, 157n5
Dorfman, Rachel, et al., 7, 79
Doty, Alexander. 159–160n6
Dow, Bonnie J. 12, 27, 38, 136, 160, 161–162n16
Drawn Together, 49, 52, 87
Deuce Bigelow: European Gigolo, 169n49
Duggan, Lisa, 16, 39, 40, 158, 84, 93, 99, 110, 152, 166n2
Dumbledore, Albus, 1–2, 4, 7, 15
Dyer, Richard, 25, 34
Dynasty, 23, 36–7

E
Edelman, Lee, 10, 17, 56, 60, 83, 88, 93, 113, 119, 142, 152
Ellis, Alan L., 5, 6, 7
Empty Bed, 68, 122
Erni, John Nguyet. 27, 44, 114, 160n13, 161n15

F
Fallibilism., 43, 44, 162n18
The Family Stone, 87
Far From Heaven, 123–126. 127, 145, 146
Fejes, Fred, and Kevin Petrich. 15, 23, 29, 33–34, 38, 57, 159n4, 167n21
Fejes, Fred, 12, 27
Ferguson, Roderick A., 104, 110
Fiske, John. 159n2
Foster, Guy Mark, 108
Foucault, Michel, 12, 106, 158n7, 160n7
Fox, Ragan Cooper, 26, 66, 78
Freddy Krueger, 48–49, 56, 61, 64, 76, 79
Freebie and the Bean, 33
Freud, Sigmund, 59
Friend, R. A., 157n5
Friends, 109
Fuss, Diana, 158n7
Future; gay male site of fear/doom, 8, 48–49, 56–61; tied to aging and queer critique 13, 41; more about past 28; defined 157n2; uniquely human, 31; ties to heteronormativity 41, 58–59, 60, 63–64, 82; identification with, 82, 88; defined as marriage/child, 85

Futurity., 17, 45, 79, 80, 117, 119, 121; in relation to future, 60

G
Gabbay, Sarah G., and James W. Wahler, 5, 6
Gamson, Joshua., 98, 158n8
gay; use of term in study 158n7
gay male aging; as culturally distinct process, 5–7; as loss, 8, 64, 77; as tragic/symbolic punishment, 16, 47–49, 69, 74–76; complications facing 6, 7, 13; negative mythologies, 3,6,7,8; pedophilia, 65–66, 69–70; positive findings, 7; arrested development, 59–60; coding of older gay male body, 66–67; invisibility, 68, 70–72; contained, 77
gay male culture.; absences in Hollywood representations, 45, 113, 154, 157–158n6, 160n14; consumerist critiques 12, 27; linked to HIV/AIDS, 9; relationship to media and representation 12, 21, 22, 23, 24, 26–27, 28; youth/value connected to beauty, 8, 62-3; youthism 6, 7, 57–8, 73–80, 123, 128, 136; ageist/youthist binary, 78–9, 143; drug use, 52–3, 163; relationship to death 55–6; rejected by assimilationist, 90–1; constructed as shallow, 97; cosmopolitanism, 107–108, 116
gay male youth; negative meanings of aging 3; lack of role models, 8, 24, 26, 66; self-destructive tendencies, 10; upholding notion, 173n28
gay representation; pre 90s, 3, 12, 20, 29, 31, 32–33, 40–41, 159; post 90s, 3, 12, 15, 20, 24, 27, 28, 34, 38, 160; "normal"/identifiable/assimilationist gay male, 80, 81–111; notions of progress, 20–21, 47; self-loathing, 33–4, 97–8, 168n35; misogynist/patriarchal, 109–10
generativity, defined 8, 128; absence in gay culture and representation 26, 45; tied to future meaning; queered, 130–31, 136–142, 152–3
Gever, Martha, John Greyson, and Pratibha Parmar., 160

Gilbert, Daniel, 28, 31, 92, 150, 151
Goltz, Dustin B., 5, 6, 7, 15, 30, 43, 48, 77, 141, 153
Gorman, Michael E, and Keith Nelson., 5, 6, 8, 26
Groomsmen, 54, 85, 98, 101
Gross, Larry., 11, 15, 23, 24, 27, 28, 29, 31, 38, 41
Guide to Recognizing Your Saints, 163n21

H
Hajek, Christopher, and Howard Giles, 3
Halberstam, Judith.17; emergence of queer time 9, 129; queer politics 158n8; adult/youth binary, 141, 153, 158n9, 167n15, 173n27, 174n31; gay shame, 110, 162n17; straight time & queer time, 60, 72, 113, 117, 130, 135–136, 143–144, 149–150
Hall, Stuart, 12, 23, 159
Happy Endings., 54, 98, 107, 167, 115, 116, 118, 141
Hart, Kylo Patrick R., 2–3, 9, 38, 40–41
Hellbent, 65, 77
Hegemonic Masculinity, 32, 42, 168
Herdt, Gilbert H., and Brian de Vries, 5
hetero/homo binary, 35, 36, 42, 94–96
heteronormativity, 35; and aging 7; assumed naturalness/perfection 7, 24, 26, 33, 47, 50, 69, 83, 98, 117; generativity 8; temporality, 9, 10, 92, 118, 122; as queer temporal punishment (tragedy)16–18, 29, 40, 47–9, 79; orientation of, 30, 36, 37, 39, 42; marriage/child systems 83, 84–92, 171n3; violence 41, 103, 169n55; gendered dimensions, 42; intersectionality, 125–6, 160n9, 161–162n16; explicit critiques, 166n2; and narrative, 141–2
HIV, *See* AIDS
The History Boys, 137–40
A Home at the End of the World, 54, 115, 128, 129–130, 131, 145, 167
homonormativity. 105, 110, 118, 126, *See* Duggan
Homophobic violence., 33, 49–51; as parody 52, 163n16
hooks, bell, 23, 159n2

Hornby, Nick, 51
Hostetler, Andrew J., 6, 7, 157n5
The Hours, 67, 70, 72, 79, 123, 125

I

I Now Pronounce You Chuck & Larry, 101
ideological critique., 14–5, 43, 158–159n10
intersectionality, 35, 36, 38, 39, 84, 103–111, 116
Isherwood, Christopher, 28–9, 56, 60, 64

J

Jackson, Ronald L., 106
Jagose, Annamarie, 44, 160n7
Johnson, E. Patrick, 35
Jordan, A. B., 159n2

K

Katz, Jackson, 147, 159n2
Katz, Jonathon Ned., 158n7
Kellner, Douglas., 12, 23, 160–161n16
Kelly, J., 6
Kertzner, Robert, Ilan Meyer, and Curtis Dolezal, 5, 6, 7
Kilbourne, Jean, 159n2
Kimmel, Douglas C., 5, 128
Kinsey, 92, 142, 144
Kiss Kiss Bang Bang, 69
Kissing Jessica Stein, 87
Kooden, Harold, and Charles Flowers., 5, 6, 8, 64

L

L.I.E., 53, 66, 69–70, 76
Lacey, Nick., 117–8, 172n14
Lacroix, Celeste, and Robert Westerfelhaus, 20
Lantana, 72
Laramie Project, 50
Latter Days, 51, 98, 130, 142
Lee, John A., 5
lesbian aging., 5
Little Miss Sunshine, 51, 74, 90
Locke, Brian., 159n2
Love and Death on Long Island, 6
Luciano, Dana, 21, 123, 124–5, 152
Lucky Number Slevin, 51, 85

M

Making Love, 23
Mambo Italiano, 90, 91, 95, 97, 98

Mamma Mia! The Movie, 152, 167n32
Manalansan, Martin F., 37, 99
Manchurian Candidate, 22
Maupin, Armistead., 122, 128, 132, 135, 151, 172n18
McIntosh, Peggy, 108
McKerrow, Raymie, 12, 43, 116, 161–162n16
Mean Girls, 169n49
media effects, 22, 23, 161–162n16
The Mexican, 69
Midnight Cowboy, 33
Milk, 151–153
Miss Congeniality, 108
Mitchell, Danielle, 145
Morrison, Linda, and Jeff L'Heureux, 10
Muñoz, José Esteban, 1, 17, 35, 110; futurity 10, 60, 142, 143, 152; potentiality, 44, 119, 166n2; whiteness, 108, 143–144
musement., 43, 44
My Best Friend's Wedding, 24, 109, 171
Mysterious Skin, 50, 54, 66, 77

N

Nero, Charles, 108
The Next Best Thing, 54, 72, 89, 109
Nicholas, Jonathon, and John Howard, 10
The Night Listener, 72, 90
Nightmare on Elm Street, *See* Freddy Krueger
Nine Dead Gay Guys, 67
Noah's Arc, 88, 89–90, 104; violence 50, 51; HIV/AIDS 55; queer romance, 133; aging and, 136–7, 173n24
normativity, 31, 34; and deviance, 37; in gay representation, 37, 38–40, 41

O

Ono, Kent A., and John M. Sloop, 43, 116, 161–162n16
Ott, Brian L., and Eric Aoki, 32, 50, 66

P

Peele, Thomas, 29, 30, 31, 41, 160n13
Perez, Hiram, 37, 107, 110, 158n8
Philadelphia, 20, 35, 87, 91
Pieterse, Jan Nederveen., 23, 159n2
Police Academy, 67

Porfido, Giovanni, 32
Poseidon, 68–69, 122
The Producers, 67, 107, 169n49

Q

Queer as Folk, 4, 20, 46, 102, 103, 132, 155; youthism. 47, 73–75, 165n83; aging as loss/punishment, 61–63, 70–2. 73, 76; gay violence 50, 51, 52–53; death/illness flirtations, 53–54, 55, 67; gay misery, 56, 58; marking of old/young 60, 76; older gay body, 67; saintly older gay, 77; drug use, 163–164; pedophile myths, 88; heteronormative scripts, 91, 167n27; parody of "Gay as Blazes," 93, 102, 167n27; political limitations, 99, 104, 106, 126–127; whiteness, 106–107, 108; misogyny, 109; Brian Kinney finale, 112–113; Queer romance/marriage, 133, 134–135; queer family, 172n8

Queer Eye for the Straight Guy, 4, 39, 86, 91, 101, 107–108, 116
queer, 129; use of term, 158n8
queer audiencing., 25, 26, 28, 45–46, 52, 118–119, 154, 159–160n6
queer media criticism, 38, 44, 161–162n16
queer theory, 35, 41, 44
Quinceañera, 126–7, 130, 171n4

R

Rand, Ayn, 105
Rawls, Todd W., 5, 7
Rechy, John, 136
Reid, John, *See* Andrew Tobias
Remafedi, Gary, 10
Reno 911!, 67, 169
Rent, 78–9, 87, 146
Rick & Steve: The Happiest Gay Couple in the World, 109, 144
Rofes, Eric E., 51
Román, David, 9
Ross, Marlon, 106
Rowling, J.K., *See* Dumbledore, Albus
The Rules of Attraction, 47, 52, 60, 107
Running with Scissors, 59, 150
Russo, Vito., 3, 20, 21, 23, 26, 28, 29, 30, 31, 32, 33, 34–5, 40–41, 49, 65

S

Sandoval, Chela, 166n5
Saved!, 90
Schiappa, Edward. 161–162n16
Sedgwick, Eve Kosofsky., 25, 44, 96, 166n2
Seidman, Steven, 20, 23, 27, 28, 29, 31, 33, 38, 40, 42, 85, 93, 96, 97, 102, 103, 133
Sender, Katherine, 12
Sex and the City, 59, 73, 74, 84, 87, 90, 95, 107, 132, 145, 170–171n77, 172n17
Shepard, Matthew, 32, 49, 50, 66
The Shield, 50, 54
Shock to the System, 58, 97
Shome, Raka, 106, 159n2
Shortbus, 51, 59–60, 98, 140, 173n25
Shugart, Helene A., 12, 27, 38, 109–110, 120, 131, 136, 161–162n16
Six Feet Under, 16, 96, 99, 164n44; gay linked to violence, 49, 50; HIV/AIDS 55; gay misery, 57; youthism, 75–76; heteronormativity idealized, 86–87, 88–89, 92; identification via shame, 98; whiteness and race, 108; patriarchy, 109; finale, 111; queer family, 172n8
Sloop, John M., 13
The Sopranos, 49, 50, 85, 90, 98
South Park, 52, 99
Spin City, 60, 99, 108
Spring Awakening, 94, 96
Storey, John, 14
Suddenly Last Summer, 20
Sweet Home Alabama, 29, 86, 96, 107, 167n32

T

Talladega Nights: The Ballad of Ricky Bobby, 87, 107
Thomas, Kate, 125
Three to Tango, 101, 171n1
Tobias, Andrew, 21, 24, 94, 96, 102, 104, 106, 119, 159n1, 170–171n56
Tompkins, Phillip K., and George Cheney, 81
Touch of Pink, 85, 95, 142
Trick, 67
tragedy, 21, 47, 53, 78–80
Tropiano, Stephen., 23, 27, 31

Trujillo, Nick. 159n2

U
Ugly Betty, 95, 107

V
V for Vendetta, 70
Vaid, Urvashi, 41
Villarejo, Amy, 37

W
Walters, Suzanna Danuta., 23, 26, 27, 28, 29, 31, 38, 40, 41, 42, 70, 93, 96, 97, 157n6
Wander, Phillip, 15, 43
Warner, Michael, 12, 30, 31, 35, 102, 133, 166n2
Wedding Wars, 86, 100, 108
Wilde, Oscar, 61, 67
Will & Grace, 4, 16, 20, 24, 38, 39, 46; gay misery 59; aging anxiety, 63; heteronormativity idealized; 86, 87, 89, 91–92; "normal" gay, 97, 134; apolitical, 100; desexualized, 102; whiteness, 107; finale, 111, 145–146; Karen Walker, 167n30; misogynist, 171n77
Williams, Raymond, 14
Wilson, Clint C., and Félix Gutiérrez, 23
The Wire, 49, 95, 147–150. 151, 155, 174n37, 174n41
Wonder Boys, 74, 163

Y
Yep, Gust, 30, 34, 35, 40, 41, 103, 166, 169, 125, 132
Yep, Gust and John P. Elia, 136, 166n2
Yoakam, John R., 6, 7, 12, 26, 44–5

Z
Zook, Kristal Brent. 159n2

Printed in Great Britain
by Amazon